FINANCIAL REPORTING AND AUDITING

FINANCIAL REPORTING AND AUDITING

Bridging the Expectations Gap

Edited by

Gerard McHugh
and David Rowe

Oak Tree Press

Dublin

Oak Tree Press
Merrion Building
Lower Merrion Street
Dublin 2, Ireland

© 1996 Gerard McHugh and David Rowe

A catalogue record of this book is
available from the British Library.

ISBN 1-872853-70-6

All rights reserved. No part of this publication may be reproduced or transmitted in any form or by any means, including photocopying and recording, without written permission of the publisher and the individual contributors. Such written permission must also be obtained before any part of this publication is stored in a retrieval system of any nature. Requests for permission should be directed to Oak Tree Press, Merrion Building,
Lower Merrion Street, Dublin 2, Ireland.

Printed in Ireland by Colour Books Ltd.

Contents

ABOUT THE CONTRIBUTORS ix

INTRODUCTION xv
Gerard McHugh and David Rowe

1. THE AUDIT ENVIRONMENT 1
   Gerard McHugh
   Introduction 1
   The Modern Company Audit 3
   The Auditing Profession in Ireland 6
   Current and Emergent Trends 8
   Conclusion 17

2. FINANCIAL REPORTING REFORMS — RECENT
   DEVELOPMENTS IN THE UK 19
   Ruth King
   Introduction 19
   Development of the System 21
   The Current Regulatory Structure 23
   The Search for a Conceptual Framework 26
   Big GAAP/Little GAAP 33
   Conclusion 39

3. FINANCIAL REPORTING REFORMS
   — AN IRISH PERSPECTIVE 41
   Paul O'Connor
   Introduction 41
   New Structures for Setting Accounting Standards 44
   The Irish Profession's Response 47
   The Responses to the Report of the Ryan Commission .. 50
   Conclusion 53

4. FRAUD AND THE AUDITOR 55
   Gerard McHugh and Eugene McMahon
   Introduction..55
   Defining Terms..56
   Fraud 57
   Fraud in the Republic of Ireland...59
   Characteristics of the Fraudster...60
   Investigating and Prosecuting Fraud.................................62
   Auditors and Fraud..64
   Preventing Fraud...66
   Conclusion 69

5. AUDITORS AND THE LAW 71
   Laurence Shields and Arthur Moran
   Introduction...71
   The History of the Law in Relation to Audit.....................71
   The Function of Audit..74
   The Duties of Auditors..75
   The Standard of Care 78
   The Auditor's Duty to Third Parties...................................79
   Insuring Audit Liability Exposure 87
   Conclusion 89

6. DIRECTORS AND THE LAW 91
   Michael Forde
   Introduction...91
   Sources of Law 91
   Who is a Director?...92
   Rights and Duties Generally...93
   Directors' Duties in Special Contexts.................................96
   Unlimited Liability — Reckless Trading............................99
   Extent of Liability..102
   Exoneration 102
   Conclusion 102

   Commentary: Alex Spain 104
   Qualities of a Director 106
   Reliance on Executives 107
   Reckless Trading 108
   Conclusion 108

7. AUDITORS AND DIRECTORS 109
   Denis O'Hogan
   Introduction...109
   The Working Relationship 110

Contents   vii

    The Respective Responsibilities of Directors
    and Auditors 111
    Directors' Influence on the Appointment and Removal
    of Auditors 114
    The Structure of Irish Business 115
    New Influences on the Relationship between Auditors
    and Directors 118
    Conclusion 125

  Commentary: Sir Desmond Lorimer   126
    Shareholders: How They are Served 126
    An Extended Auditor's Report...127
    Shareholders' Nominee on Audit Committee 130
    Reducing Shareholder Apathy 130
    Auditors' Independence 131
    Economic Pressures and Audit Tendering 132
    The Prevention and Discovery of Fraud 132
    Conclusion 133

8. AUDIT FAILURE   135
  Edward Cahill
    Introduction..135
    The Objectives of Financial Reporting 136
    The Audit 137
    Authority for Audit 138
    Audit Failure and its Consequences 140
    The Determinants of Audit Failure...................................143
    Has There Been Audit Failure in Ireland? 147
    Towards a Wider Definition of the Scope of Audit 150

  Commentary: Brian Conroy   152
    Users'/Stakeholders' Reaction 152
    The Audit Profession's Failure 153
    Structure of Financial Reporting 157
    Conclusion 158

9. THE AUDIT OF SMALL COMPANIES   159
  Cecil W. Donovan
    Introduction..159
    The Small Company..160
    The Early Debate, 1979–81 161
    Lifting Burdens, 1985–88 168
    Conclusion 177

10. SUBSTANCE OVER FORM   179
    Robert Kirk
        Introduction and History..179
        The True and Fair View 181
        The Development of a Standard on Substance 183
        The Application of the Concept of Substance over Form
        in Practice..187
        Conclusion 194

11. A CRITICAL AFTERWORD   197
    Ronan Keane

REFERENCES   201

About the Contributors

EDWARD CAHILL is Professor of Accounting at University College Cork. He trained as a chartered accountant with Kennedy Crowley & Co. (now KPMG Stokes Kennedy Crowley), qualifying in 1964. Subsequently, he worked for industrial and banking concerns prior to joining Trinity College in 1977 as a full-time academic.

He earned his masters degree and doctorate at Trinity College, Dublin and has been the recipient of a number of research fellowships and awards. He is author of *Corporate Crisis — Paradoxes in Entrepreneurial and Mature Organisations in Ireland*, to be published by Gill and Macmillan in the near future.

BRIAN CONROY is a partner in Bastow Charleton, Chartered Accountants, with special responsibility for audit services. He was educated at University College Dublin and graduated in 1972 with a masters degree in business studies. He qualified as a chartered accountant in 1975 with the unique distinction of achieving first place in each of his Institute examinations.

Subsequently, he worked in Canada and the UK with well-known firms of Chartered Accountants. He has written and lectured on a wide range of accounting and auditing topics. He served for a number of years as Chairman of the Final Admitting Examination Board of the Institute of Chartered Accountants in Ireland.

CECIL DONOVAN is a fellow of the Institute of Chartered Accountants in Ireland and an associate of the Institute of Taxation in Ireland. He recently retired from partnership in the Dublin office of Deloitte & Touche but continues as a consultant to that firm.

He joined Butler Chance (now Deloitte & Touche) as an articled clerk in 1954 and then rejoined them from Price Waterhouse, London in 1962, and was admitted to the partnership in 1964. As a partner in the firm, he had overall responsibility for the firm's quality assurance procedures.

He was a member of the Council of the Institute of Chartered Accountants in Ireland from 1977 to 1989 and was the Institute's President for the year to May 1987. He was Chairman of the working party that formulated the successful practice review system of the Institute, which was introduced early in 1988. Between 1981 and 1985, he was Chairman of the Institute's Education and Training Committee. He lectures widely on auditing and accounting matters.

He has been a member of the International Federation of Accountants (IFAC) Education Committee since May 1988 and was appointed Chairman on 1 January 1993. He has been nominated to continue as Chairman for a second term until 31 December 1997.

MICHAEL FORDE is a senior counsel and practises at the bar, principally in Dublin (Law Library) and in London (Gray's Inn). He is the author of numerous books on aspects of Irish Law, including *Company Law* (2nd ed. 1992), *The Law of Company Insolvency* (1993) and *Commercial Law in Ireland* (1990).

RONAN KEANE is a judge of the High Court. He was educated at University College Dublin where he earned his Bachelor of Arts degree. He went on to study at Kings Inns and was called to the bar in 1954. He was called to the inner bar in 1970. In 1979, he was appointed a judge of the High Court and has been a President of the Law Reform Commission.

In addition to his court work, Justice Keane has contributed numerous papers to legal journals. He is the author of a number of books on company law, equity and the law of trusts and local government law in the Republic of Ireland.

RUTH KING is a lecturer in accounting and financial management at Loughborough University Business School. She trained as a chartered accountant with Deloitte Haskins & Sells (now Coopers & Lybrand), qualified in 1980 and remained with the firm for several years as a client manager. She then worked for a short period as Principal Finance Officer at Trent Polytechnic (now Nottingham Trent University) during its transfer to corporate status, before taking up her current post in 1989.

She teaches on a variety of undergraduate, postgraduate and post-experience programmes, and her main research interests embrace aspects of financial reporting and issues in accounting education. She is Executive Editor of *Accounting Education: An International Journal* (Chapman and Hall).

ROBERT KIRK is Professor of Accounting and Finance at the University of Ulster. An economics graduate of Queens University Belfast, he trained as a chartered accountant with the Belfast office of Price Waterhouse. He qualified in 1976, achieving first place in the Institute's final examination. Subsequently, he spent two years as a financial controller with a subsidiary of Shell (UK).

He later became a lecturer at Queens University where he was in charge of both the University's Diploma in Accounting and of the Institute of Chartered Accountants in Ireland's Final Admitting Examination programmes.

In addition to professional journal articles, he has published two books on company law in Northern Ireland, the most recent of which was a joint publication with Coopers & Lybrand. He co-authored the first *Survey of Irish Published Accounts*. He has just completed a book on accounting standards for the Chartered Institute of Management Accountants and edits a quarterly professional journal, *Irish Company Reporting,* published by the University of Ulster.

SIR DESMOND LORIMER is Chairman of Northern Bank Limited and Lamont Holdings plc, a director of National Australia Group (UK) Limited, Irish Distillers plc and a number of other companies.

Until 1974, he was a practising chartered accountant and was President of the Institute of Chartered Accountants in Ireland for the year 1968–69. He has also served on the Listed Companies Advisory Board to the London Stock Exchange.

As Chairman of Northern Ireland Electricity plc, he led that company through privatisation. Other public interests included responsibility for the establishment of the Northern Ireland Housing Executive and the Industrial Development Board for Northern Ireland.

GERARD McHUGH is a lecturer in accounting and financial management at Trinity College Dublin. He trained as a certified accountant with the Dublin office of Deloitte, Haskins and Sells, qualifying in 1980. In 1983, he returned to full-time study at the University of Sheffield, where he earned his masters degree in accounting and financial management. He returned to Dublin to take up his present post at Trinity College in 1985.

He has published in the professional and academic journals on research methodology, auditing and financial reporting and is co-author, with Professor R.M.S. Wilson, of *Financial Analysis: A Managerial Introduction* (Cassell). He is an associate editor of *Accounting Education: An International Journal* (Chapman & Hall). His research interests are in auditing and financial reporting, and he is currently pursuing doctoral work at Loughborough University.

EUGENE McMAHON is an audit partner in the Dublin office of the European audit specialists, Rawlinson Hunter Mazars, whose head office is in Paris. He trained as a chartered accountant with a small Dublin firm of chartered accountants and, after qualifying, spent some time with Deloitte Haskins & Sells.

Prior to joining his present firm, Eugene worked for five years with the Institute of Chartered Accountants in Ireland, where he initially had overall responsibility for the Institute's audit quality assurance programme known as *Practice Review*. He also headed up the Institute's *Practice Advisory Service* and is widely acknowledged as an expert on practice management.

He has lectured widely at conferences and seminars on both audit quality issues and practice management matters. He has provided many training courses, including an extensive programme delivered to officers of the Garda Síochána Fraud Squad.

ARTHUR MORAN is a partner in Matheson Ormsby Prentice, Solicitors, in Dublin. He studied modern languages at Trinity College, Dublin, and law at the Law Society of Ireland. He qualified as a solicitor in 1975, and in 1977 was appointed a partner in his present firm, where he practises company and commercial law. He is a member of the Law Society's European Union and International Affairs Committee.

PAUL O'CONNOR is a manager with Craig Gardner/Price Waterhouse, Chartered Accountants. He is a chartered accountant by profession and in 1991 was seconded on a full-time basis as Secretary to the Commission of Enquiry into the Expectations of Users of Published Financial Statements (the "Ryan Commission"). Since then he has maintained an active interest in financial reporting matters, advising clients on corporate governance and the requirements of the Cadbury Code of Best Practice. He is a member of the Main Committee of the Leinster Society of Chartered Accountants.

DENIS O'HOGAN is the Technical Partner in the Dublin office of Ernst & Young, Chartered Accountants. He holds a B.Sc. in mathematical science from University College Dublin, an M.Sc. in statistics and operations research from Trinity College and a B.Sc. in information technology from Dublin City University. He joined Arthur Andersen in 1971 as an articled clerk and qualified as a chartered accountant in 1974. He moved to Arthur Young & Company in 1978, was admitted to partnership in 1980 and has stayed with that firm through the subsequent mergers that resulted in the present firm of Ernst & Young.

He has been involved with accounting education for many years and was an examiner in the Final Admitting Examination of the Institute of Chartered Accountants in the early 1990s. He served with the Parliamentary and Law Committee (South) of the Institute and as one of the CCAB-I advisers to the Government during the negotiation of the EC Seventh Company Law Directive on group accounts.

DAVID ROWE entered the small Dublin firm of Forsyth & Co. in 1937, and qualified as a chartered accountant in 1942. He was admitted to partnership in the following year and remained with that firm through its subsequent mergers, in the first place with Kennedy Crowley & Co., forming what ultimately became KPMG Stokes Kennedy Crowley. During the last 10 years up to retirement in 1980, he was the Technical Partner in the firm.

He has had a long involvement with accounting education. He helped to set up the multi-subject approach in the Final Admitting Examination of the Institute. After retirement, he helped to establish the Centre for Accounting Studies in Lesotho, on behalf of the Department of Foreign Affairs. He edited *The Irish Chartered Accountant 100, Centenary Essays 1888–1988*.

Charitable activities involved him in the 1980s as Director of the Dublin Samaritans; and at present he is President of An Taisce. He has maintained contact with third-world aid activities, being for a period Chairperson of the Agency for Personal Services Overseas, and associated still with APSO as a member of the Senior Services Overseas working party.

LAURENCE K. SHIELDS is a Senior Partner in L.K. Shields & Partners, Solicitors. He was educated at University College Dublin where he obtained a Bachelor of Civil Laws. He qualified as a solicitor in 1972 and, in addition, is an associate of the Institute of Taxation in Ireland and a fellow of the Chartered Institute of Arbitrators. He has lectured extensively, including a period as lecturer and examiner in Company Law and Partnership for the Law Society of Ireland. He is a

Council Member of the Dublin Solicitors Bar Association and was President in 1983–84. He was a member of the judging panel for the Leinster Society of Chartered Accountants Published Accounts Awards from 1987 to 1990. He is currently a member of the Council of the Law Society of Ireland and Chairman of its Finance Committee, and was Junior Vice President in 1993–94. He contributed to the chapter on Ireland in *European Product Liability*, published by Butterworths in 1992. He is a director of a number of companies.

ALEX SPAIN is Chairman of DCC plc, National Irish Bank Ltd., and Granville Development Capital. He is a director of National Australia Bank (UK) Ltd., UMS Group Ltd. and other companies.

A chartered accountant by profession, he became a partner in KPMG Stokes Kennedy Crowley in 1960. From 1977 to 1984, he was the Managing Partner of that firm. He was President of the Institute of Chartered Accountants in Ireland in 1975 and Chairman of the Financial Services Industry Association 1988–89.

He is a member of the Irish Government's Efficiency Audit Group and a member of the Irish Government's International Financial Services Centre Committee.

Introduction

The origin of this book can be attributed at first remove to the labours of the late Edmund Grace FCA. For a number of years before his death he was developing his ideas about corporate governance, about the basic philosophy underlying the existence of companies, and the functions of, and interconnections between, directors, executives, auditors, shareholders, and exterior parties. Eddie's primary academic effort was directed towards building bridges of understanding between these various interests.

To support him in his work, the AIB and the Institute of Chartered Accountants in Ireland provided research funding which was administered by a small committee. At the time of his death Eddie had amassed a large amount of written material, which required extensive editing, organising and annotating. The committee considered the matter at great length, and decided eventually that it would not be possible to complete Eddie's work without his guiding hand and vision.

So, a radical new approach was agreed upon, which would recognise Eddie's work, but would not in any way pretend to complete it. It was decided to request a number of eminent lawyers, accountants, academics and company directors to contribute essays on various subjects, which paralleled the issues that Eddie had been examining. The emphasis of the collection is on presenting many points of view and — in keeping with Eddie's ambitions — on creating the building blocks upon which a more informed debate about what has now become widely referred to as the "expectations gap" in financial reporting and audit might be conducted. Hence the book's subtitle.

In the context in which the book was born it is perhaps appropriate to summarise some of the trends of thought which were emerging from Eddie's work. Directors have two major areas of responsibility — entrepreneurial and custodial. The thrust of Eddie's work in his last years was devoted to understanding and improving the latter.

He viewed the control structure of a company as an integrated one, involving both internal and external elements. The internal system comprises *inter alia* the system of internal checks and segregation of duties, internal audit, and board supervision. The main external control is imposed by market through its comparison of achievements with expectations. The Annual Report is an important source of information in making this assessment. Eddie had argued for many years that the Annual Report should be akin to a modified "prospectus", year by year, to enable meaningful evaluations to be made. The external auditor is a key part of that control mechanism, ensuring that the directors fulfil their disclosure obligations to the market. It was Eddie's abiding hope that the relationship of trust and openness so essential between the directors and the auditors should be fostered and improved.

THEMES

To some degree these themes are taken up in the essays herein. But many others are touched upon: important changes are taking place which will shape the future practice of financial reporting and auditing; and critical questions are being asked and need to be answered. For example:

- **Negligence Claims**: Increasingly, those who have relied to their cost on misleading financial information are attempting to fasten the fault on the negligence of auditors (Chapter 1: The Audit Environment, Gerard McHugh). Will this lead to more demanding standards imposed on, or accepted by, auditors? Or will it lead to a defensive attempt by the profession to tighten and confine the area of responsibility of the auditor, and to lobby to have that accepted by the business community?

- **Duty of Care**: It is uncertain whether the law is tending to expand or reduce the classes of person to whom the auditor owes a duty of care. The English *Caparo* case drew the line at a fairly conservative level, but will this case necessarily be followed in Ireland? (Chapter 5: Auditors and the Law, Laurence Shields and Arthur Moran.)

- **Cost of Insurance**: Increased litigation has led to higher insurance premiums, touching levels that are beyond the means of some practitioners. Is it likely that practitioners and clients may be allowed to negotiate agreed limits of liability? (Chapter 5: Auditors and the Law.)

- **The Regulatory Framework**: Ireland lacks active and transparent regulatory mechanisms, such as are now established in some other countries. Is this a contributory factor to audit failure? Is self-regulation sufficient? (Chapter 8: Audit Failure, Edward Cahill.) Is legislative backing for standards and for monitoring on the way? Following the recommendations of the Ryan Commission, and the lead given by the British Government (Chapter 2: Financial Reforms — Recent Developments in the UK, Ruth King), it seems likely that accounting standards, and the establishment of an Irish Financial Reporting Review Panel, will gain statutory support (Chapter 3: Financial Reporting Reforms — An Irish Perspective, Paul O'Connor). For better or for worse, it seems inevitable that the days of ad hoc accounting decisions, and latitude in judgment are over.

- **The Expectations Gap**: That such a gap exists appears to be beyond question (Chapter 1: The Audit Environment, Gerard McHugh). But whether the gap can be bridged by educating the public in what the profession believes it *ought* to expect, or whether more needs to be done in the area of "whistle-blowing", remains a matter for discussion. Undoubtedly, there are steps that management can take to minimise the possibility of fraud, but whether there is much that the auditing profession itself can do in this regard is not at all clear (Chapter 4: Fraud and the Auditor, Gerard McHugh and Eugene McMahon).

- **The "Value" of Audit**: Cost-conscious managements examine all aspects of expenditure to ensure that each "adds value". Audit fees have not escaped this scrutiny. It may not be easy to persuade clients that endorsement of financial statements by a reputable auditor adds value through enhanced confidence. Are there other possible by-products of the audit which more obviously add value? (Chapter 7: Auditors and Directors, Denis O'Hogan). Is it likely in the foreseeable future that the audit reporting remit will be widened, to include, for example, reporting on the adequacy of internal controls, and of management planning and control? (Chapter 8: Audit Failure.)

- **Audit of Smaller Companies**: Recent British legislation exempts smaller companies from the audit requirement (with certain exceptions). It seems likely that Ireland will enact similar legislation in the near future. How is this move likely to affect audit practitioners? And indeed, what effect will it have on the companies concerned? Could it be that audit will be replaced in some cases by a Revenue-driven, or creditor-driven, system of alternative verification? (Chapter 9: The Audit of Small Companies, Cecil Donovan.)

- **Auditor Independence**: The critics who claim that auditor independence is at risk by virtue of a too cosy relationship between auditing firms and their clients have been vociferous in recent years, and have sought a total separation of the audit function from the provision of any other services (Chapter 1: The Audit Environment, and Chapter 7: Commentary on Auditors and Directors, Sir Desmond Lorimer). Other "remedies" have also been suggested, such as the rotation of auditors. Will this argument prevail in the future? And if it does, what are the implications for the profession in Ireland? (Chapter 8: Commentary on Audit Failure, Brian Conroy.)

- **Audit Committees**: The creation of audit committees of non-executive directors has aided the independence of auditors. There remains an anomaly that more extensive reporting to a sub-group of directors has not been matched by any equivalent in-depth reporting to shareholder representatives, for whom the auditor is supposed to be acting (Chapter 7: Auditors and Directors, Denis O'Hogan).

- **Service to Shareholders**: Is the audit report an adequate medium of communication between auditors and shareholders? Are shareholders inhibited from positive participation in the governance of their company? (Chapter 7: Commentary on Auditors and Directors, Sir Desmond Lorimer.)

- **Directors' Remuneration**: The British Cadbury Report's recommendations for very detailed reporting of directors' remuneration appear to have been watered down here by agreement with the Stock Exchange. Are more stringent requirements likely in the future? (Chapter 7: Auditors and Directors, Denis O'Hogan.)

- **Reckless Trading**: The 1990 Companies Act opened the possibility of unlimited liability for directors who trade "recklessly". The prospect is frightening, but so far the courts have interpreted the provisions with sense and pragmatism (Chapter 6: Directors and the Law, Michael Forde and Alex Spain).

- **Substance over Form**: It has become generally accepted that reporting on the substance of transactions should take precedence over their legal form (Chapter 10: Substance over Form, Robert Kirk). In this connection, one may also ask whether the process of European integration is likely to alter further the relationship between financial reporting and the law in this country? (Chapter 4: Auditors and the Law, Arthur Moran and Laurence Shields).

- **Competition within the Auditing Profession**: Competition between practising firms is increasing the pressures upon auditors (Chapter 1: The Audit Environment, Gerard McHugh). Will this lead to the cutting of corners, the taking of risks, in order to retain clients and profits? (Chapter 6: Commentary on Auditors and Directors, Sir Desmond Lorimer).

The foregoing listing is selective, concentrating on those issues which appear to indicate the sharpest trends, and to raise questions of major importance for directors and auditors, and indeed for government and the public. Their range, when accumulated, is startling, and indicates the profound changes that have been taking place in recent years, and are at present evolving. The number of unanswered questions suggests that we may expect quite fundamental developments in the future, probably leading to greater transparency, more useful information, more effective accountability and tighter monitoring. If these enormous advantages can be achieved without overloading industry and the profession with bureaucratic regulations, then we can only welcome them.

We would like to thank all our contributors, who have generously given their time and their creative thinking, and have been most patient and co-operative when we sought revisions. Particularly we thank Justice Ronan Keane for his incisive assessment of the contributions and of the possible impact of the book as a whole. A number of organisations assisted Eddie Grace in his research work, including: AIB, Deloitte & Touche, KPMG, Pannell Kerr Roster, Coopers and Lybrand, Oliver Freaney & Co., Matheson Ormsby Prentice, L.K. Shields & Partners, Eugene F. Collins & Son and the Irish Accountancy Trust. We gratefully acknowledge their continued support for the present volume. We would like also to record our appreciation for the continued backing and encouragement of Niall Crowley, Cecil Donovan, Arthur Moran, Laurence Shields, John Keogh, and Dick Lane.

Gerard McHugh
David Rowe

1
The Audit Environment

Gerard McHugh
Trinity College, Dublin

INTRODUCTION

Thirty years ago, who could have predicted that company auditors would become one of the most controversial professional groupings in commercial life? The idea that the practices of a crusty, male-dominated profession whose expertise involved the arcane task of checking financial books and records would become the subject of high-level Review Commissions, Government Reports and Senate Investigations (in the US) would have seemed fanciful and remote. Yet, this is precisely what has occurred and the past 20 years have probably been the most traumatic ever experienced by the auditing profession, both nationally and internationally.

In Britain and in Ireland, many practising auditors will trace the birth of this "modern era" to the 1960s, a period during which serious criticism of the accounting profession began to appear on the public agenda. In 1969, the late Professor Edward Stamp penned his famous letter to the editor of *The Times*, in which he criticised the accounting profession for failing to develop a codified system of accounting rules. The debate he provoked is widely acknowledged to have provided the stimulus for the formation of the Accounting Standards Steering Committee, in 1970, and the Auditing Practices Committee, in 1976. Both bodies exist today in reincarnated forms as the Accounting Standards Board, and the Auditing Practices Board. Thus began the most intensive period of regulation yet experienced within the auditing and accounting communities.

It was also in the 1960s that the large audit practices began to internationalise in earnest — forming strategic alliances across continents and expanding into greenfield regions. Building on their powerful audit base, public accounting firms diversified into management consulting and came to dominate the markets for taxation advice, insolvency and receivership services, growing to become very profitable enterprises. With profitability and size came power; in many western and eastern bloc economies, public accounting firms have come to rival merchant banks as advisers to national governments.

Success has brought its share of hostility, however. It is argued that granting a statutory audit monopoly to certain professional accounting institutes has given auditors an unfair advantage when competing for other business assignments, such as management consulting, taxation advice and pensions consulting. It is further suggested that providing business-advisory services alongside the audit has compromised the independence of audit firms — an allegation that is vehemently denied by the profession. Others claim that in some instances audits are not being performed with the competence one might reasonably expect of professional experts — in other words, that work is performed negligently.

Increasingly, the users of audit services are seeking legal recourse against auditors, and the "auditor negligence claim" has become the crisis of the 1990s. According to Jake Netterville, past chairman of the American Institute of Certified Public Accountants, the liability crisis in the US is "far and away the most important problem facing the profession".[1] Closer to home, the spectre has been raised of orphans and widows of deceased partners of large audit firms starving in the street because the value of deceased partners' assets could not be determined pending the outcome of litigation against their firms.[2]

By comparison with the auditing profession in America, Canada and Britain, the Irish auditing profession has remained relatively unscathed. But there is every reason to believe that its immunity will be short-lived. The Institute of Chartered Accountants in Ireland, which represents most professional auditors in this country, has acknowledged the potential seriousness of increased litigation against auditors, and has assured its members that it will continue to press Government to change the law, which it claims maintains this "unfair situation".[3]

This focus on the roles, functions and competence of the auditor in the financial reporting process has generated a debate that has spread far beyond the professional enclosure. The term "audit expectations gap" has been coined to refer to the perception that auditors are performing in a manner at odds with the expectations of those for whose benefit the audit is conducted.[4] We are now seeing the beginnings of the reform process being put in place by the accounting profession itself in common-law countries — the United States, Britain,

Ireland, Canada, Australia and New Zealand.

In a sense then, the next 20 years look like being as eventful for the auditing profession as the past 20. In this chapter, we consider the impact that the broad international developments are having, and are likely to have, on the profession in Ireland. Before we turn to consider these issues, some preliminary context-setting remarks seem appropriate.

THE MODERN COMPANY AUDIT

Many people are understandably confused about the organisation of the accounting/auditing profession and the relationship between accounting, financial reporting and auditing. Crudely put, *accounting* refers to the activity of *recording* economic/financial transactions, and *financial reporting* refers to the activity of *preparing and disseminating* accounting information to interested users. When such information is in the form of the statutory financial statements, those statements must be audited (in the checking sense of the word), and must be accompanied by an auditor's opinion. Those who perform the audit function must, by law, be qualified accountants (i.e. full members of certain recognised accounting institutes or associations).

Although the practice of audit (qua third-party investigation) existed as early as 8,000 BC, the origins of the modern audit can be traced to nineteenth century British companies legislation. It is widely assumed that the rationale for introducing audit legislation lay in the need to protect investors in public companies — however, this gives a less than complete picture of the development of the audit requirement. From 1856 until 1900, there was no statutory audit requirement whatsoever for companies incorporated under the joint stock companies legislation — permitting incorporation with limited liability to be obtained with a freedom amounting almost to a licence.[5] In reality, the development of audit in the nineteenth century was more closely associated with the "regulated companies", such as the railways, gas producers and banks, which were all required under their incorporating legislation to undergo annual audit.[6] The motivation for the requirement had as much to do with protecting creditors, controlling monopoly pricing and ensuring standards of public safety, as with the protection of investors. The UK Companies Act, 1900 extended the audit requirement to companies established under the general companies acts. It was even later again that the auditing profession secured the legal right to monopolise the provision of audit services among certain specified professional bodies (introduced in 1948 in the UK and in 1963 in Ireland).

The most famous manual of auditing, which educated a whole generation of auditors from 1971 onwards — V.R.V. Cooper's *Student's Manual of Auditing*[7] — defines auditing rather plainly:

> The object of the audit is to enable the auditor to report on the truth and fairness of the financial position shown by the balance sheet and of the profit or loss shown by the profit and loss account. The auditor is required to state unequivocally in his audit report whether or not, in his opinion, the accounts show a true and fair view. Where he cannot give an affirmative opinion in this respect he must, of necessity, qualify his report in such a way as to show quite clearly why he considers that a true and fair view is not presented and, where applicable, in what respects and to what extent he considers the accounts to be misstated. (p. 1)

The popular notion of the auditor as an investigator (qua detective), entering a company's premises to unearth financial wrongdoing, is somewhat fanciful. The belief probably stems from auditing practices of earlier years when the emphasis was very much on the extensive checking of documents. In fact, even as late as 15 years ago, it was often considered important that "signs" of the audit work (in the form of markings and stamps) were imprinted all over the client's books and records — as proof to the client that checks had been performed. The emphasis has changed since then towards more analytical and systems review, but it is almost certain that the practices of earlier decades have left many with the impression that when the auditor "signs off" everything is "correct".

In practice, the modern audit team is composed of a number of trained and partly-trained accountants carrying out test examinations of books and records, with a view to determining whether the financial statements prepared by the directors present a true and fair view of the results for the period. At the junior level, the task demands a thorough understanding of accounting and information-recording systems, and consists of a fair amount of routine. The senior staff spend a higher proportion of their time managing the high-risk dimensions of the audit, and it is they who deal with any contentious aspects of the client's financial reporting, such as valuations.

Auditing also calls for a high degree of diplomacy: the audit team needs to maintain satisfactory relationships with a number of constituencies whose interests in the outcome of its work may be quite different. For example, the company's senior management selects the auditor — maintaining a good working relationship with that group can ensure the smooth progress of an audit and re-appointment.[8] The auditor also has a statutory duty to report to shareholders on the truth and fairness of the financial statements presented by that same senior management group — hence, the need for a certain "detachment" from senior management. Auditors may also find themselves in the role of "broker" with financial institutions — that is, a client's bankers may wish to place reliance on the work of the auditor before granting or renewing financing facilities. Auditors may also find that the Revenue Authorities place a special reliance on their work in order to assess a company's taxation liability. Maintaining all these relationships is difficult — the demands and expectations are high and the pressures can be intense. Figure 1.1 below gives some sense of the relationships mapped in terms of the *proximity* between the auditor and other constituencies.

FIGURE 1.1: THE AUDITOR'S RELATIONSHIP WITH THIRD PARTIES

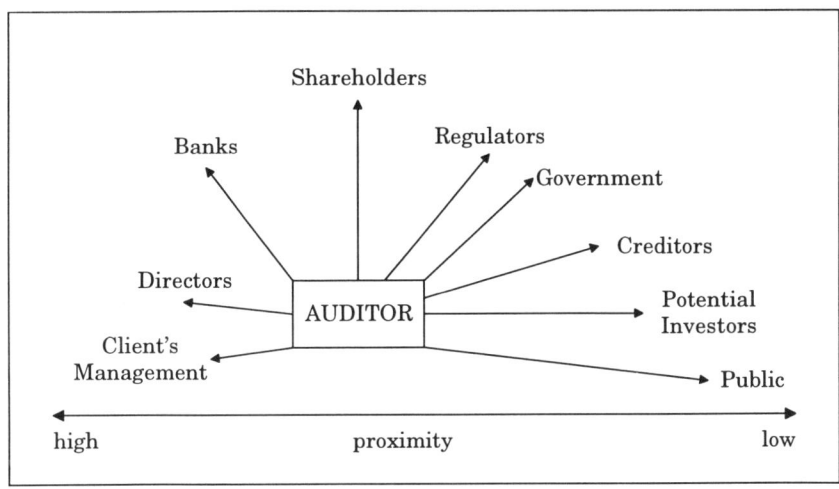

By and large, all of these constituencies have some interest in the audit process, but these interests are not the same, nor are they static over time. At its core, auditing is a "political" activity; the function of audit, the domain of audit, the interests it serves and the relationships between those interests are inherently contestable. For example, as has already been stated, it was the creditor, and not the shareholder, who featured most prominently in the minds of the legislators who drafted the earliest reporting and auditing requirements of companies. Throughout the twentieth century, the perceived importance of the creditor has reduced somewhat and the shareholder and investor have assumed a higher prominence. At the time of writing, the profession in Ireland has been involved in a huge public controversy over the unwelcome attempt by the Minister for Finance to impose a *duty* on auditors (among others) to report tax fraud to the Revenue Commissioners. The accounting profession mounted a huge lobby against the relevant Section 153 of the 1995 Finance Bill, and succeeded in persuading the Minister to modify the "whistle-blowing" provisions — see Section 172 of the Finance Act, 1995. However, had the original Section 153 remained, it would have changed the nature of auditing in this country.

THE AUDITING PROFESSION IN IRELAND

Ireland's auditing and financial reporting traditions are inextricably bound with those of Britain, both in their origins and in current practice. Ireland and Britain also have much in common with the audit and financial reporting environments of the Commonwealth and former Commonwealth countries such as Australia, New Zealand and Canada, and with traditions of the US. The structure of the accounting and auditing professions in all of these countries is much the same. The major difference in the UK and the Republic of Ireland is the proliferation of accounting bodies. It is probably fair to say that, even today, Britain and Ireland look more to the US than to Europe in accounting and auditing matters.

There are roughly 12,000 accountants working in Ireland. Four bodies — the Institute of Chartered Accountants in Ireland (ICAI), the Chartered Association of Certified Accountants (ACCA), the Institute of Certified Public Accountants in Ireland (ICPAI) and the Chartered Institute of Management Accountants (CIMA) account for over 90 per cent of professionally qualified accountants. These four bodies are also widely known as the "recognised" accounting bodies, in the sense that they are all members of the Consultative Committee of Accountancy Bodies, an umbrella organisation, which is acknowledged to represent the profession in its relationship with external constituencies. Three of these four bodies; the ICAI, ACCA, and ICPAI are specified under the Companies Acts, 1963 to 1990, as qualified to conduct the audit of incorporated bodies.

The Institute of Chartered Accountants in Ireland, founded in 1888, is the oldest of the bodies. The Chartered Association of Certified

Accountants is a British-based body dating back to 1905. It has a worldwide membership of 47,000, of whom 2,000 work in Ireland. The Institute of Certified Public Accountants in Ireland was formed in 1943 and currently has 1,100 members. Of the total membership of these bodies, approximately 4,000 members (35 per cent) are engaged in public practice. Of that number, close to 3,500 are directly engaged as audit practitioners. Table 1.1 below presents some up-to-date figures on growth trends and current membership working in Ireland for each of the bodies.

TABLE 1.1: MEMBERSHIP OF THE PROFESSIONAL ACCOUNTING/ AUDITING BODIES WORKING IN IRELAND

Professional Body	founded	1964 Members	1974 Members	1984 Members	1993/94 Members	1994 Students
ICAI	1888	1,473	2,400	4,140	6,482	2,000
ACCA	1905	210	610	1,109	2,032	4,293
ICPAI	1943	155	190	462	1,100	1,600
Total		1,838	3,200	5,711	9,614	7,893

TABLE 1.2: NUMBERS WORKING DIRECTLY IN PROFESSIONAL PRACTICE

Professional Body	1964	1974	1984	1994
ICAI	627	1,106	2,154	2,899
ACCA	63	183	330	706
ICPAI	70	100	230	320
Total	760	1,389	2,714	3,925

The accounting profession has grown significantly in recent years, and the audit profession, as an element of that, has grown also. Table 1.2 shows that over the 30-year period from 1964 to 1994, the numbers engaged in audit practice grew by over 400 per cent, a compound annual growth rate of just over 5.5 per cent.

The most dramatic expansion in audit numbers occurred between 1974 and 1984. During that time, Ireland's industrial base and industrial output expanded. Ireland's relative success in attracting foreign industry through a series of tax holidays drove up the demand for the services of accounting professionals including auditors. Concomitant with this change, the large international firms of accountants developed associations with existing Irish firms or set up independent partnerships.

Today, the major international firms are all represented in Ireland, and the standard and quality of work and advice is comparable with best practice elsewhere. As in other countries, the audit profession takes its legitimacy from the State.[9] In Ireland, the Companies Acts, 1963 to 1990, recognise three bodies — ICAI, ACCA and ICPAI — as competent to conduct statutory audits and it is left to the bodies themselves to license their members.

CURRENT AND EMERGENT TRENDS

The environment facing the auditing profession today is a complex one and it cannot be comprehensively surveyed in this chapter. In the view of this author, however, the two issues discussed below capture the essential features of that environment. These are the changing nature of competition within the auditing industry, and the declining confidence in "audit" as a product. In a sense, the discussion that follows provides a backdrop for understanding many of the other dimensions of the auditor's world presented in the chapters that follow.

The Changing Nature of Competition within the Auditing Industry

It has become clichéd to say that we live in a competitive business world. Business has always been competitive; what has changed is the *degree of competitiveness* and the *arena of competition*. For practising auditors, selling the audit service has always been competitive. However, since the late 1970s the degree of competitiveness has increased appreciably, as has the size of the *competition arena*. Probably the clearest manifestation of these trends has been the extent to which "competitive battles" are now often fought quite openly in public. Nonetheless, claims by audit firms that the industry has become intensely competitive need to be interpreted very cautiously. A relatively short time has elapsed since the audit industry emerged from what, in competitive terms, can only be described as a gentleman's club in which advertising and poaching of clients were expressly forbidden.

The initial impetus towards "opening up" the competitive space was, ironically, Government-imposed. In 1976, the advertising restrictions of the accounting profession were the subject of a critical report by the UK Monopolies and Mergers Commission. Fearing that anti-competitive pricing was occurring, the report concluded that the advertising restrictions operated against the public interest. In 1981, the Office of Fair Trading forced some relaxation in the restrictions and, in 1984, the UK accounting bodies removed their ban on members advertising services. The Irish profession, recognising the inevitability of this proposal being adopted by the Irish Government, removed its ban at the same time.

Along with the removal of the advertising restrictions, two further features of the industry have played a significant role in raising the competitive stakes. The first is the industry's cost structure: professional staff represent a high fixed cost to audit practices. Effective utilisation (in the sense of time charged out) is a critical component of profitability. In Britain and Ireland, controlling these costs has been difficult because, as yet, there is no tradition of letting-go excess staff.[10] Thus, audit firms are engaged in a continuous search for new clients in order to achieve efficiency gains. We see clear evidence for this in the competition to serve the newly industrialising countries of the eastern bloc. Secondly, for many years now, accounting has been seen as a highly desirable career option, and there is mounting evidence that there is an oversupply of accountants at present. A by-product of this oversupply has been a relative shortage of senior promotional opportunities within the career structure of larger firms. As a result, there has been a significant growth in the number of new small practices, typically formed by senior staff who have been trained in the larger firms. These smaller firms are often well placed and very willing to gnaw at the small and medium-sized clients of larger practices.

The market for audit services has two segments: the small and medium-sized companies with turnovers of less than £2.5 million, and the larger companies with turnover in excess of that figure. The demand for audit in the smaller market can be supplied by almost any audit firm, regardless of size. It is a relatively stable market, which has experienced low growth in recent years. Prices have become more competitive recently as clients overcome traditional fears about the costs of switching. A recent UK survey by Fearnley and Beattie has found that smaller clients are now more likely to change auditor than larger ones, and in most cases the reason is a reduction in the fee.[11]

The second segment of the market is a good example of classical oligopoly. It is dominated on the supplier side by six large audit firms (the "Big Six") and, for the most part, the smaller audit firms are unable to compete in this market. International studies of market concentration, conducted in America, Australia, Britain and Denmark, all suggest that this market is becoming more concentrated. The only research yet published concerning Ireland is contained in the National Economic Research Association's study of Competition in European Accounting.[12] This confirms the dominance of the Big Six in the Irish audit market — 63 of the top 100 companies are audited by the Big Six. The increase in concentration is partially a result of the increase in merger activity between large firms, and is also related to the very successful "branding" by the large accounting firms. Purchasers of audit services firmly believe that the quality of audit performed by a large international partnership is superior to that performed by other firms.

However, despite the increasing level of concentration, all the evidence on pricing policy points away from the existence of oligopolistic or monopolistic pricing activity. Information in Ireland[13] is very poor but American and Australian research indicates that the audit market is best described as *loosely oligopolistic* — meaning that although the level of concentration in the market is high, it is not high enough to permit collusive price-fixing to occur. In a curious way, the merger-mania of the 1980s, which has resulted in a smaller group of similar-sized international audit firms, seems to be generating more, rather than less, competition.

There is plenty of anecdotal and some systematic evidence to support the claim. Most systematic evidence comes from US research. Simon and Francis found evidence of price-cutting on initial audit engagements that persists through the third year of the engagement.[14] Their estimate for the first year discount is 24 per cent, and 15 per cent for the next two years. A UK survey of more than 300 companies uncovered evidence of widespread undercutting in audit-tender negotiations — over a third of tender prices were more than 20 per cent lower than the current fee.[15] If anything, competition in the audit industry is set to intensify further in the 1990s.

This intensification of competition within the industry is likely to have a number of consequences for the auditing profession. One certain outcome is that opportunities for professional employment in audit practices are likely to be fewer as firms increase their investment in information technology, and as margins are cut by the increased competition. This will reduce the attractiveness of careers in the auditing profession, and perhaps the accounting profession more generally, as we approach the year 2000. Already, the high number of accountants on the market has depressed salaries. The profession's response to this needs to be well thought through. The knee-jerk reaction of some professional accountants — controlling the labour market by restricting student registrations and controlling the qualification pass rates — simply cannot operate in a democracy such as ours.[16]

On the assumption that Ireland will tend to follow both American and British trends, it seems likely that companies will switch auditor more regularly than before. An increasing number of large companies have begun opening their audit appointment to tender. At the small-company level, the evidence is also mounting that the lifelong personal relationship between small-business people and their accountants is under threat. If these shifts within the audit market occur without impacting on quality, they should be good for the consumer.

There is, however, a third and more parlous possibility. Some auditors worry that too much competition within the industry may cause quality to decline. Within the firms, senior accountants, managers and partners are under constant and increasing pressure to contain costs on audit engagements. The traditional response to this pressure from young ambitious accountants has been to under-record time involvement on client assignments.[17] In effect, this means that clients are not billed for the true level of time spent on their audit.[18] If these pressures build to a point where young accountants in charge of audit engagements and their junior staff begin to "sign-off" as having performed procedures that they have not in fact performed, the consequences for the auditing profession will be catastrophic. The profession has yet to face this problem head-on. In 1991, when it was reported that Price Waterhouse in the UK had offered a discount of £900,000 to secure the audit of Prudential Assurance plc, the President of the Institute of Chartered Accountants in England and Wales (ICAEW) defended its action commenting that "we live in a world based on competition", and that "there was no evidence that low-balling — the practice of undercutting an incumbent firm's audit fee — has led to a firm doing a rotten job".[19] This may be wishful thinking of the most naïve kind.

The Declining Confidence in the Audit Product

At its most basic, the audit is a "credibility good" — it enhances the credibility of the financial statements prepared by management. To the extent that we can say that there is a demand for audit, that demand is predicated on three fundamental characteristics of the audit product. Firstly, demand rests on the belief among shareholders that a strict independence is maintained between the auditor and the management of the enterprise that is being audited. Secondly, demand rests on the belief among shareholders that a chosen auditor is acting in their interests and will inform them when those interests might be at risk. Thirdly, demand rests on the belief that an audit engagement is performed professionally and competently.

One reading of the criticisms levelled against the profession over the past 20 years (albeit not one that the profession cares to face up to), is that "purchasers" of audit services are less confident in these beliefs than before. The accusations of complicity with management, failure to "blow the whistle" and negligence are now being heard with an intensity and regularity never before known. That is not to say that such accusations were unheard of before now, but rather that such criticism has taken on a particular resonance in the 1990s. We deal with each of these criticisms in turn:

Independence

The allegation that auditors and client managements develop a cosy economic relationship that compromises auditor independence is a plausible one that has been around for a long time, and refuses to go away. Independence is a founding principle upon which the whole notion of audit relies — where it breaks down, the audit loses its meaning. The criticism of the profession essentially turns on what constitutes a breakdown of independence between auditor and client. Taking the general case, those who claim that the relationship between auditors and management has become too cosy argue that the effective performance of audit requires a level of detachment between the auditor and the management that is not evident in current practice. They point out that the typical auditor views the company's management as the "real" client, relegating in priority the shareholder, the creditor and public, for whom the statutory audit provisions were designed. Perhaps the specific criticism that is most commonly made is that auditors have been too compliant and even complicit in permitting management to report misleadingly. Even where creative accounting devices are permitted (or rather, not prohibited) under generally accepted accounting principles, accounts-users feel betrayed by auditors who condone such financial reporting practices.

It is alleged that this cosy relationship is fostered by audit firms to enable them to cross-sell a range of other business services to their clients, such as taxation advice, consulting advice, business-policy advice, accounting-systems design and internal-control design. In other words, the motivation is pure self-interest and at odds with the public-interest orientation traditionally understood to be a distinguishing feature of a profession. Among the most powerful advocates of this view are Abraham Briloff in the US and Austin Mitchell, MP, in the UK. In its most radical form, their argument concludes with the recommendation that audit firms be forbidden to engage in any activities other than audit — in effect, these commentators envisage a profession of public auditing that does simply that and no more.[20] This is the situation in France and other European countries.

Clearly, professional audit firms have a significant vested interest in ensuring that there will be no change to the status quo — which permits auditors to act in a variety of capacities for the companies they audit. The profession argues that the provision of advisory services is entirely compatible with the provision of independent audit, and that internal arrangements within the firms ("Chinese walls" and such like) ensure that conflicts of interest do not arise.

Critics find these assurances unconvincing, and are becoming increasingly vociferous in their criticism. They continue to campaign for the prohibition of auditors from offering services other than audit. The profession knows that these are powerful arguments that have a strong appeal to regulators from Washington to Brussels — but the profession cannot admit this openly. The profession realises that it must respond to these criticisms and it does so, usually in the form of increased self-regulation to indicate that, as a profession, it cares seriously about the issues that are being raised. However, it refuses to confront the central issue, and the critics refuse to remain quiet. Positions are so well entrenched that a kind of stalemate now exists.

If there is a middle ground here — and it is not at all clear that there is — it would seem to be in extending existing professional ethical guidance to prohibit firms from acting as auditor where they are also providing other services. While less radical than the "Briloff" proposal, it is more likely to gain the approval of the accounting/audit firms because it does not hamper their freedom to compete in the non-audit market and leaves the playing field reasonably level for all participants. However, if this is to be done, the guidelines must be drawn up very carefully in order to ensure that simple avoidance techniques, such as separate incorporation of audit and consulting services, are also prohibited.

User Expectations on Service

A second reason for the decline in confidence in the audit product is the existence of an expectations gap. This fine-sounding term refers to the notion that auditors are not delivering the service that users expect of them in relation to such matters as the detection of fraud and irregularities, warning of impending failure, and whistle-blowing.

The profession across the English-speaking world has responded to these concerns by establishing high-level commissions to investigate the source of the problem. In Ireland, in 1991, the ICAI established the Ryan Commission on Financial Reporting. Invariably, all the reports have found a high level of public and business misunderstanding of the auditor's role. In addition, each report has recommended ways of reducing the level of misunderstanding.

By and large, the reaction to these deliberations has been lukewarm. Company directors have been cautious in their welcome — acknowledging that something must be done, provided that it does not impose a new regulatory burden on business. Here in Ireland, the late Desmond Traynor, former chairman of one of the largest domestic companies, could scarcely hide his frustration with what he called growth business in "corporate governance". In his annual statement to shareholders, he commented:

> I must say personally I feel that the overall emphasis appears to be more on control and monitoring than on what should be the responsibility of directors, to ensure growth, profitability, adequate return on investment and increased value for shareholders. Nothing proposed will improve commercial judgment or increase productive drive. The inclusion of a statement on directors' responsibility in the annual report in no way changes directors' responsibility. They have always been responsible for all of the matters proposed for inclusion in a responsibility statement. The suggestion that the inclusion of such a statement would somehow sharpen the focus of directors would I believe be insulting to my colleagues.[21]

Auditors have been more receptive, but this may not be so surprising given that most reports have concluded that the expectations gap is primarily a problem of misunderstanding on the part of the accounts-users. Nor is it surprising when the composition of many these commissions is examined. For example, of the nine people appointed to the Irish Commission on Financial Reporting, eight were chartered accountants, and, although submissions were invited by the Group, no attempt was made to measure empirically the extent of a user-expectations gap in Ireland. It would seem that the president of the ICAI had already made up his mind on the matter. In an open letter to members, published before the Commission (which his Council had established) had even met, he said:

> All these changes and legislation mean fundamental change for our profession and in the manner in which we operate. But will it satisfy our critics? I doubt it. *We need positive and sustained action from our profession to answer the unjustified comment and unrealistic expectations often arising out of ignorance and misunderstanding of the financial statements which we prepare and audit* [author's italics].That is why our Council decided to establish a Commission of Enquiry into the expectations of users of published financial statements in the Republic of Ireland.[22]

The belief among professional auditors that the criticisms of them are rooted in public ignorance of their role has a long history. Over 100 years ago, in 1888, the president of the English Institute, in an address to London chartered accountants dealing with similar criticisms, opined:

> It appears to me to be the rooted opinion of an unenlightened public and of the ignorant portion of the press that an auditor must have failed in his duty if a fraud has been effected, whether it is eventually discovered or not.... The result of this ignorance has been that in cases where such frauds have been discovered, an immediate outcry is raised for the dismissal of the auditor. Without any careful investigation or enquiry into the facts, his utter ruin is decreed and the whole profession is attacked and menaced.

As an explanation, *public ignorance* can bear only some weight. Nobody denies that many professional activities, accounting and audit included, often give the impression of objectivity and rigour to activities that still call for subjective judgment. But frankly, it is asking too much to suggest that the current crisis in auditing is the result of widespread ignorance. Moreover, it can lead nowhere in terms of developing a solution to the problem. What is more worrying, it serves to divert attention from what may be real failings in the performance of this important public function. This matter is examined in more detail in Chapter 8 on Audit Failure — suffice to say here that unless the profession openly acknowledges that the *performance of audit* stands in need of as serious and thorough an examination as the *level of user understanding*, we are unlikely to make progress towards solving current difficulties. It is also likely that the level of public and managerial cynicism, with regard to the sincerity of the auditing profession in addressing the problem, will increase.

Allegations of Negligence

The third factor contributing to a decline in confidence is the belief that audits are being performed with less diligence than one might reasonably expect from professional experts. No doubt this belief is itself fuelled by the extent of litigation against auditors at the present time. A survey conducted by the American Institute of Certified Public Accountants showed that claims against public accounting firms, other than the Big Six, rose by 66 per cent between 1987 and 1991. Of those firms, 40 per cent could no longer afford insurance and are now "going bare". In November 1990, the seventh largest accounting firm in the US, Laventhol and Horwath, filed for bankruptcy. On a global scale, it is estimated that accounting firms worldwide face £20 billion in damage claims.[23]

In Britain and Ireland, litigation against auditors on the scale experienced in the United States has not occurred yet, though there is evidence that such a situation may be around the corner. In October 1993, the Irish practice of the former Ernst & Whinney reached an out-of-court settlement of $135 million (IR£77 million) in a negligence claim arising out of the spectacular collapse of the Insurance Corporation of Ireland, a large publicly quoted insurance company. Cases awaiting hearing include the action being taken by the administrator of PMPA against the company's former auditors, and by Aer Lingus, also against its former auditors.

Whether the increasing level of litigation against auditors can be taken as evidence of an increased level of negligence in audit work is itself questionable. The truth is that we really know very little about the quality of audit work: there has been little systematic research. The profession claims strenuously that the quality of audit work is rising all the time. In its eyes, the rise in litigation against auditors is not a sign of increasing negligence, but rather is a direct result of the level of insurance cover carried by auditors and the joint and several liability system in tort, which makes it possible for an injured party to seek redress against one party for the wrongs of others. Thus, what needs to be changed, according to the profession, is the law of tort or, alternatively, company law, which at present prohibits auditors from entering into arrangements with client companies to limit their liability exposure. The profession in Britain and Ireland is lobbying hard to persuade governments to adopt the latter policy.[24]

The auditors may protest too much: the public image they promote of the doomsday scenario facing auditors must be interpreted very carefully. Only a small proportion of what are widely reported as claims against auditors are related specifically to audit work. A recent analysis, carried out by the American Institute of Certified Public Accountants of claims against its professional-liability insurance plan, shows that taxation and accounting assignments account for almost 60 per cent (in value) of malpractice claims, audit assignments account for about 22 per cent, business and investment advice 14 percent and the balance, management consulting. Many of these pending actions have little foundation and are unlikely to result in successful action. Others will be settled or awarded amounts significantly lower than the legal claim suggests. Moreover, in listening to the persistent complaints of the profession, it is easy to lose sight of the very stiff judicial requirement that plaintiffs should be able to establish both that a duty of care is owed to them by the auditor and secondly that the auditor was, in fact, negligent. Thus, a great deal more analysis and public discussion of the real exposure of auditors needs to take place before legislators allow themselves to be persuaded by the current lobbies.

CONCLUSION

The audit industry is in a process of radical transformation. As competitive pressures increase, revenues are being driven down; as litigation for negligence increases, costs are rising; and as technology improves, unemployment begins to loom. At the same time, attempts to prise open the profession to public scrutiny are gaining momentum. For the first time, the very private relationship between auditor and client is being made public. As society begins to understand more fully the nature of this relationship, it begins to demand more of auditors. Whatever might be said about the practicality or constitutionality of the "whistle-blower" provisions contained in Section 153 of the 1995 Finance Bill (which were substantially watered down in the revised Section 172), there can be little doubt that the Minister for Finance, Mr Quinn, had the overwhelming support of the electorate in his attempt to redefine (for that is what it amounted to) the statutory audit function. As the debates over the role of auditing in our society reach some degree of closure, we can see the very essence of auditing changing before us. The remaining chapters in this book attempt to consider what the new landscape might look like.

2

Financial Reporting Reforms — Recent Developments in the UK

Ruth King
Loughborough University
Business School

[The] pain of change [is] ... resisted by all who are disadvantaged by it and only passively supported by those who benefit.

Sir Ron Dearing
FRC, *The State of Financial Reporting: A Review*
London: FRC, 1991: 7

INTRODUCTION

There is little doubt that financial reporting has undergone more extensive and more rapid change in the past 20 years than ever before. New accounting and financial devices have been developed, some more straightforwardly than others, and there has been considerable growth in the number and types of individuals becoming interested in publicly available accounting information, its preparation and presentation. Although there is some support for a free market in financial information, it is widely held that the provision of such information cannot be left solely to market forces. There is considerable inequality among its users in their exposure to and understanding of the complexities of modern business practice and methods of accounting for it. There is wider stakeholder interest in published financial reports than just that of the shareholders who effectively pay for them. Increasingly, calls for social responsibility and accountability are heard and are being taken note of by those responsible for regulating the publication of accounting information.

Against this background, and in the context of a growing raft of legislative and other reporting requirements, mounting criticism of the accounting profession and its part in financial reporting is apparent. Frequently, this results from a financial disaster where the losers naturally look for a culprit and the cry often heard is "Where were the auditors?" But they are, of course, only the last part of a complex story. Much has been written about the audit "expectations gap", the part it plays in the problems of financial reporting in the late twentieth century and its potential solutions.[1] It is axiomatic that such a thing exists, but it is clear too that this is only partly in respect of what auditors can and cannot (or do not) do. There is also a gap in respect of what accounting information is and is not, as regards the purpose of financial reporting and whether or not this is achievable. The debate is likely to continue for some time, not least because the accounting profession has yet to agree wholeheartedly on what are the desirable and achievable objectives for financial reporting. Indeed, perhaps the accounting profession is not the most appropriate interest group to be making this decision. At the extreme, the answer could be imposed by the legislature. However, British systems, not just in accounting, tend to avoid so far as is possible the detailed and rigid legal frameworks that exist in other parts of the world, and rely instead on "the profession" to regulate itself. This has naturally led to some accusations of the promotion of self-interest (for example, the compromise answer devised to keep company management (who pay the fees) content; the making of complex rules in order that only accountants can apply, understand and interpret them).

It is difficult when some such conflicts of interest undoubtedly exist to determine who should set accounting standards. A detailed legislative framework should have the benefits of objectivity and adequate powers of enforcement. However, it could prove to be excessively rigid, preventing the evolution of accounting practice. Furthermore, experts who wish to do so can soon devise ways of avoiding regulations by designing transactions that fall just outside the undesirable parameters. This has, amongst other things, fed the ongoing "substance over form" debate in the UK (for example, where does the distinction lie between transactions that are legitimate management tools and those that are devices designed to deceive?) and led to the issue of FRS 5, 'Accounting for the Substance of Transactions' (April 1994). A more appropriate interest group could be the users: they may know what they would ideally like from a set of accounts but may have inadequate expertise to determine what is feasible. Conversely, preparers of accounts have the expert knowledge (or can buy it), but as the balance of power essentially lies with this group, their dominance in determining the financial reporting framework would effectively revert to a "free-market" situation.

The UK system has evolved in a way that reflects its culture and history, whilst attempting to address the conflicting interests of various stakeholder groups — perhaps with differing degrees of success. The legislative framework is essentially that of outline guidance amplified by professional standards. It contrasts quite starkly with the detailed and rigid legislative framework that exists elsewhere in the world, for example in Germany and Japan.[2] The current UK approach is built on a desire for a framework of principles within which any transaction can be fitted, rather than detailed rules (the "cook-book") dictating the treatment for each type of item.

The remainder of this chapter is structured in five sections. The first addresses the development of the system in more detail and is followed by a description of the current regulatory framework. Then follow two selected areas of controversy, being the search for a conceptual framework and the "Big GAAP/Little GAAP" debate. Finally, there are some concluding remarks.

DEVELOPMENT OF THE SYSTEM

The regulation of financial reporting other than by law has been relatively recent and there have been considerable advances over the past 25 years. Prior to the recent changes involving the establishment of the Financial Reporting Council (FRC) in 1989, standard setting had been primarily the responsibility of the professional accounting bodies in the UK. In 1970, the Institute of Chartered Accountants in England and Wales (ICAEW) formed the Accounting Standards Steering Committee (ASSC), but until then, very little in the way of formal consideration of appropriate and consistent accounting practice existed. Several financial disasters of the late 1960s focused attention on the shortcomings of financial reporting as it then operated. Indeed, there is a view that if the ICAEW had not taken this lead in the process of change, further regulation may have been imposed on financial reporting by force of law. By 1976, all the institutes of the Consultative Committee of Accountancy Bodies (CCAB)[3] had joined, and the body was renamed the Accounting Standards Committee (ASC). During its life, the ASC issued 25 Statements of Standard Accounting Practice (SSAPs) (some having since been amended or superseded), most of which addressed specific areas of assets, liabilities or the measurement of profit where choice, uncertainty or controversy existed. Despite its success in narrowing the areas of difference in certain aspects of financial reporting, the ASC was subject to increasing criticism over its life, a fact which is illustrated by there having been three separate review committees — Watts (1978), McKinnon (1983) and Dearing (1987/8). Criticisms of the ASC and the shortcomings of the regulatory framework enacted by that body are well documented elsewhere.[4] It is perhaps worth noting, however, that it was not until the Dearing Committee reported that significant steps were taken to change the standard-setting process. There is an implication, in the words of Sir Ron Dearing (below), that the problems brought on by the recession, following hard on the heels of the confidence (perhaps over-confidence) of a period of boom, activated the reform process.

> The corporate confidence developed during the 1980s' boom, the associated readiness by banks to lend and by companies to borrow, the growth of innovative accounting practices (e.g. off balance sheet financing and the development of hybrid financial instruments) sometimes designed solely to avoid an increase in reported company gearing, coupled with a framework of accounting standards that was being outpaced by developments, have made the recession which followed a correspondingly more chastening experience for bankers, creditors and shareholders, as well as for financial reporting itself.[5]

The key recommendations of the Dearing Committee Report,[6] which reflected the findings of the earlier reviews, were as follows:

- *The Need for a Conceptual Framework*. Historically, the standard-setting process had been criticised as something of a "fire-fighting" activity, reacting in a seemingly ad hoc way to each new problem or controversy as it arose. As a result, some inconsistencies existed and, perhaps more importantly, new standards were required as new accounting and financial devices were invented. There was also a recognition that standards formulated too specifically can be susceptible where accounting innovations are concerned. Such problems can be minimised in the context of a framework within which each new problem can be considered and a solution devised. The Committee therefore recommended that further work should be undertaken on a conceptual framework, and that regardless of the outcome, new accounting standards should be accompanied by a statement explaining the principles behind them.

- *Quality as Opposed to Quantity*. Relatedly, the Committee considered that standards should not necessarily be issued to cover every eventuality, but that they should provide "quality" guidance on best practice, reducing available options and promoting compliance.

- *Exemptions from Standards on the Grounds of Size.* It has been noted that many standards are designed primarily for large public companies and the Committee recommended that the costs and benefits of compliance for small companies should be examined — the so-called Big GAAP/Little GAAP debate.

- *Applicability of Standards to Public-Sector Organisations.* The Committee concluded that it was equally valid to apply accounting standards to public as well as private-sector organisations.

- *Enforcement.* The Dearing Committee recommended that legal backing for standards should be increased so that enforcement was more effective. Two of the Committee's specific recommendations were enacted in the Companies Act, 1989, although two further recommendations were dropped. Those enacted were firstly the requirement that published accounts should include a statement of compliance with accounting standards, and secondly, most importantly, that there should be power for the courts to require the revision of accounts held not to show a true and fair view. This latter is a significant change in the law, giving standards a weight they previously lacked. It is a power which would be exercised, should the need arise, through the Financial Reporting Review Panel (FRRP) as described below.

- *Structure of the Standard-Setting Body.* The Dearing Committee recommended a restructuring of the standard-setting body, in part as a response to the criticism that the ASC failed to represent adequately the interests of most, except the members of the accounting profession. This structure is described in detail in the next section.

THE CURRENT REGULATORY STRUCTURE

The regulatory structure for the setting and enforcing accounting standards is show in Figure 1 below.

The Financial Reporting Council (FRC) was established in May 1990. Its subsidiary bodies are the Accounting Standards Board (ASB) (August 1990) and the Financial Reporting Review Panel (FRRP) (February 1991). The FRC is "the over-arching and facilitating body for the new arrangements, through which appointments to the operational bodies are made and financial support to them is channelled."[7] Its chairman and three deputy chairmen, drawn from accountancy, industry and commerce and the City, are appointed jointly by the Secretary of State for Trade and Industry and the Governor of the Bank of England. There are 24 further members and observers, and the chairmen of the ASB and the FRRP are ex-officio members. The FRC's funding is provided through sponsors, these being the CCAB, the Stock Exchange, the Banks, the Institutional Investors and the Department of Trade and Industry, together with the National Audit Office and the Northern Ireland Department of Industry and Commerce.

FIGURE 2.1: REGULATORY STRUCTURE FOR THE SETTING AND ENFORCING OF ACCOUNTING STANDARDS

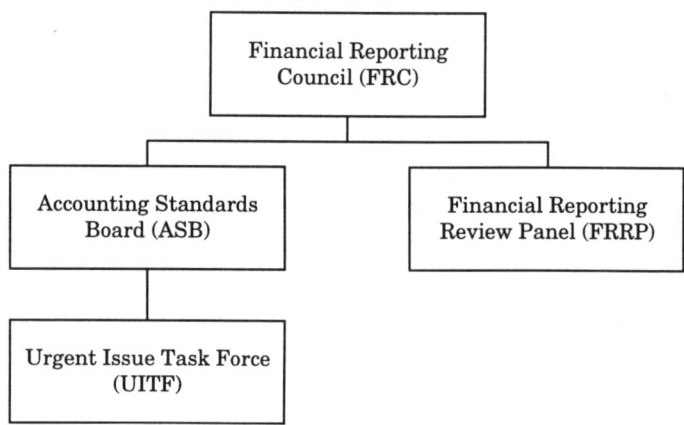

The ASB is constituted to make, issue and amend accounting standards. It comprises a full-time chairman and technical director and seven further voting members. It initially adopted the 22 extant standards developed by the ASC, and since that time has issued eight Financial Reporting Standards (FRSs), some of which replaced or amended existing SSAPs. It has also issued its draft Statement of Principles (in seven chapters), several discussion papers and exposure drafts for proposed standards. Aside from its membership composition, one of the key changes in its operation compared with that of the ASC is that the ASB is empowered to issue standards on a majority decision. The ASC required consent from all its constituents, making the standard-setting process potentially very lengthy, and one that might end with a compromise solution rather than that which was theoretically or technically the most sound. FRS 3, *Reporting Financial*

Performance, has been so issued, together with an explanation of the dissenter's opinion. This does not appear to have had any noticeable or adverse effect on the credibility of the ASB, although a good deal of discussion as to the efficacy of FRS 3 was generated at the time of its issue, in the general business press and in accountancy journals. Indeed, Sir David Tweedie noted in his first report on the operation of the ASB that although wider consultation with interested parties was taking place, "a consensus achieved at the expense of principle would not be worth having, and would quickly bring the system into disrepute".[8]

The main business of the FRRP is to look into material departures from accounting standards. Where it believes that the departure is not justified and that the accounts therefore do not show a true and fair view, it seeks to remedy the situation. It will first try persuasion, but if necessary it has power to take court action to set the matter right. Its remit covers public and large private companies, any others being dealt with by the Department of Trade and Industry. Each case is examined by a group of five or more individuals, drawn from the membership of the FRRP, which currently stands at 24. Up to the date of the annual report at the end of 1994, the FRRP had considered the accounts of 169 companies (and written to 240 other public companies which had failed to state that their accounts complied with generally accepted accounting standards, as newly required by the Companies Act, 1989). Fourteen cases were still under consideration at the end of 1994, the others having been concluded. Public statements were issued in 25 cases, indicating that some remedial action was required — most were remedied with the inclusion of additional notes in the following year's accounts, with only one requiring a full corrective note in the year in question. The FRRP has thus far remedied all defects without court action — its powers have therefore yet to be tested to the full. However, its Chairman, Edwin Glasgow, believes that "[The FRRP's] very presence has ... been instrumental in deterring the adoption of, or leading to the abandonment of, a number of doubtful accounting practices."[9]

The Urgent Issues Task Force (UITF) was created in March 1991 as a "sub-committee" of the ASB, "to assist it in areas where unsatisfactory or conflicting interpretations have developed or seem likely to develop."[10] (Some changes to its membership and streamlining of its operation took place in September 1995.) Each topic is dealt with by reaching a consensus of the membership, normally 11 of the 15 members voting with no more than two of those dissenting. The membership comprises up to seven senior representatives from the largest accounting firms, one member from a medium-sized accounting firm, four members from industry or commerce, and up to three further members chosen on a personal basis. This latter group currently includes one academic. The UITF has to date issued 13 Abstracts (interpretations of accounting standards) dealing with issues ranging from the thorny problem of goodwill, through the transfer of current assets, to fixed assets to lessee accounting for reverse premiums. (Some have been superseded by the issue of FRSs.) The ASB has said that compliance with UITF Abstracts will normally be required in order to give a true and fair view.

There also exist two bodies which act in an advisory capacity to the ASB: these are the Financial Sector and Other Specialised Industries Committee and the Public Sector and Not-for-profit Committee (formerly called the Public Sector Liaison Committee).

Many problematic issues have been and are being addressed by the FRC and its subsidiary bodies and there are many remaining to be dealt with. A review such as is contained in this chapter might cover a multitude of interesting and topical issues, but it would be impossible to do them all justice in the limited space available.[11] The next two sections therefore cover selected topics which reflect some of the author's particular interests. These are, firstly, the search for a conceptual framework for financial reporting and, secondly, the applicability of standards to "small" companies — the "Big GAAP/Little GAAP" debate.

THE SEARCH FOR A CONCEPTUAL FRAMEWORK

The idea of a conceptual framework for accounting is not a new one, although its exploration in the UK. has been relatively recent. The search for a theory of accounting has been more actively pursued in the US for a longer period, largely, it seems, because of the earlier acceptance there of business education as a legitimate academic pursuit.

One of the main purposes of developing a conceptual framework for financial accounting is to enable the development of standards on a consistent and coherent basis. Furthermore, it should facilitate the development of broad standards based on accepted principles, and so avoid the prescription of detailed legalistic rules. Such a framework should also counteract the "where does it say I can't do that?" approach and enable accountants to place new devices in the relevant part of the framework to decide upon their appropriate treatment, rather than having to develop new standards for each new device.

The first real attempt in the UK to develop a theoretical framework for financial reporting was a Discussion Paper issued by the ASSC in 1975, *The Corporate Report*.[12] In the same year, the Inflation Accounting Committee appointed by the government reported in the *Sandilands Report*.[13] Both of these reports took as their starting point the information needs of users, but the *Sandilands Report* focused specifically on the impact of inflation on the decision usefulness of financial reports. The next step was a consultative document issued by the ASC in 1978, entitled *Setting Accounting Standards*,[14] in which it recognised the criticisms made regarding the lack of a conceptual framework for the setting of its accounting standards. Although there appeared to be a certain reticence within the ASC, it commissioned a review from Professor Richard Macve, whose report, *A Conceptual Framework for Accounting and Financial Reporting: The Possibilities for an Agreed Structure*,[15] was published in 1981. The report identified conflicts of interest as a key factor in the standard-setting process, and in particular, the susceptibility of the process to politics and compromise. Regrettably, no immediate steps were taken to pursue this project in the UK.

In 1988, the Research Committee of the ICAS issued a discussion document entitled *Making Corporate Reports Valuable*.[16] This was the result of a project which considered the nature of financial reporting from first principles. Its proposals were somewhat radical but were designed to stimulate discussion rather than to provide definitive answers. The report concluded that, in addition to the problems caused by the lack of a consistent conceptual basis for the preparation of accounts, financial reports were deficient in a number of other respects. In summary, these were the preference for reporting of legal form at the expense of economic substance, the emphasis on profit rather than wealth and on cost rather than value. It proposed an alternative system of financial reporting which could reflect economic reality. The paper identified, as did previous reports, the various needs of different user groups, but went further in suggesting the range of information that could usefully be included in published reports. It also resurrected the discussion on alternatives or supplements to pure historic cost accounting.

The Solomons Report, commissioned by the Research Board of the ICAEW, and published in 1989, also addressed the issues surrounding the need for a conceptual framework for financial reporting.[17] Many aspects of this work can be seen reflected in the ASB's *Statement of Principles*, which is discussed below. In addition to the purposes and users of published accounts, Professor Solomons' report discussed their "elements" and the balance-sheet approach versus profit and loss account approach debate. In essence, the balance-sheet approach focuses on the determination of the amounts at which assets and liabilities are stated in the balance sheet; the profit (or loss) for the period is then necessarily the difference between the opening and closing balance-sheet totals. The alternative view is to take determination of revenues and expenses in the profit and loss account as the starting point; the balance-sheet amounts then naturally follow — for example, assets being expenditure not yet written off to the profit and loss account. Solomons concluded that the balance-sheet (or assets and liabilities) approach was the most sound; he considered that the profit and loss account approach was susceptible to income smoothing, and that in that scenario, the balance sheet was potentially seen as that which is left over, rather than as a statement of financial position. The report also discussed at some length the defects of the hybrid accounting basis used by many entities in the UK — that is, historic cost contaminated by, for example, irregular revaluations of fixed assets and by the use of the closing-rate method for the translation of some balances denominated in foreign currencies. Solomons advocated a model based on value to the business of its assets, and the maintenance of real financial capital. The ICAS and ICAEW subsequently published jointly *The Future Shape of Financial Reports*[18] which amalgamated the main proposals of *Making Corporate Reports Valuable* and *The Solomons Report*. However, the different approaches of the two original reports to the measurement of items in the financial statements were unresolved.[19]

The most recent attempt at the shaping of a framework within which future standards can be developed has been the issue by the ASB of its *Statement of Principles*. This comprises seven chapters on different aspects of the nature and purpose of financial reporting. The separate chapters have been gradually released in draft form and a combined Exposure Draft has recently been published.[20] The ASB has apparently made extensive use of the earlier research reports formulated in the UK, and the US Federal Accounting Standards Board's Conceptual Framework project.[21] The seven chapters are summarised and briefly discussed below.

Chapter 1 — The Objective of Financial Statements

This Chapter states that "the objective of financial statements is to provide information about the financial position, performance and financial adaptability of an enterprise that is useful to a wide range of users in making economic decisions". It concludes that although the many stakeholder groups have different needs, a set of financial statements that satisfies the needs of investors is likely to satisfy most of the needs of other user groups.

It is an essential preface to the development of a workable framework for financial reporting that its purpose is established. Unless it is known for what end and for whom accounts are prepared, there cannot be compiled information which can be expected to meet anyone's requirements satisfactorily. However, there are conflicting views as to the appropriateness of the "decision usefulness" approach adopted by the ASB as the objective of financial reporting. This broad view was first formalised in the UK in *The Corporate Report*, as noted above, and has appeared in most other explorations of the need for a conceptual framework for accounting and reporting. However, there is still a view, consistent with the origins of the legal framework of financial reporting, that it should be concerned primarily with stewardship and accountability — that is, the reporting by management to the owners of the equity.[22] The approach taken by the ASB extends the purpose beyond this fairly narrow definition. It recognises the belief that other parties have legitimate interests in financial aspects of business organisations. These parties can include banks and other lenders of capital, customers and suppliers, employee groups, government agencies and society at large. In the absence of (or as well as) other sources of information, these groups will make use of that which is publicly available, being the financial statements filed at Companies House. One option might be to include a "health warning" with published accounts, stating that they are prepared to meet shareholders' needs only, but there is an increasing willingness to recognise that companies and their accountants have responsibilities to the wider public. (There is of course the separate but related issue of the possible need for a "health warning" for shareholders' use of published accounts in recognition of the financial reporting expectations gap identified earlier, but it is beyond the scope of this chapter to investigate the expectations gaps.)

There are cogent arguments in favour of both the narrow accountability view and the wider decision-usefulness view. However, whichever is subscribed to, the information included in financial reports must be of use, and it is the question "What makes accounting information useful?" that the second chapter sets out to answer.

Chapter 2 — Qualitative Characteristics of Financial Information

Once over the materiality threshold, Chapter 2 identifies relevance and reliability as the two key characteristics possessed by information which is useful for decision-making, noting that more of one may lead to less of the other in both individual items or collated sets of information. For example, historic cost information on amounts relating to land and buildings may be reliable, but not particularly useful. In contrast, information on valuation of land and buildings may be more useful but is less reliable. The chapter goes on to develop further levels of the attributes of usefulness, and presents them diagramatically. Taken on its own, this is a relatively uncontroversial chapter and is consistent with most previous work on conceptual frameworks.

Chapter 3 — The Elements of Financial Statements

The ASB has defined seven component parts of financial information, which it calls elements. These are assets, liabilities, equity, gains, losses, contributions from owners and distributions to owners. Fundamentally, it argues that all aspects of the financial statements stem from the first two, that is the determination of assets and liabilities. It is therefore essential that the framework contain workable definitions and "rules" for their recognition and measurement. This is the chapter which essentially sets out the ASB's view, consistent with the position adopted by Solomons and outlined above, that the key to the financial statements is the determination of balance-sheet amounts. The profit (or loss) for the period will follow as the difference between opening and closing balance sheets (adjusted for injections of capital). The alternative, which takes determination of revenues and expenses in the profit and loss account as the starting point, is consistent with the view that any business entity is essentially undertaking a series of transactions, which needs to be summarised into a set of financial statements for periodic reporting purposes. In contrast, the former view embraces the possibility that a balance sheet might represent some view of an entity's value. Although there is evidence that many users of accounting information are under this misapprehension, the balance sheet patently does not currently do this. It will take a fundamental rethink of the way in which accounts are prepared to achieve this result. However, it is perhaps with this in mind that the ASB has developed Chapter 5 of the Statement of Principles on measurement, discussed below, and has issued a related Discussion Paper on valuation.

Chapter 4 — Recognition of Items in Financial Statements

Three criteria for recognition are identified. These are that the item meets the definition of an element as set out in Chapter 3; that a change in assets or liabilities has occurred; and that the item can be reliably measured. It again draws on definitions and concepts identified in the earlier research noted above — for example, in the Solomons Report.

Chapter 5 — Measurement in Financial Statements

The arguments surrounding the use of different bases for measurement are debated in this chapter. The ASB acknowledges the problem in dealing with measurement bases other than historic cost, but concludes that a principle of "value to the business" could be applied in preparing accounting information. The chapter details the way in which such a value might be arrived at for both assets and liabilities. It also addresses alternative capital maintenance concepts. There is further exploration of these issues in the ASB's Discussion Paper, *The Role of Valuation in Financial Reporting*. The paper concludes that the current hybrid accounting basis (historic cost modified by ad hoc revaluations of certain assets) is unsatisfactory, and it describes three alternative solutions. These are a return to purely historic cost accounting, a move to a current value system, or a modified historic cost basis which addresses the existing anomalies. It is the last of these which appears to be preferred by the ASB, using the "value to the business" principles noted above. These proposals are a radical departure from the historic cost basis of financial reporting which has been used in the UK until now. As noted earlier, previous attempts to move away from this basis have not been successful — for example, the attempt to account for the effects of inflation in the 1970s and early 1980s, and the proposals put forward by ICAS in *Making Corporate Reports Valuable*. However, the ASB seems intent on raising alternative bases for discussion, as witnessed by the very recent issue of its Discussion Paper on the treatment of taxation. This proposes that companies should make full provision for deferred tax in company accounts, but should discount the amount shown in the balance sheet — a considerable departure from the historic cost basis of accounting.[23]

Chapter 6 — Presentation of Financial Information

The main statements to be contained in a set of financial statements are described in Chapter 6. The new feature here is the Statement of Total Recognised Gains and Losses, which is prescribed as an additional primary statement by FRS 3. This statement is an attempt to bring movements on reserves to a more prominent position in the financial statements, rather than their being, as some felt had hitherto been the case, "hidden" near the end of the notes to the accounts. This has generally been welcomed as a move against "reserve accounting" and possible exploitation of certain options in the existing framework to take some profits and losses straight to reserves, in particular where this can lead to inconsistent treatment of what are "related" transactions (for example, in the treatment of exchange differences on translation of some foreign currency amounts).[24]

Chapter 7 — The Reporting Entity

This last chapter deals with the types of entity which should prepare and publish financial information. It appears to broaden the scope to include not only those organisations for which there is a legal requirement to account to providers of capital for the utilisation of their resources, but also those with obligations to broader groups of stakeholders who would otherwise not have access to financial information. It does, however, state that such obligations only arise where the benefits of providing the information outweigh the costs of its preparation. This chapter seems to be consistent with the "Big GAAP/Little GAAP" debate (discussed in the next section) and with the ASB's views on the application of standards to public-sector bodies. The chapter concludes by addressing the preparation of group accounts and the treatment of associates and joint ventures.

The search for a conceptual framework in the UK has been considerably progressed by publication of the ASB's draft *Statement of Principles*. Whilst there is some disagreement over elements of its detail, and in particular regarding the proposals on valuation, it has been generally welcomed.

The next section deals in further detail with the applicability of standards to "smaller" companies.

BIG GAAP/LITTLE GAAP

Relief of the statutory and other regulatory burdens on smaller companies has long been the subject of debate. The government and other bodies have acknowledged this as a concern for some time, and although there have been several studies around the world[25], there has in practice been relatively little to alleviate the situation in the UK, particularly in respect of financial reporting requirements.

As regards published accounts, the Companies Act, 1985, allows most small and medium-sized companies to file abbreviated accounts on public record at Companies House. It should be noted, however, that if a company chooses to take up this option, it faces an *increase* rather than decrease in its administrative burden. Despite a further Statutory Instrument of November 1992 (SI 1992/2452) which introduced a small number of exemptions in relation to the statutory disclosures demanded, all companies are still required to produce a full set of statutory accounts for their shareholders. Note also that the Statutory Instrument is drawn up on a negative basis, rather than as an inclusive list — that is, it is a catalogue of things which need *not* be disclosed. The preparer of the accounts still needs to know what the full requirements are before the non-obligatory items can be omitted.

In his budget of November 1993, the then Chancellor, Kenneth Clarke, announced that small companies would be exempt from audit. This possibility had been raised by a working party of the Auditing Practices Committee (APC) set up in 1977, but no further action resulted at that time, and the timing of the announcement took many by surprise. The Chancellor specifically stated that those companies with a turnover of less than £90,000 and net assets of less than £1.4 million would no longer be required to be audited, while those with a turnover of between £90,000 and £350,000 and assets no greater than £1.4 million would require an "independent accountant's report" (now known as a "compilation report") rather than a full audit. It was estimated that some 300,000 companies (about 21 per cent of all limited companies) would consequently be exempted from audit, and a further 200,000 (around 14 per cent) would require only the compilation report. Note, however, that the size limits for these regulations are not the same as those of small and medium-sized companies for the purposes of filing abbreviated accounts.

With regard to the applicability of accounting standards, at present there are exemptions on the grounds of size written into three standards. The first two of these, created under the régime of the ASC, are SSAP 13 (Revised), *Accounting for Research and Development* (mainly as regards profit and loss account disclosure requirements), and SSAP 25, *Segmental Reporting*. Exempted companies can, in these cases, be quite large, since they are defined in those standards as entities which are up to 10 times bigger than the limit for "medium-sized" companies as defined by the Companies Act, 1985. This currently embraces companies with a turnover of up to £112 million and total assets of up to £56 million! The ASB subsequently exempted "small" companies from compliance with the requirements of FRS 1, *Cash Flow Statements*. There, the ASB uses the Companies Act, 1985 definition of "small". So, despite the fact that only three standards are thus far specifically affected, there appears to exist a lack of clarity in the thinking behind the applicability of standards to "small" companies.

One could therefore ask whether or not these efforts have actually helped. It seems that regulations designed to relieve the burden simply add to the complexity of financial reporting: the business person needs to know all the "rules" in order to sort out which aspects of which regulations apply to their organisation.

How, then, could this problem be tackled in respect of accounting standards? Three possible positions could be adopted. The first is that since there is an underlying assumption that all accounts which show a true and fair view must apply generally accepted accounting standards,[26] there can be no exemptions from their requirements. The second is that where standards are unduly burdensome (that is, the costs of application outweigh the benefits), small companies could or should be excluded from their requirements. The third position argues that since small companies present what is a unique set of characteristics, a separate set of standards should be developed for them. Currently, only the Australian and New Zealand professions are exploring this latter option, although it is one discussed by Davies et al.[27]

The ASB recognised the "Big GAAP/Little GAAP" debate as one of some importance early in its life, and, at its behest, a CCAB Working Party on the subject was established. It has recently published its report exploring the issue of exemptions from standards on the grounds of size or relative lack of public interest.[28] The phrase

Financial Reporting Reforms — Recent Developments in the UK 35

"relative lack of public interest" is a comparatively new one in the debate, which has in the main centred on "small" companies. However, the phrase seems to recognise that even in small companies there are wider stakeholder interests which may need to be catered for, and that this extra dimension should be recognised in the discussions.

The principle arguments in the UK centre on the first two of the options described above — the "true and fair view" position and the cost/benefit argument. However, it is worth exploring here the more radical approach put forward by, for example, Davies et al.[29] They argue that the dilemma should start with a consideration of the objectives of financial reporting — effectively a first principles approach. In other words, it is not a question of whether standards impose a burden on companies, but rather whether those reporting standards are of any value for decision-making purposes. Davies et al. posit that some standards are necessary, but that the existing framework does not necessarily produce information which is of use for decision-making purposes. They further argue that "small" companies, with a limited number of members all of whom are also managers, should be able to incorporate under a different regulatory structure of limited liability, and that subsequently a different financial reporting framework could be developed to suit their needs better. The users of the financial statements of "small" companies are likely to be different in many respects from those of large plc's — the information which is of use to them is different, and it therefore seems sensible to propose a different reporting framework.

Fundamentally, the need for accountability to the owners from those with stewardship disappears when these persons are one and the same. This seems to be the position being explored by the accounting professions in Australia and New Zealand. There is also some consistency of this proposal with the stance adopted in Germany and other countries where the banks and other stakeholders have a closer relationship with what are essentially privately owned business entities, and have more of a long-term interest in their survival. However, the draw-back of this argument is the need to provide for any legitimate interests of wider stakeholder groups who have no other means of access to financial information and whose needs will be different from those of the owner/manager group. There may be, as the terms of reference of the Working Party suggest, a *relative* lack of public interest in such entities, but there is, theoretically at least, a range of possible stakeholders whose interests might not be catered for in this scenario. This could include employees, suppliers, the local community, and perhaps social or environmental "pressure groups".

In a way, it seems strange that the CCAB Working Party does not appear to have more explicitly adopted this decision-usefulness approach, since this is what the ASB's draft Statement of Principles (SOP) sets out in its first and second chapters. If the users and the information that is useful to them are different for "small" companies, then surely this should be recognised in the standard-setting framework as a matter of principle. The Working Party does address user groups and their requirements, and it acknowledges that the user groups for the accounts of "smaller" companies are likely to be different in some respects from those of larger companies, particularly plcs. It notes that problems will exist because at least some of these groups are likely to have conflicting needs and interests. But despite identifying a number of distinctive characteristics regarding the purpose and users of the financial statements of "small" companies, this "first principles" approach to the problem was not taken explicitly.

The Working Party points out that there is a recognition in the UK that, in some cases, publicly available information is not expected to give a true and fair view. Specifically, this applies to the abbreviated accounts of small and medium-sized companies filed under the provisions of the Companies Act, 1985, and which are generally not required to make the disclosures that would only be required for compliance with accounting standards. In other words, if these accounts are not required to show a true and fair view, there is no reason why they should necessarily comply with all accounting standards. What this argument apparently fails to consider is that *all* companies are required to prepare accounts which show a true and fair view for their shareholders (even though "small" companies are not required to file them on public record), and that legal opinion holds that the courts would look to compliance with accounting standards as prima facie evidence of truth and fairness.[30] This argument against the "true and fair" justification for applying all standards to small companies is therefore to some extent a spurious one under current legislation. Furthermore, a case could be made that there is a failure even under the existing framework to provide for the legitimate interests of wider stakeholder groups, even though there may be relatively less public interest in smaller companies than in larger ones.

As regards the cost/benefit argument, the ASB explicitly states in its "Aims" that its standards should take account of the balance of expected benefits against expected costs. In this, they include the applicability of standards to smaller companies. The costs can include not only the gathering, processing and auditing of data in an appropriate form, but also a possible loss of competitive advantage. It could be argued that the burden of compliance is a reasonable cost of limited liability. Further, it is difficult to envisage how such costs and, more particularly, the benefits, might appropriately be measured, especially since those benefits experienced chiefly by the wider stakeholder groups (public-interest groups) may be long term and perhaps intangible. However, allied with this, the Working Party identifies complexity as a problem, perhaps a disbenefit. Much of the requirement of the regulatory framework relates to disclosure and leads to what may be considered complex explanatory notes to the published accounts. It may be difficult for a user to identify what is important. Such problems are of course not unique to "small" companies. However, many recent standards have been driven by the needs of, and the uses and abuses by, large and complex organisations, and may be inapplicable to smaller entities. The Working Party further argues that comparability (with the accounts of other companies) may be less important in the smaller company provided that the user is able to understand what is going on. This implies a potential trade-off of comparability for lack of complexity and ease of comprehension.

The CCAB Working Party concluded that, in general, the costs imposed by compliance with standards outweighed the benefits obtained for less complex organisations. It is not clear how the costs and benefits were measured and compared in arriving at this conclusion. There is also some question of inconsistency with the findings of a 1988 study conducted by Carsberg for the ASC[31]. That study found that there was not a major concern amongst small companies regarding any burden of compliance, although Carsberg suggested that this might have been because of a lack of awareness. It could also be argued that the complexity of financial reporting has perhaps increased since the date of that report. In fact, the ASC and the ASB did subsequently exempt some companies from aspects of three standards, on the grounds of size, as noted above. Nevertheless, the Working Party's conclusion accords with the desires of the ASB and what is generally perceived to be the view of some "small" business managers and advisers.

Having reached the conclusion that full compliance is unnecessary for "less complex" organisations, the questions of the extent of exemption and the definition of "less complex" need to be addressed. Taking complexity first, it is axiomatic that any cut-off point will essentially be arbitrary. Complexity is abstract, and the perception of its level varies with an individual's experience and knowledge. It means different things to different people. The Working Party therefore concluded that size was a practical and adequate proxy for complexity. Notwithstanding the fact that some small organisations are complex and some large ones essentially straightforward, they selected the Companies Act definitions of "small". As regards requirements for compliance, the Working Party distinguishes four possible approaches:[32]

- "Top down" — whereby exemptions would be made for individual standards as necessary, or less complex requirements substituted. This would involve the least change to the existing situation.

- "Bottom up" — where core standards would apply to all entities, and others only to non-exempt entities. This option would require reconsideration of existing standards and a continuing deliberation, although the Working Party indicates that there should be an initial presumption of exemption.

- Complete exemption — all small companies would be exempt from applying all standards. This seems inappropriate in the current legislative framework.

- Special standards — a completely new set of standards would be designed specifically for small companies. This approach goes part way towards the recognition of a different framework; however, it could difficult to apply in isolation — that is, without a complete rethink of the regulatory framework for such businesses.

The Working Party favours the bottom-up approach on the grounds that this gives standard setters more opportunity to provide users with what they need. They hold that the requirements of Company Law are sufficient in most cases to provide useful published accounts without the need for full compliance with accounting standards. Where necessary 'a more straightforward treatment, accompanied by appropriate explanation, may be all that is required' to produce appropriate benefit for an appropriate cost.[33]

As a final thought, the Working Party also recommends the provision of a management commentary to provide further useful information. This seems to parallel the Operating and Financial Review recommended by the ASB as best practice for bigger companies.[34] However, problems of commercial confidentiality would seem to cast considerable doubt on the feasibility of this suggestion. The Companies Act already requires a review of the year and expectations for the future in the Directors' Report, but in most cases this contains the briefest and blandest of statements. It is difficult to envisage improvements of any magnitude.

In some ways it does seem that an opportunity may have been lost. A fundamental examination of the distinctive characteristics of different types of corporate structure and the appropriateness of the same reporting framework for all could have been undertaken alongside work on a conceptual framework. This is the more so since the ASB is considering a fundamental departure from another aspect with which financial reporting is imbued, namely the historic cost basis. The CCAB Working Party seems to have approached the problem initially from the perspective of user needs, but has not grasped the principal issue: it has not started with a clean sheet for these "small" or "less complex" companies, or those with a lower degree of public interest. Indeed, the Working Party concludes that it is not possible to look at the presence of public interest in individual cases, nor the needs of potential users, and argues that size is a more objective criterion for exemptions. Any relief of the regulatory burden, therefore, seems destined to remain firmly tied to the existing structure.

CONCLUSION

So how is the new system doing? There is no doubt that the revised structure under the FRC has addressed several of the thorny issues which have been troubling the world of financial reporting for a number of years. A great deal has changed in a relatively short time. Broadly speaking, the system seems to have more credibility, even though the legal powers of the FRRP have yet to be tested in the courts. Further, the changes introduced by the ASB have been generally welcomed, despite continuing debates over various aspects of their detail. The ASB does recognise that standards may need to be reviewed, and indeed is currently doing so with FRS 1, *Cash Flow Statements*.

Perhaps the most controversial area for debate in the near future will be the basis of balance-sheet valuation for financial reporting. In this respect, the ASC seems to be moving more towards what is perceived by the "non-accounting" users of accounts as "useful information", although most other areas of the world are still rooted in historic cost as the basis of accounting. This may highlight a further issue for serious consideration, namely the extent to which international harmonisation is necessary, desirable and achievable. The ASB seems to recognise merits in international harmonisation of accounting practice.[35] However, harmonisation is an area fraught with difficulty, and there are already considerable barriers to its success. It is axiomatic that the current regulatory environment in the UK is strongly coloured by its history and culture and will continue to be so. Other influences have been felt, but the remaining structure is essentially rooted in the UK's past. The most startling contrast is perhaps between those countries with a detailed legislative framework (for example, Germany, Japan) and those which rely on a smaller legal structure, amplified by non-statutory regulations (the Anglo-American influence). Given the continuing debates within the UK, let alone the international differences, harmonisation must be a very long-term objective.

3

Financial Reporting Reforms — An Irish Perspective

Paul O'Connor
Price Waterhouse

INTRODUCTION

Financial reporting in Ireland is in the throes of change. Company financial reports from even 20 years ago are almost unrecognisable when compared with those presented today. Much of the change that has occurred has been in response to criticism about the limitations of financial statements. These criticisms came mainly from the various users of financial statements such as investors, financial analysts and employee groups.

The late 1980s saw the criticisms reach a new level of intensity as the general economic downturn was accompanied by an increase in the number of corporate failures. Companies' financial statements were criticised for not displaying enough information, or for giving insufficient prominence to certain information. Users criticised a process which enabled potentially significant information to be relegated to footnotes, rather than appearing in the primary statements. In the case of the UK company Polly Peck, currency translation losses suffered on its "soft" currency investments were accounted for as reserve movements while the income from those investments was included in the profit and loss account, thus artificially inflating earnings per share (EPS). Users were unimpressed with the accountancy profession's response to these criticisms, which suggested that it is impossible to reflect the financial affairs of complex entities in one page and that the financial statements should be read in their entirety.

Financial statements were criticised also for failing to provide adequate information to enable users to anticipate likely future trends, concentrating as they do on historical information. What help, it was asked, was a balance sheet in assessing the value of an entity's assets when it contained historical values which often dated from 20 or more years prior to the balance-sheet date? The profession's abortive attempts to deal with *current values* in financial statements were instanced as indicative of its inability to address the inherent defects in historical cost accounting. In the same context, users failed to understand how a company could produce financial statements, showing it to be in a healthy profitable position, yet collapse without warning a year later. The public surprise in Ireland attendant upon the collapse of the Cambridge Leasing Group in 1993 is a case in point.

Some of the criticism of the financial reporting process was directed at Accounting Standards, those statements of best practice which set out the means by which the figures in the financial statements should be determined. Accounting standards were criticised for allowing too much flexibility in the range of options — permitting companies to influence their reported results through judicious selection. Where options existed, users recognised that preparers tended to gravitate towards the option which produced the best result, notwithstanding its appropriateness. For example, the fiasco surrounding the classification of extraordinary and exceptional items permitted Irish Press plc in its 1989 accounts to post EPS of £2.08 (1988; EPS loss £1.65) despite incurring an operating loss for the period of £1.75 million. Moreover, accounting standards had no legal status and users criticised the inability of the accounting profession to enforce compliance on directors who ultimately are responsible for preparing financial statements.

Users were also unhappy about the absence of guidance or standardisation on many other controversial financial reporting matters. In these instances it seemed that preparers could be as "creative" as they liked, without restraint. This appeared to stem from the lack of an overall conceptual framework for accounting to which preparers and users could turn in instances of doubt. In areas such as income recognition, little definitive guidance was provided. Faced with complex transactions often spanning several years, users were presented with a wide range of alternative accounting treatments.

One area singled out for special criticism was *acquisition accounting*. The flaws in acquisition accounting became all the more visible with the increase in the number of company takeovers during the mid-1980s. Under the extant acquisition accounting rules, the acquirer could write down the asset values of an acquired entity and account for these write-downs through reserve movements (as opposed to taking them through profit and loss account) by way of goodwill write-off. Any subsequent profits on disposal of those assets would of course be accounted for through the profit and loss account in future years, again artificially inflating subsequent years' EPS.[1] The motivation was clear; the acquiring company, often paying for the acquisition with its own share capital (paper), needed a continual profit growth to support its share price and the attractiveness of its offer. Excessive asset write-downs charged to reserves could only help in this regard. The ability to engage in this form of income manipulation has now been greatly curtailed by the recently issued FRS 6: *Fair Values in Acquisition Accounting*.

Brand accounting, which openly contravened the extant accounting standards, was another area where differing treatments prevailed. Proponents of brand accounting argued that brands were both tangible and measurable and should therefore appear on company balance sheets. Groups faced with weak balance sheets and low net-asset values were attracted by the notion of boosting their net assets through brand accounting. A key problem with brand accounting was the huge variation in approaches which companies adopted because of the absence of regulatory guidance.

The auditing profession, considered by some to be the last safeguard provided to the investing public, also came in for criticism. Users complained that financial statements containing material misstatements bore audit opinions deeming them to be "true and fair". Users also failed to understand how serious weaknesses in controls, often facilitating fraudulent activity, could go undetected by the audit.

All of these criticisms amounted to a serious attack on the credibility of the financial reporting process. More worrying for the profession, the "flaws" in the financial reporting process, and the companies that abused them, became the subject of media mockery. A series of books cataloguing the accounting machinations of large companies also appeared on the market — see for example Terry Smith's *Accounting for Growth*, variously described as the DIY guide to the manipulation of financial results, or the health warning to investors, depending on one's perspective.[2] Curiously, financial reporting rarely attracts the same attention or criticism in the Irish financial press as it does in the UK and the US. Many of our financial journalists seem happy to reprint the blurb from the public relations consultants uncritically.

NEW STRUCTURES FOR SETTING ACCOUNTING STANDARDS

The accounting profession in these islands showed a willingness to tackle the criticisms levied at financial reporting with the establishment in 1990 of the Dearing Committee. This independent committee was set up to investigate and make recommendations on the structures for the development and enforcement of accounting standards.

Traditionally, the process for setting accounting standards in the United Kingdom and Ireland had been the preserve of the accounting profession. Until 1990 the umbrella body of the accountancy bodies, the Consultative Committee of Accountancy Bodies (CCAB), through its Accounting Standards Committee (ASC), was responsible for setting accounting standards. In theory, these standards, once established were to be enforced by the respective professional bodies.

The report of the Dearing Committee[3] was published in 1991 and it recommended significant changes to the standard setting process including:

- Creating an independent body — the *Financial Reporting Council*, with wide representation from all parties interested in financial reporting, to monitor the standard-setting process

- Creating a separate standard-setting body, with the authority to issue standards in its own right — the Accounting Standards Board (ASB)

- Enacting legislation to back the ASB standards

- Creating a watchdog — the *Financial Reporting Review Panel* — to monitor companies' compliance with accounting standards and to compel companies to comply.

The United Kingdom Government endorsed the recommendations of the Dearing Committee and implemented the necessary changes in United Kingdom company law. The accounting standards issued by the ASB are now given statutory backing under the United Kingdom Companies Acts. Directors must state in their report whether they have complied with all accounting standards in preparing financial statements and must give reasons for any material departures. The Financial Reporting Review Panel is legally empowered to compel directors of companies who present defective accounts to rectify them. In certain cases, the directors who approved the defective accounts may be made personally liable for the costs of preparing and distributing revised accounts. Moreover, where the Review Panel identifies a defect in a company's accounts, which has not been referred to in the auditor's report, the Panel will draw this fact to the attention of the auditor's professional body for investigation and possible disciplinary action. The message from the UK is clear: in cases of the issue of defective accounts, all of the relevant parties will be asked to account for their actions.

In addition to providing statutory support for the new régime, the United Kingdom Government agreed to contribute a share of the required funding, which is considerably more than required previously. The ASB has a full-time executive, unlike its predecessor; and the Financial Reporting Review Panel, in addition to funding for its ongoing activities, has been endowed with a substantial "war-chest" to fund any court action necessary to compel directors to amend defective financial statements.

The Irish Government was less willing to endorse the recommendations of the Dearing Committee with financial and legislative support. Notwithstanding this lack of support, the Irish Government indicated a desire to maintain the alignment of accounting standards in the Republic of Ireland with those in the United Kingdom. It was agreed that accounting standards in this country would continue to be promulgated by the Institute of Chartered Accountants in Ireland (ICAI). These standards would be the Financial Reporting Standards devised by the ASB, as amended for the purpose of their application in the Republic of Ireland. They would lack the legal backing that accounting standards in the United Kingdom enjoyed. Moreover, the Financial Reporting Review Panel would not operate in the Republic of Ireland.

To date, the ASB has issued seven Financial Reporting Standards. Each of these standards deals with an area about which there had previously been considerable criticism. The ASB has also issued drafts of six of the seven chapters of a proposed Statement of Principles, a high-level document setting out a conceptual framework for financial reporting. It is hoped that this framework will provide the necessary guidance in situations where no specific guidance exists.

In addition to setting accounting standards, the ASB, through its sub-committee, the Urgent Issues Task Force (UITF), issues consensus pronouncements on areas where unsatisfactory or conflicting interpretations of standards and law have developed, or seem likely to develop. It also considers areas where no guidance yet exists but is judged necessary. The UITF has issued 12 consensus pronouncements to date.

The Financial Reporting Review Panel has also been active. Since its creation, it has reviewed the accounts of a number of companies and published the results of those reviews. When the Panel was established, it was suggested that the very threat of legal action, and the publicity attaching to it would be sufficient to compel compliance. This comment has proven to be well-founded.

Among the more notable companies whose accounts have caused some controversy are Trafalgar House and the Royal Bank of Scotland. In the case of Trafalgar House, the Review Panel disagreed with the treatment of property write-downs charged to reserves in the 1991 accounts of the company and also with the treatment of advance corporation tax. The directors of Trafalgar House agreed to restate the comparative figures in its 1992 accounts, treating the property write-down as a charge to profit.

In the case of the Royal Bank of Scotland, the Panel was dissatisfied with the Bank's capitalisation of expenses incurred in the establishment of its direct banking operation. These expenses, charged in prior years, were restated and capitalised in the 1992 accounts, with a resultant gain in the profit and loss account following the reinstatement. As with the Trafalgar House case, the directors agreed to restate the comparative figures in the 1993 financial statements. So far, the Panel has yet to take a legal action against a company to secure rectification of defective accounts, although in the Trafalgar House case legal proceedings had been initiated when the directors reluctantly accepted the Panel's findings. In most cases, the Panel has been satisfied with the level of publicity that has been accorded to its pronouncements, and, accordingly, directors have not been requested (or legally compelled) to provide additional information or revised financial statements.

Each of the actions undertaken by the Panel has further enhanced its reputation and its moral authority. It has quickly become a recognised force in the financial reporting process in the United Kingdom. In drawing up accounts, companies do appear to heed the threat of action by the Panel, and that threat has given added backbone to accounting standards. Companies are also aware of the reaction of share prices in response to announcements from the Panel. The announcement that the Panel has taken issue with a company's financial statements has often resulted in a sharp decline in share price.

Progress under the new régime has been considerable. The accounting standards and other guidance issued by the ASB, while not completely free from criticism, have been broadly welcomed in both the UK and the Republic of Ireland (where they have been promulgated by the ICAI). In fairness, the ASB probably deserved a honeymoon period as it tackled the obvious accounting abuses of cash-flows, EPS and acquisition accounting. Recently, however, some dissent has begun to surface. The view from some quarters is that by focusing on the balance sheet, with the implicit assumption that profit is a measure of the difference between two balance sheets, the ASB has been putting undue emphasis on the balance sheets to the detriment of the profit and loss account. In tackling the profit and loss account, the ASB appears to have focused on presentation rather than measurement. A further cause for concern has been the delay in putting in place the *Statement of Principles*, the conceptual framework underlying accounting standards. Many see this as crucial in providing support to existing standards, and guidance where standards do not exist. One can only hope that the ASB, as is its stated intention, takes time out from its standard-issuing crusade to complete the *Statement of Principles* in the near future. Other concerns relate to the length of standards that have veered from being principle-based to being highly prescriptive. An over-regulated profession with little scope for professional judgment is in no-one's interests.

The UITF pronouncements have also faced some criticism, principally as a result of the lack of consultation prior to their issue. The ASB has accepted this criticism and has already amended its procedures for issuing UITF consensus pronouncements to include a consultation period.

The position in Ireland has been somewhat different, primarily because of the absence of legal backing for accounting standards. Although no company has taken a stand against the ASB standards, as promulgated in Ireland by the ICAI, it is clear that these standards do not enjoy the same level of authority as is provided by the United Kingdom régime. The fear that the Review Panel can evoke in "would-be miscreant directors" does not exist in this country.

THE IRISH PROFESSION'S RESPONSE:

The Commission of Enquiry into the Expectations of Users of Published Financial Statements (The Ryan Commission)

The inaction of the Irish Government in providing a statutory framework for accounting standards as outlined in the Dearing Report prompted the ICAI to establish an independent Commission, under the chairmanship of Professor Louden Ryan, to enquire into the extent to which published accounts of Irish companies met users' expectations. The terms of reference of the "Ryan Commission" covered not only financial reporting standards, but extended to the entire financial reporting process. The Ryan Commission published its report in January 1992.[4]

Perhaps the most substantial recommendations in the report deal with the development of financial reporting standards and their enforcement. The Ryan Commission had no doubt that the same financial reporting standards should apply in the Republic of Ireland as in the UK, and that those standards should be devised by the ASB. It recommended that, as is the case in the UK, these standards be recognised in law, and that all companies be required to state that the accounts had been drawn up in compliance with them. It further recommended that there should be an enforcement mechanism along lines similar to the UK Financial Reporting Review Panel. The Commission also recommended that in the event that legal backing was not forthcoming, consideration should be given to establishing a *Voluntary Panel*, and that this Panel should seek to operate in conjunction with the Irish Stock Exchange and other regulatory authorities.

The Ryan Commission welcomed the work of the ASB in seeking to revise financial reporting standards, to develop new standards where none existed and to develop a conceptual framework for financial reporting. It supported the intention to reduce the number of options within financial reporting standards and to give clearer guidance on the circumstances in which particular options should be used. The Commission argued that there should be clearer and more detailed disclosure of accounting policies to assist users in comparing accounts of different companies. It recommended that an Irish Financial Reporting Review Panel should be enabled to take action where an enterprise's statement of accounting policies was considered deficient.

The Ryan Commission found that there was widespread public confusion about where responsibility lay for financial reporting, and recommended that directors should acknowledge their responsibilities in a *Directors' Responsibility Statement*. This statement, which should be included in the annual report of *all* companies, would confirm the discharge of their responsibility for the financial statements and also for the systems of internal control within the company. The Ryan Commission stressed the key role that audit committees could play in assisting the board of directors to understand and fulfil their responsibilities for financial reporting. It recommended that, where practical, companies should establish an audit committee to oversee the company's system of internal controls and the financial reporting process.

The Ryan Commission made a number of recommendations for additional information to be provided in annual reports. It recommended that the Chairperson's Statement included in the annual report of listed companies should contain a statement of the company's objectives and its strategic plan. The statement should also contain details of changes in accounting policies during the year, together with the reasons for them and their effect on the current year's results. It was recommended that the Chief Executive's Review should give more detailed commentary on the results and the financial position of the company. Interestingly, not long after the Commission reported, the ASB issued non-mandatory guidance on many of these issues in its statement, *Operating and Financial Review*.[5]

The Ryan Commission felt that a requirement to link the results to plans would assist users in assessing the performance of management. In the same context, it also recommended that users be given more information on the rewards that are paid, by disclosing the remuneration of the chairperson and the highest-paid director, together with an indication of the range of payments to other directors.

For most users of accounts, the interim statement and the preliminary profits statement provide information that is more timely than the published accounts. The content of these statements is regulated by the Stock Exchange. Given their importance to users, the Commission recommended that the rules on Preliminary and Interim Statements should be amended to require additional information. In the case of Interim Statements the Commission recommended that auditors should carry out a limited review and report on these statements. In respect of Preliminary Statements, the Commission recommended that the auditors give their approval to the publication of the figures and the form in which they are presented.

The Ryan Commission considered that some of the criticism of the role of the auditor stemmed from a lack of understanding of that role and the nature of the audit process. The Commission believed that this misunderstanding, which extended even to some company directors, could be removed by clarification of responsibilities within the financial reporting process and of the nature and scope of the audit process. In addition to better communication, the Ryan Commission recommended extending the scope of the audit to provide users and companies with assurances on key areas such as internal controls, by requiring the auditors to report to the directors on the system of controls, and to an appropriate authority on discovery of fraud.

Other recommendations of the Ryan Commission on the role of auditors in the financial reporting process included a reduction of the period within which a company must hold its AGM and file its financial statements, disclosure of non-audit fees, further restrictions on auditors on the fees they can earn from a single client and more lay representation on, and open reporting from, the internal disciplinary procedures of the profession.

The report of the Ryan Commission received a fair degree of popular acclaim from most interested parties. Whilst some parties may have expressed reservations regarding certain of the recommendations, or the extent of others, the broad thrust of the report was widely welcomed as a meaningful contribution to the debate on improving financial reporting in the Republic of Ireland. The recommendation attracting the most publicity — the creation of a Review Panel in Ireland — was widely favoured among the accountancy profession. Almost a year after the publication of the Ryan Commission report, we saw the publication of the report of the UK-based Committee on the Financial Aspects of Corporate Governance (the Cadbury Report)[6]. Both reports covered much of the same ground and contained similar recommendations in a number of areas, such as directors' responsibility statements, audit committees, reporting on results, disclosure of remuneration, interim statements and preliminary announcements. The Cadbury Report has received greater publicity than the Ryan Commission report for two main reasons: firstly, the relative sizes of the UK and Irish economies; and secondly, and more importantly, the endorsement by both the UK and Irish Stock Exchanges of the Cadbury Committee's *Code of Best Practice*. Public companies listed on these exchanges must include a statement of compliance with the Cadbury Code.

THE RESPONSES TO THE REPORT OF THE RYAN COMMISSION

In response to the Ryan Report, the ICAI also issued two Statements of Best Practice: *Companies Reporting in the Republic of Ireland*,[7] and, *The Audit of Companies Reporting in the Republic of Ireland*.[8] These Statements endorsed many of the recommendations of the

Ryan Commission and recommended them to the profession. Issued by the Council of the ICAI, the exact status of these statements is somewhat indeterminable, as they are not part of the handbook of formal guidance issued by the ICAI to its members. The Council of the ICAI has stated that it expects its members to have regard to the statements. The Statements are, however, clearly subordinate to the baseline professional guidance currently promulgated. Best practice has always been a concept that causes confusion among preparers of accounts. Insufficiently important to warrant mandatory status, yet at the same time representing the most up-to-date and appropriate treatment, "best practice" is a non-sequitur which renders the guidance ineffective. Problems in financial reporting have not typically been encountered at the end of the financial reporting spectrum where companies that endorse best practice are found. Indeed, the ICAI's own attitude in preferring a statutory *Review Panel* as set out below would appear to be at odds with the issuance of Statements of Best Practice.

The ICAI[9] also made a submission to the then Minister for Industry and Commerce seeking legislative backing for accounting standards, for a Directors' Responsibility Statement and for the establishment of an *Irish Financial Reporting Review Panel*. The ICAI did not favour a non-statutory Review Panel as it felt that such a body would be ineffective.

The Irish Government's response to both the Ryan Report and the submission from the ICAI was initially disappointing. Whilst welcoming the Report, the Department of Industry and Commerce, with an understaffed Company Law Division and a backlog of EU directives to enact in local law, ruled out the promise of legislative backing in the medium term, as it had done earlier with respect to the Dearing Report. Underlying the response was an apparent belief in the Government, that the auditors, if properly carrying out their duties, should in their audit report draw attention to non-compliance with accounting standards.

The accountancy profession showed a willingness to persist with the call for reform. In September 1993 the Chartered Association of Certified Accountants issued the report of a working party, which it had established to consider how the Ryan Commission recommendations might be advanced.[10] Recognising the Government's attitude to funding a Review Panel, the report advocated a *Financial Reporting Ombudsman* as an interim measure. The Working Party advocated a similar role for the Ombudsman as the Ryan Commission intended for the Review Panel. The Working Party report also focused on the particular aspects of small and medium companies and suggested how the Ryan recommendations could be tailored to cater for the particular needs of such companies, which were not directly within its terms of reference but are greater in number in Ireland.

In the intervening period, significant changes have occurred, both at ministerial level and in the reorganisation of the Government department responsible for company law in the Republic of Ireland. In October 1993 the new Department of Enterprise and Employment began a process of reviewing the recommendations of the Ryan Commission. The Department contacted a number of interested bodies, including those bodies directly affected by the recommendations contained in the Ryan report, and sought reaction to the recommendations and proposals to advance them. In April 1994, the Minister for Enterprise and Employment launched a Company Law Review Group to review and make recommendations on company law in the Republic of Ireland. The Group was specifically directed to review the recommendations of the Ryan Commission and to consider the merits of those recommendations which would require changes in company law. The Group reported to the Minister for Enterprise and Employment in December 1994.[11]

The Company Law Review Group supported the majority of the recommendations of the Ryan Commission requiring changes in company law. It also highlighted areas such as directors' responsibility statements where a combination of the Cadbury Code and best practice has led to a situation where most companies now include such a statement.

The Review Group made a firm recommendation that financial reporting standards be recognised in Irish company law. It recommended that accounting standards be defined to mean such standards of accounting practice as issued by such a body or bodies as may be prescribed by the Minister by regulation. This very sensible proposal effectively means that the Minister could authorise the accounting bodies in this country to continue to promulgate the standards of the ASB, thus giving legal backing to what is at present observed voluntarily.

The Review Group recommended the establishment of a *Financial Reporting Review Panel* along the lines of that currently existing in the UK. For obvious reasons, the Review Group envisages a more modest operation than that currently operating in the UK. It recommends that the Panel should confine itself to the more serious and material cases of non-compliance with financial reporting standards.

The Review Group does not go as far as designing the structure for such a Review Panel. However, the benefits of a fully fledged Irish Financial Reporting Review Panel would probably not justify the costs. Moreover, the small size of the Irish business community may cause particular difficulties for the operation of a Panel. Notwithstanding these issues, the overriding need for an effective enforcement mechanism still exists. A simple mechanism would be to empower the Minister for Enterprise and Employment to appoint an Inspector if a company's financial statements seem to be seriously defective. Relevant parties should be able to refer cases to the Minister. Such an Inspector should operate in a manner similar to an Inspector appointed under Part II of the Companies Act, 1990. The Minister should be empowered on receipt of the Inspector's report, to request the directors to rectify the financial statements at the company's expense, and to apply to the Court, if necessary, for an order compelling rectification of defective accounts at the directors' expense.

The Review Group also recommended that the law be changed to require a company to hold its AGM within six months of the financial year end and to file its annual return (including financial statements) within 35 days of the AGM. While this is not as strict as the Ryan Commission recommended (i.e., 14 days) it is a marked improvement on the current nine-month AGM requirement and further 60-day filing requirement.

Other recommendations of the Ryan Commission with which the Company Law Review Group concurred include the regulation of the auditing profession, disclosure of non-audit fees and reporting by auditors of fraud. The Review Group disagreed with the proposal to increase the statutory disclosure of directors' emoluments, on the ground that most listed companies were voluntarily making the additional disclosures set out in the Cadbury Code, or the Irish Association of Investment Managers' albeit less onerous statement.

CONCLUSION

The developments in the financial reporting process as outlined above have primarily taken place at the behest of the accounting profession and user-representative bodies. It now falls to the Government to act. Suggestions that a further commission should be established, to set out how those Ryan Commission recommendations accepted by the Company Law Review Group can be enacted, must surely be greeted with exasperation. Informal consultations should take place. However, formal response should be on foot of publication of a Bill.

If the Irish Government wishes to be seen to take financial reporting and corporate governance seriously, it must enact the legislation proposed by the Company Law Review Group as a matter of great urgency. The traditional links that Ireland has maintained with the accounting profession in the UK have maintained its position at the vanguard of developments in the financial reporting process. Although these links still persist on a restricted scale, and are dependent on voluntary backing in this country, only equivalent legislation will restore full co-operation. This is all the more important in the context of a global capital marketplace, where funds for economic activity are becoming increasingly mobile. If the Irish marketplace is viewed as less regulated than that of our competitors, the international funds that represent so much of the capital employed in this country may be diverted into better-regulated markets. It would be extremely disappointing if the lack of decisive action on the Government's part were to cause this to happen. Indeed, it would be disastrous for both the country and the Government.

Moreover, in taking the required action, the Irish Government should consider extending financial reporting regulation to non-corporate entities. Traditionally, the regulation of financial reporting by these bodies has been limited. Yet building societies, co-operatives, trades unions, charities and other non-corporate entities are some of the largest economic entities in this state and should be subject to the same reporting standards as the corporate sector. Reforms in company law should therefore be extended to cover these bodies. Such a bold step would then put this country where it belongs, at the vanguard of developments in the financial reporting process.

4
Fraud and the Auditor

Gerard McHugh
Trinity College, Dublin

Eugene McMahon
Rawlinson Hunter Mazars

INTRODUCTION

> Twelve senior executives of the collapsed Bank of Credit and Commerce International were yesterday sentenced in Abu Dhabi to serve a combined total of 61 years in prison and ordered to pay $9 billion for their involvement in one of the biggest frauds in history. [*The Irish Times,* 15 June 1994]

The BCCI executives may well breathe a sigh of relief that they were not convicted in China. In 1992, eight financial executives — mainly accountants — were executed in China for defrauding a national bank of more than 30 million yuan. It is not an overstatement to say that the extent and cost of crime in the workplace is staggering. One recent estimate places the annual cost of corporate crime in the United States at around $200 million (Petersen and Farrell 1986),[1] while losses from employee theft are estimated to run to $120 billion annually.[2] In the UK, losses from fraud against corporations are estimated to run at £14 million daily.[3] A recent survey of Ireland's top 500 companies conducted by accountants KPMG suggests that fraud levels in Ireland are on the increase and have never been higher.[4] Reports such as these must strike fear in the heart of any corporate investor, and confirm to even the most sceptical that corporate crime is a factor of everyday business life.

Of course, fraud has always been with us: George Robb's recent work *White-collar Crime in Modern England: Financial Fraud and*

Business Morality, 1845–1929, presents a fascinating catalogue of deceit and corruption in the late nineteenth and early twentieth centuries, a reminder to us that there is nothing new under the sun.[5] But fraud is on the increase and many observers link its growth to a perceived decline in moral standards and a consequent rise in our acceptance of dishonesty. This chapter sets out to explain the nature of fraud and the principal ways in which it manifests itself within business. Having identified dishonesty and deception as being central to its existence, we go on to profile the fraudster. To the extent that any policy implications can be taken from the analysis presented here, it is proposed that seeking to identify the criminal in advance is probably too difficult and unreliable, and accordingly it is recommended that the concentration of effort should be on the development of a management ethos which gives high priority to effective internal controls, designed to inhibit the would-be criminal, and to a corporate ethos, which is seen to be observed at the highest level.

Recognising that the weight of recent financial scandals has drawn criticism upon the statutory auditor, this chapter also seeks to examine the nature of the statutory auditor's role, and the inherent difficulties which corporate crime poses for statutory auditors. While acknowledging that the auditing profession has endeavoured to respond to its critics, it is suggested here that more can be done in terms both of preventing and of discovering fraud. In the final analysis however, the business community in particular, and society itself in general, must also play their parts.

DEFINING TERMS

In discussions of fraud, terms abound and confuse: embezzlement, racketeering, economic crime, blue-collar crime, white-collar crime, occupational and organisational misconduct are just some of the terms commonly used. In this chapter, our concern is essentially with what is more commonly referred to today as white-collar crime — that is, fraud perpetrated by trusted employees on their employer organisations. Before proceeding, however, two important distinctions need to be drawn; the first is between fraud, which by definition is a crime, and "sharp" or unethical behaviour involving no criminal act. It has become increasingly commonplace in public discourse to confuse "sharp" business practice and fraud. This is certainly in error and must in part be a result of careless media reporting of some of the activities of high-profile business people. For example, a case in point is the debacle in 1992 surrounding the executives of the former Irish Sugar Company (now Greencore plc) who were removed from office following revelations of alleged personal gains made from transactions which were deemed to be in conflict with their duties as company directors. The report of the Government-appointed investigator into the series of transactions points to no fraud having been committed despite widespread public censure of the individuals involved. Similarly, Mr Dermot Desmond's and Mr Michael Smurfit's part-ownership of the property which was planned to house the head office of Telecom Éireann involved no fraud, despite the public scandal it gave rise to.

The second distinction worth drawing is between occupational crime and organisational crime. Occupational crimes are crimes carried out by employees, typically for their own gain. Organisational crimes are crimes committed by organisations. Of course, crimes in this latter category involve individuals also, but the actions expose the organisation to criminal charge. The primary focus of this chapter is on that category of occupational crime *against* the organisation, committed by managers or others in trusted positions. However, organisational criminality cannot be ignored; it may be expected that large-scale organisational crime such as EU fraud, money-laundering and illegal arms sales will continue to be carried out by corporations and will probably increase.[6]

FRAUD

There is no simple definition of fraud in any Irish statute, nor is there any specific legal offence of fraud. Where "fraud" charges are brought against an individual, it is typically under legislation contained in, for example, the Falsifications of Accounts Act, 1875, the Forgery Act, 1913, or the Larceny Act, 1916 (as amended). Leaving aside these legal technicalities, in this chapter we use the term fraud to refer to:

> crime for financial gain committed by means of deception by persons in entrepreneurial, professional or semi-professional positions utilising their special occupational skills and opportunities.

Deception is at the heart of fraud, and the secrecy that surrounds deception makes the crime difficult to understand fully and even harder to quantify — not least because the victims may be unaware that they have even suffered. Even when such crimes are discovered, there is a reluctance to highlight the losses because adverse publicity may reflect badly on the senior management of the organisation itself. But the problem does not end there: only a tiny proportion of detected and alleged fraud is ever proven to the satisfaction of a court of law. Perhaps arising from these difficulties, many organisations believe frauds to be an inevitable fact of commercial life, and work to keep them within "acceptable" limits. However, when considering what might be "acceptable", it is worth remembering the adage that "there are no immaterial frauds, just ones which have had insufficient time to grow"!

The secrecy surrounding fraud has given crime an aura of mystery, which fascinates many in our society who enjoy a good detective novel. Often it is the sheer enormity of the amounts defrauded that fascinates us, but we also yearn for information on the mechanisms used and the uses to which proceeds are put. Fraud can yield very substantial illicit benefits to the fraudster and, perhaps ironically in an increasingly violent society, does so without any actual or implied physical threat. Mistakenly, it is often assumed that the execution of the crime relies on the ingenuity of the criminal. Rarely, in fact, is this the case, and, as we shall see, most frauds are perpetrated in circumstances where adequate control procedures are either not in place or are not operating effectively.

Fraud may be perpetrated in a variety of ways. The crudest form is probably simple and straightforward theft from an employer organisation of cash or other "negotiable instruments", such as cheques and property. The former Head of Internal Audit at AIB plc explained it rather colourfully: dismissing the "cloak and dagger" image of fraud, he observed that in many cases there is no series of false documents — "the fellow just literally takes the money".[7] In this context, expenses fraud is perhaps a slightly more sophisticated form of theft, usually involving the forgery or alteration of documents. However, over the past 20 years we have witnessed an appreciable increase in the sophistication of schemes of embezzlement, such as dummy accounts, price-fixing, kickbacks and phoney invoices, to name but a few.

Where accounting systems are very complex and understood by only a few, as for example in money markets and derivatives markets, there may be ample opportunity to perpetrate crimes which remain invisible for long periods of time. Probably the most infamous of the sophisticated frauds was that perpetrated by the management of the Equity Funding Corporation of America. In an effort to hide declining profitability, the management began a series of accounting machinations to increase income. In essence, they generated phoney insurance policies, recorded income and laid a well-devised scheme to fool the auditors. It was a kind of pyramid scheme and was facilitated by computer technology. If anything, the advances in information technology, which continue to place low-cost sophisticated computer power within easy reach of growing numbers of individuals, present new opportunities for the criminal to exploit computer power for illegal gain.

FRAUD IN THE REPUBLIC OF IRELAND

The Republic of Ireland is no different from the rest of the world in experiencing a growth in both the incidence and costs of corporate crime. The KPMG survey referred to earlier found that 40 per cent of respondents admitted having experienced fraud in the immediate past. Forty-four per cent of respondents regard fraud as a major problem for Irish business today and 63 per cent believe that it is becoming a more serious problem. The survey revealed some interesting data on the cost of fraud: 29 per cent of all fraud detected involved sums in excess of £10,000, while 2 per cent of the survey respondents revealed losses or potential losses in excess of £1 million. Finally, almost 70 per cent of frauds were dealt with by dismissal, but only 28 per cent resulted in a criminal prosecution. Add to this the incidence of fraud against the EU and the extent of tax evasion revealed by the two "tax amnesties", and we can see that there is certainly no cause for complacency in Ireland.

In 1992, recognising the growing public concern about the effectiveness of the State's response to the problem of serious fraud, the then Minister for Justice, Mr Pádraig Flynn, secured Government approval for the establishment of a Government Advisory Committee on Fraud. The Report of that Committee, published in December 1992, is a further testimony to the growing problem of serious fraud in Ireland. Table 4.1 shows recent statistics from the files of the Garda Fraud Squad,[8] which are cited in the Report.

The Report quotes the Garda Fraud Squad's assessment that, in its largest 50 investigation files open in 1992, the total amount potentially at risk was approximately £26 million, with the top 20 cases each involving sums of money in excess of £100,000. The Report goes on to note that in 1989, 1990 and 1991 an average of 33 commercial fraud cases were referred to the Director of Public Prosecutions by the Fraud Squad.

TABLE 4.1: CLASSIFICATION OF ALL FRAUD REPORTED, 1989–91

Year	Number of Cheques and Credit Card Complaints	Number of Commercial Fraud Complaints
1989	1,569	234
1990	2,524	242
1991	1,708	383

All that the above information can tell us with certainty is that there is a fraud problem in this country, and that the monetary sums involved can be very significant. Undoubtedly, it understates the scale of the problem. The secret nature of the crime means that many incidents of fraud go unreported. Moreover, even where the Gardaí are invited to investigate a fraud, they are often hampered by the lack of legally admissible evidence, which ultimately can militate against achieving successful convictions.

CHARACTERISTICS OF THE FRAUDSTER

Who commits fraud and why do they defraud? Do fraudsters share characteristics and personality traits? Can we say anything about the nature of the fraudster? How do fraudsters behave when they are discovered? These are just some of the questions that are being asked by professionals in fields including psychology, personnel selection and recruitment, criminology and auditing. All the evidence available, both nationally and internationally, indicates that if there is such a person as the typical fraudster, he (for they are usually male) is not easy to spot. Almost all fraud investigators agree that, on discovery of a fraud, the victim usually expresses astonishment at the identity of the perpetrator.

Psychological studies are beginning to provide some clues about the nature of the white-collar criminal mind. A recent study carried out among gaoled white-collar criminals in the US revealed large, statistically significant differences between white-collar offenders and non-offenders.[9] The pattern of score differences revealed that offenders had greater tendencies towards irresponsibility, lack of dependability, and disregard of rules and social norms — the researchers termed it an absence of "social conscientiousness". However, researchers are a long way away from devising reliable tests that could identify such tendencies in persons in advance of their committing crime!

Two common factors are present in most fraud — motive and opportunity.

Motive

Financial gain is the most common motive, but white-collar criminals rarely commit crime just to accumulate wealth. They are usually committed to financial obligations that they cannot meet. Undoubtedly, there are those who commit fraud who are not in financial need. However, in such cases patterns of spending change, and ultimately the fraud must be continued in order to sustain enhanced lifestyles. The motive may also be retaliatory: that is, the employee may be annoyed or frustrated with some aspect of the job and seeks to inflict damage which may or may not provide personal financial rewards. Computer crimes such as programming viruses, causing physical damage to equipment and blocking access to information are commonly associated with retaliation.

A Perceived Opportunity

The decision to commit fraud inevitably involves an assessment of the risk of detection. Where the risk of detection is low, the incidence of fraud increases. The primary organisational safeguard against fraud is the system of internal control. Controls may breakdown for a variety of reasons but most commonly when there is pressure on profitability, when organisational restructuring is taking place, and during periods of staff shortages because of holidays, illness and, increasingly, down-sizing. In some enterprises, systems are designed to tolerate errors up to certain limits, or an aggregation of errors over a period of time. This can mean that the fraudster who is neither too greedy nor too careless, becomes almost impossible to detect.

When fraud has been detected, researchers find that the perpetrators typically deny the charge. The early denial of a fraud gives the perpetrator time to lose, alter, destroy, or conceal valuable documents and records.[10] It also results in lost time, which can mean confused witnesses and lost evidence. Denial can also anger those investigating fraud and may on occasion incite investigators to insult, harm, slander, libel, or terminate employment without due cause. Such reactions can have a price!

When denial cannot be maintained any longer, the criminal may attempt to rationalise and even justify the dishonest act. The notion here is that the perpetrator's motivation was really "not all that bad":

fraudsters decriminalise their acts or minimise the crime. They may suggest that they are merely "borrowing" the money to cover a short-term financial difficulty and intend to repay it in the near future. Fraudsters may even point to the perceived dishonesty in the dealings of their peers: the notion that "they are all at it"! This type of rationalising behaviour is, in a sense, understandable. Most people who commit fraud are first-time offenders and would not commit other types of crime.[11] In a curious way, disappointment and embarrassment felt by the victim can in some instances give rise to a sense of sympathy for the perpetrator, which persuades the victim not to report the crime.

INVESTIGATING AND PROSECUTING FRAUD

If white-collar crime is difficult to detect, it is even more difficult to prove, to prosecute and to secure convictions. A very high proportion of detected fraud goes unprosecuted. However, the tide has begun to turn. Some countries have made sweeping advances in their criminal law codes to ensure a higher rate of convictions. In 1987, for example, a special *Bank Fraud Task Force* was established in Dallas, Texas, to examine the white-collar crime involved in the collapse of the savings and loan institutions. At its peak in 1991, the task force had 150 federal officers; 260 people had been charged as a result of its investigations into the failure of 43 financial institutions, of whom 211 had been convicted and 15 acquitted.[12] In the UK, the Criminal Justice Act, 1987, set up the Serious Fraud Office (SFO) to investigate suspected offences involving serious or complex fraud. Although many feel that the UK legislation in the area of fraud is still in need of radical reform, there is little doubt that the SFO represents an improvement on what went before.

Here in Ireland, revised legislation is urgently needed if fraud is to be tackled seriously. In addition, the resources available to the Fraud Squad of the Garda Síochána must be augmented, as cases cannot be investigated quickly enough and delay always acts to the advantage of criminals. The Report of the Government's Advisory Committee on Fraud informed us that the Fraud Squad's access to accounting expertise was almost non-existent and the absence of computerisation in the Fraud Squad of the Garda Síochána rendered it effectively impossible even to compile statistics on the number of convictions for serious fraud (para: 2.4). Since the Report was published, the resources of the Fraud Squad have been slightly augmented but by no means sufficiently to make a serious impact on bringing cases to trial more speedily.

At the time of writing, a number of high-profile fraud actions await hearing. A subsidiary of the national airline — Aer Lingus Holidays Ltd. — went out of business in 1990 after losing £10 million over the previous five years. Two men have been charged with conspiracy to defraud the company of £500,000. However, as the case has yet to be heard, we cannot say whether any fraud in fact took place. The liquidator of the investment brokerage company, Mark Sinnott Life and Pensions Ltd., traced investor funds of £50,000 which were directly lodged into the personal account of Mark Sinnott Jnr. Details of this transaction are contained in an affidavit lodged in the High Court by the liquidator of that company, Mr Desmond Guilfoyle of Coopers & Lybrand. However, a replying affidavit from Mr. Sinnott denied that there was any intention to defraud or misappropriate the funds. This case has yet to go to trial — it is clear therefore that the time-scale in which enquiries are carried out by the Fraud Squad and cases are subsequently brought to trial is very lengthy indeed, and such delays do nothing to allay the concerns of innocent investors.

In the UK, the Serious Fraud Office has encountered many teething problems and has failed to secure convictions in a number of high-profile cases where convictions were expected. However, in revising our legislation we can learn from their experience.[13] As a first step though, the recommendations contained in the report of the Advisory Committee on Fraud must be advanced to the draft-legislation stage. The essence of the Advisory Committee's recommendations is worth repeating:

- There should be a statutory duty on every person to report reasonable suspicion of serious fraud to the Gardaí or, where appropriate, the Revenue Commissioners.

- A National Bureau of Fraud Investigation should be established within the Garda Síochána to replace the Garda Fraud Squad.

- Serious fraud enquiries should be conducted by investigating teams comprising Gardaí from the National Bureau, accountants and lawyers.

- The Director of Public Prosecutions should have a realistic increase in staff not only to assist in serious fraud enquiries but to prosecute serious fraud offences.

- The fraud-related offences that are currently found throughout the statute books should be consolidated into a single, modern statute.
- New pre-trial procedures should be established so that as many procedural and related issues as possible may be dealt with before a serious fraud trial commences, either by agreement or by direction of a judge. Only those matters genuinely in dispute should be left to be determined by the jury.
- Juries in serious fraud trials should be enabled to draw proper inferences from the silence of an accused on being questioned where exculpatory evidence is put forward at the trial which could reasonably have been made available to the Gardaí at the investigation stage.

In May 1995, the Government announced the creation of a National Bureau of Fraud Investigation, and, by June 1995, new fraud legislation was being prepared, which would consolidate offences of dishonesty. It is to be hoped that this legislation will not be too long in preparation.

AUDITORS AND FRAUD

Discussions of fraud rarely exclude the auditor. When fraud is uncovered in an enterprise, the auditor usually receives the first telephone call: "Why didn't you discover this?" When the auditor discovers the fraud, the question is slightly different: "Why didn't you discover it earlier?" The auditor cannot win. However, the search for the auditor's blood very often illustrates a profound misunderstanding of the respective responsibilities of directors, management and auditors. Moreover, if there is a degree of confusion between auditors and their immediate clients with respect to their roles regarding the prevention and detection of fraud, it is hardly surprising that those further removed from the auditor, particularly the financial press and public generally, are even more perplexed, and hence even quicker to point the finger when news of financial wrongdoing becomes known.

A number of issues must be teased out here: the nature of the statutory audit, the responsibility for fraud prevention, the responsibility for fraud detection, and the responsibility for reporting discovered fraud. Some of these issues are aired in other chapters in this volume and are addressed here only briefly in order to ensure completeness within this essay.

The Statutory Audit and the Responsibility for Fraud-Prevention and Detection

Company law envisages the auditor reporting on the truth and fairness of the annual financial statements prepared by the directors of a company. Strictly speaking, the law does not envisage the auditor having a primary responsibility to detect fraud, although the abiding belief of many is that the auditor's primary role is to do just that. The auditing profession has responded to public calls for it to accept a greater responsibility for fraud detection. The latest guidelines, issued in 1995, are contained in the Auditing Practices Board's *Statement of Auditing Standards 110: Fraud and Error*. Paragraph 2 of the Standard requires auditors "to plan and perform their audit procedures and evaluate the results thereof, recognising that fraud and error may materially affect the financial statements". Para 25 goes on to state that based on their assessment of risk, "auditors should design audit procedures so as to have a reasonable expectation of detecting misstatements arising from fraud or error which are material to the financial statements".

In terms of defining the role of the statutory auditor more explicitly, this is probably as far as the audit profession can go. In the final analysis, company directors are responsible for the stewardship of a company's affairs, the safeguarding of its assets and the prevention of fraud. There is no doubt either that the primary responsibility for fraud detection rests with the directors, and company law supports this. Auditors plan their work so that they have a reasonable expectation of detecting material misstatements in financial statements or accounting records, resulting from irregularities or fraud, but their examination cannot and should not be relied upon to disclose all irregularities and frauds that may exist. The detection of fraud by auditors will inevitably be limited by the extent and range of tests that they carry out to discharge their statutory responsibilities.

If the foregoing suggests that the statutory auditor is somewhat powerless in the face of a well-concealed and collusive fraud, then this is at least in part the case. However, the profession is far from complacent in this regard. The profession has embraced the concept of greater regulation for auditors, to assure the users of financial statements that the quality of audit work undertaken by practising firms meets the highest standards. Since December 1992, all those seeking to carry out the functions of a statutory auditor must first seek audit registration from a Recognised Supervisory Body. The criteria for recognition are designed to give assurance that those carrying out the audit function have the necessary integrity, competence and resources to discharge their statutory function satisfactorily. The major professional accounting bodies in Ireland have introduced a system of quality monitoring of all their members who are engaged in auditing practice. This quality-assurance programme involves an independent examination of all practising members' working papers, at least once within a five-year period, in order to ensure that work is being carried out to an acceptable standard.

Reporting Detected Fraud

Auditors are not agents of the state as are the police. The professional duty of confidentiality has always been a cornerstone of the relationship between an auditor and client organisation. A similar duty exists in other professional relationships, such as that between doctor and patient, and banker and client. But the duty of confidentiality is not absolute and, as the APB's new standard, SAS110 *Fraud and Error*, makes clear, circumstances can arise where the auditor is not bound by that duty (para. 53). For example, that duty may be overridden by a statutory duty to report criminal acts. Section 172 of the Irish Finance Act, 1995 imposes such a duty on auditors who discover tax evasion in the course of their work. The Act requires that, in the first instance, the offence should be reported to the company, which should rectify the matter. If the company does not rectify the situation or report its tax situation to the Revenue, auditors will be obliged to resign their position and report their resignation to the Revenue Commissioners.

PREVENTING FRAUD

Nothing that has been said here so far suggests that fraud is set to decline. In fact, the opposite seems to be the trend. However, it is also clear that we cannot give up trying to combat such crimes. The fight against fraud will always involve the concerted and combined efforts of the Gardaí, the auditing profession, company management and the Director of Public Prosecutions. As has already been said, legislative action on the investigation and prosecution sides is urgently required of Government. In this final section, therefore, we focus on four mechanisms that can be effected by organisations in order to minimise the effects of crime.

Internal Controls

More than half of all frauds occur because of poor internal control. A triennial survey conducted by the UK Audit Commission found that the majority of computer-aided frauds discovered in 1990 were discovered by mere chance and that the role of internal control in detection had declined — see Table 4.2 below.[14]

TABLE 4.2: METHODS OF DISCOVERY OF COMPUTER-AIDED FRAUD

Method of Detection	1981		1984		1987		1990	
	No.	%	No.	%	No.	%	No.	%
Internal Control	8	42	40	52	48	41	17	23
Internal Audit	4	6	9	12	13	11	9	13
External Audit	1	2	—	—	—	—	1	1
Other Means	34	50	23	30	52	44	44	60
Not Disclosed	—	—	5	6	5	4	2	3
Total	47	100	77	100	118	100	73	100

Source: Survey of Computer Fraud and Abuse, Audit Commission (UK) 1987 and 1990.

This is an extremely worrying trend for those involved in the design of control systems and for auditors. Accounting, financial and operational controls, frequently checked and effectively supervised, can play an important role in preventing corporate fraud. Auditors must continue to drive this message home to company directors.

Corporate Culture

Many commentators on fraud believe that the foundation for building an honest workforce lies in the corporate culture. Interestingly, the National Commission on Fraudulent Financial Reporting in the US,[15] more commonly known as the Treadway Commission, identified corporate "tone at the top" as the essential element in establishing an environment for proper financial reporting. It recommended that corporations set the appropriate moral tone, by use of corporate codes of conduct and self-assessment techniques designed to indicate risks of fraud, while emphasising the need for a better-controlled environment. While one would not wish to dispute the essential reasonableness of this notion, we should be very clear about the difficulties. In competitive business and job environments there are strong pressures to choose the "easy" answers. For example, a recent US case, TI Group, the American specialist aerospace company, has been accused of defrauding the US Air Force of more than $20 million by fraudulently overcharging labour and overhead elements on defence contracts. Earlier this year, the reputable Lucas Industries was fined $18.5 million after admitting that its staff falsified quality certificates for gearboxes.[16] Thus, establishing an ethical climate involves unremitting effort. Moreover, the ethical climate of organisations is extremely fragile and the grapevine quickly communicates situations in which executives have chosen the expedient action over the right one.[17] Thus, a clear management style embracing good personnel practices needs to be reinforced through action rather than pronouncement.

Recruitment and Selection Policies

Although we have said that it is very difficult to identify criminals in advance, organisations can minimise risk by developing careful recruitment and selection policies. Various personality and integrity pre-employment tests are now in common use throughout the US and Europe. Despite the serious doubts raised about the reliability of these tests, employers continue to use and to refine them. However, even if employers are not yet prepared to incur such costs, there is still plenty of information easily available; employers should follow up references rigorously and the tone of referees' replies should be assessed.

Whistle-blowing

Whistle-blowing involves the reporting by a current or former employee of illegal, inefficient or unethical practices in an organisation to persons who have the power or resources to take action. It does not include, for example, reporting of illegal activity where reporting such activity is in fact a statutory responsibility (as is now the case for bankers who discover money laundering). Whistle-blowing may be internal or external. In the context of white-collar crime and organisational misconduct generally, there is an ongoing debate about the effectiveness of whistle-blowing in reducing or controlling organisational misconduct. Preliminary indications are that it may have a modest impact. As yet, whistle-blowing is far from a socially acceptable activity and can cause great personal hardship for those who do it. But whistle-blowing is on the increase across the globe and its proponents argue that it has enormous potential as a mechanism for exposing and controlling organisational misconduct. There are downsides for the organisation, which must be weighed up, not least of which is the effect on work practices of turning employees into monitors.

CONCLUSION

According to criminologist Professor Michael Levi, fraud may well be the modern crime "par excellence"[18] The chances of being detected, prosecuted and convicted are not high. In the absence of any change in the law and the resources of the investigators and prosecutors, organisations in this country must inevitably rely on prevention and early-warning mechanisms in order to deter would-be white-collar criminals.

The auditing profession has responded in the only way that it can, given the statutory nature of the auditor's appointment. The profession must continue to raise the standards of its own work. However, what the auditing profession cannot do, and must not do, is to accept responsibility for the growth in a crime which ultimately is both a national and international malaise. The profession must continue to press for a greater awareness in the corporate sector of the cost of fraud to companies. It must persuade business that greater investment in the prevention and detection of fraud would be in the interests, not only of each individual company, but ultimately of society itself. But even this may not be enough for its critics. The question must then be turned back to those critics to map out a radical alternative for the audit function in our society. One senses that it may involve placing even more responsibility on auditors. If that is what society wants, then so be it. But it will be expensive. For auditors to carry out their task on the basis of a presumption of dishonesty would greatly increase their workload. Indeed, one suspects that the cost of audit on such a basis would vastly exceed the cost of upgraded internal controls adequate to achieve the same result. While the business community has stated itself to be anxious to come to terms with corporate crime, it is, as yet, unclear what price it is prepared to pay to achieve this goal.

5
Auditors and the Law

Laurence Shields
L.K. Shields & Partners

Arthur Moran
Matheson Ormsby Prentice

INTRODUCTION

In November 1993, partners in the former Irish firm of chartered accountants, Ernst & Whinney, reached an out-of-court settlement of approximately IR£77 million with AIB plc and Icarom, in an action against them arising out of their audit of the collapsed Insurance Corporation of Ireland. This represents the largest such settlement to date in these islands. Reports of auditors making huge monetary settlements in actions brought by clients and others who have relied upon audited financial statements are now commonplace. Worldwide estimates of claims outstanding against auditors are staggering, amounting to billions of dollars.

This chapter is concerned with the legal aspects of the auditor's work. We examine how the statute law defines the function and duties of the auditor, and in particular how the courts have interpreted those functions and duties. We also consider the standard of care that the courts expect, and we go on to focus in depth on the auditor's duty to third parties. Finally, we speculate on the likely implications that international developments in the area of the auditor's liability might have in Ireland. Before doing this it is appropriate briefly to discuss the general character of the law in relation to audit.

THE HISTORY OF THE LAW IN RELATION TO AUDIT

A requirement for auditors to examine and report on the financial statements presented by company directors has formed part of the law relating to companies since the earliest Companies Acts enacted in 1844 and 1856. The Joint Stock Companies Act of 1844, largely the work of William Gladstone, was enacted to encourage investment for the promotion of trade in an era of industrial expansion, and provided a model which in its main outlines can still be traced in company law in Europe today. That model was completed in the 1856 Joint Stock Companies Act, which adopted the principle of limited liability and provided for the constitution of a company as a separate legal entity, which could own property and incur obligations and sue or be sued without involving its members; provision was made for compulsory registration on standard terms, as well as public access to details of the company's activities and its membership. Those early Companies Acts provided for periodic general meetings and for the auditing of the directors' accounts with a view to discouraging mismanagement and abuse of trust in the conduct of the business, and the Companies Act, 1856, set out in a Schedule, regulations for management of the company not unlike the present-day articles of association.

The audit was designed initially to protect the interests of shareholders but quickly came to serve a second function in providing the basis for taxation of companies which is reflected in a number of court cases; it was thus implicitly accepted from an early date that audited accounts would be used by third parties and not only by the members of the company to whom they were addressed. The law relating to accounts evolved slowly with the Companies Act, 1908 adding a requirement for the publication of balance sheets by public limited companies and the Companies Act, 1963 (based upon the UK Companies Act, 1948) requiring that accounts including the profit and loss account be circulated to all members of the company; the 1963 Act laid down the details which must appear in the balance sheet and profit and loss account. The most significant developments in recent years were introduced in the EC Fourth Directive which was enacted into national law in the Companies (Amendment) Act, 1986.

Auditors continue to perform an important function under the Companies Acts. In doing so, their role is in part that of providing professional services to their client (the company) and in part (by far the more important part) that of satisfying the public interest in the supervision and control, through public disclosure, of the administration by the directors of the company, of the funds placed at their disposal by or through the creditors and shareholders of the company. The law intervenes directly at two levels in the performance by auditors of their task.

First, the law provides for the auditing of financial statements by independent auditors, describes the purpose of doing so (for which reference is best made to the European Community legislation), defines the relevant standard which those statements are to reach (the true and fair view) and identifies the persons to whom the auditors' opinion on the company's financial statements is directed. At that level, the law can be said to define the legal context in which auditors perform their functions: qualified auditors have no general right to enter a company's premises and demand to see its books; and companies have no general obligation to submit their internal financial statements to the scrutiny and criticism of outsiders; therefore, it is the law that requires companies to submit their financial statements to independent audit and that, in turn, entitles the law to determine, as it has done, the responsibilities of auditors and the extent and purpose of the audit.

At the second level, in contrast, the involvement of the law is incidental to the auditor's task: it is a part of the background information that auditors must take into account. For example, for an auditor assessing the economic reality of a transaction for the purpose of determining whether or not the account of the transaction in the company's financial statements gives a true and fair view, it is clearly relevant to know how the law characterises a particular transaction and defines its legal consequences. Nonetheless, whether or not the legal characterisation of a transaction determines the assessment made by the auditor is a question that cannot be answered simply by asserting that, because it is a legal characterisation, it must be determinative. As is well known, the legal requirement is that the annual accounts of a company should present a "true and fair view". The law does not, in general, require the legal characterisation of transactions to be adopted in company accounts.

The fact that the "true and fair view" is incorporated into legislation means that it is to be regarded as a "'legal" standard, but it does not follow that, as a "legal" standard (in the sense of a standard employed by the law), it imports into the rules governing the presentation of company's accounts all the precepts of the law. On the contrary, the mere fact that the law uses the expression "true and fair view" to describe the standard to which financial statements must aspire is sufficient to put the professional adviser on guard against applying strictly legal characterisations of transactions for the purposes of company accounts. The very words "true and fair" demonstrate that particular technical legal ways of assessing transactions may have to be avoided in the interests of truth and fairness. Thus, auditors find themselves subject not only to legal rules but also to the approved practice of the profession.

THE FUNCTION OF AUDIT

The auditor of a company is placed under a statutory duty to make an independent report to the shareholders of the company on the accounts prepared by the directors. Section 193(1) of the Companies Act, 1990 requires that the auditors of a company make a report to the members on the accounts examined by them, and on every balance sheet and profit and loss account, and all group accounts, laid before the company in general meeting during their tenure in office and give an auditors' report in compliance with Section 193(4) of the Companies Act, 1990.

The statutory explanation of the function of the audit has been expanded by case law and involves, *inter alia*, the following:

- Forming and stating an opinion as to the financial position of the company as shown in the balance sheet and the accompanying revenue statements; and
- The detection of errors; and
- The detection of fraud.

There have been strong objections from the auditing profession to the requirement that auditors should be responsible for the detection of defalcations by the officers or employees of a company. However, it is apparent from the case law that the courts regard the detection of fraud as an important purpose of an audit and this has now been reflected in the professional guidelines issued to the auditors (but see discussion on pp. 76 and 77 below).[1]

The nature of the functions to be performed by an auditor will frequently turn on an interpretation of the express or implied terms of the contract between auditor and client. Because of the particular vulnerability of an auditor in carrying out an auditing function, many decided cases have turned on the question of the precise scope of a particular engagement. For example, in *The Trustee of the Property of Apfel (a Bankrupt)* v. *Annan Dexter & Co.* [1927] 70 ACT.L.R. 57, the plaintiff contended that the defendant accountant was employed to conduct an audit, but the court upheld the defendant's contention that he was engaged merely to prepare accounts for the purpose of filing income tax returns. Clearly, the nature of the engagement may affect the extent of the accountant's liability, the insurability of the risk, and the standard of care to be exercised. It is therefore essential for auditors to record their precise instructions in a confirmatory letter to their client, and these "engagement letters" are now almost universal practice.

THE DUTIES OF AUDITORS

In order to understand the developments that have occurred principally in the UK, and to a lesser extent in Ireland (which are addressed more fully later) concerning the expansion of the categories of potential plaintiffs in actions against auditors and the recent attempt to stem this tide, it is necessary to address briefly the duties of an auditor to a client.

In addition to the express contractual duties owed by auditors to their client and those imposed by law to the client and others, certain other obligations are imposed either as implied contractual terms or arising out of the fiduciary nature of the appointment. These include:

- A duty not to disclose confidential information obtained by the auditors in the course of their professional duties.

- A duty not to make a secret profit out of their position and not to place themselves in a conflict of interest. Breach of this duty will afford a remedy in equity even if auditors are acting honestly and in what they honestly believe to be the best interests of the client.

- A duty to have a knowledge of the practical rules of law that affect the carrying out of the auditing functions. This duty has been held to include a knowledge of the contents of the memorandum and articles of association of the client company. The standard of legal cognisance required of the auditors will be raised if the auditors hold themselves out as having a special knowledge of a particular area of law.

- A duty to take reasonable care of any documents entrusted to them.

The relationship between auditors and their clients is one of contract and the contract will prima facie regulate the nature and extent of the auditors' task and the standard of their performance of it. This is important in that the extent of the investigations involved in (say) an audit engagement would be greater than in the case of a more limited accountancy function. Even where the nature of an engagement is agreed to be an audit, disputes may arise as to whether the audit contract requires the taking of certain steps. These incidents of the audit contract may be spelt out in the contract itself or by statute (Section 193(4) Companies Act, 1990) or may be resolved by reference to decided case law. However, the "content" of the auditors' duty as determined in older judgments may have to be approached with some degree of caution as they concerned audit procedures and practices appropriate to much smaller and less complex organisations than those common today.

The classic formulation of an auditor's duty is set out by Stirling J. in *Leeds Estate, Building and Investment Co. v. Shepard* [1887] 36 Ch. Div. 787 as:

> The duty of an auditor is not to confine himself merely to the task of verifying the arithmetical accuracy of the balance sheet, but to enquire into its substantial accuracy, and to ascertain that it contained the particulars specified in the Articles of Association (and consequently a proper income and expenditure account), and was properly drawn up, so as to contain a true and correct representation of the state of the company's affairs.

The duty of auditors involves ascertaining and forming an opinion as to the true financial position of the company presented to the shareholders and, to this end, examining the books and records of the company and carrying out such enquiries as a reasonable and careful auditor would do. It is clearly established that an auditor is not responsible for every error and is not the insurer or guarantor of the accuracy of the audited statements. It is possible that two reasonable and careful auditors could come to divergent conclusions based on the same set of facts without being negligent. The duty of auditors is to exercise reasonable skill and care in the conduct of the audit and in the making of the report. They do not have to approach the task with a suspicious mind but if the circumstances would arouse suspicion in the mind of a reasonably careful auditor then the extent of their duty and the nature of their enquiries should be considerably more far reaching and the auditors should qualify their report if their suspicions remain unresolved.

The fact that fraud is not detected in the course of an audit does not itself prove negligence in the conduct of the audit. For example, in *Re Kingston Cotton Mill Co.* (No. 2) [1896] 2 Ch. 279, the auditor relied on a certificate of value of stock-in-trade given by the managing director of the client company and signed the balance sheet as representing a true and accurate record of the company's affairs. The Court of Appeal held that in the absence of anything to arouse the auditors' suspicion they were entitled to rely on the certificate of the managing director who was adjudged in all the circumstances to be a competent and responsible person. It follows that auditors cannot be made liable for detecting ingenious and carefully laid schemes of fraud when there is nothing to arouse their suspicion, but it does not absolve them from having to make careful enquiries and investigations. In a recent UK case, *Anthony* v. *Wright*, reported on 27 September 1994, an action against the auditors of a company by investors failed: the court found that the auditors could not be blamed for not spotting the fraudulent activity of the directors of the company, and further that there was no evidence that the investors deposited their money in reliance on the audits carried out by the defendant auditors.

In *Re Thomas Gerrard & Son Limited* [1968] 1 Ch. 455, Pennycuick J. found that the auditors breached their duty by failing to detect a fraudulent scheme instigated by the managing director, which resulted in inflated profits and enlarged dividends over a five-year period. The auditors had questioned certain post-dated invoices but accepted the explanations given by the managing director and did not qualify their report. Pennycuick J. found that the discovery of the altered invoices should have put the auditors on enquiry and they should have made further investigations by examining suppliers' statements and, if necessary, communicating with the suppliers and informing the Board of Directors of the company of their findings. The auditors were held liable for the overpayment of dividends and for the cost of recovering excessive tax paid and such amount of overpaid tax as was unrecoverable.

Whilst the judicial consensus was initially against the imposition of a duty on auditors in tort to clients, such a duty has now been recognised in *Batty* v. *Metropolitan Property Realisation Limited* [1978] Q.B. 544 and *Caparo Industries plc* v. *Dickman* [1990] A.C. 605. Many actions were framed in contract and in tort, a case in point being *Galoo Limited and Others* v. *Bright Grahame Murray* [1994] BCC 319, where the ultimate parent company of the group to which the auditors' client belonged framed its action in tort as it had no contractual relationship with the auditors. The client company sued in contract and in tort in order to support an argument for a more extended chain of causation.

THE STANDARD OF CARE

In the same way that the duty of auditors is subject to continuous change and refinement, judicial decisions can do little more than give a broad indication of the standard of care required. In this section we examine briefly some of the judgments that specifically address the question of such standards.

It has been noted previously that the standard of care will depend largely on the nature of the task undertaken. If the engagement involves an accountancy task of a more limited nature than an audit, then the degree of investigation involved may be reduced. For example, in *Meade* v. *Bell Baker & Co.* [1911] T.L.R. 269, a firm of accountants was engaged to investigate the accounts of a business to enable a person to decide whether to advance money. The consequent overvaluation in the accountants' report could not have been detected except by physical examination. The court held that the defendant had exercised reasonable care in its investigation of the accounts based on the stock sheets of the company. However, caution should be exercised in dealing with old cases, since the accountancy practices in operation at that time may not be consistent with the more complex business organisations and transactions common today.

In *Kelly* v. *Boland T/A Haughey Boland & Co.* [1989] ILRM 373, Lardner J. in the Irish High Court discussed the standard of care. Whilst accepting that an auditor cannot conduct an examination of all the company's transactions during a particular accounting period the Judge stated that an auditor must ascertain what procedures a company has made for accurate stocktaking and should test them for compliance. Whilst on the evidence the Judge found that at the time of the events in question there was no professional standard to the effect that an auditor should attend at the stocktaking, the Judge also found that it was recommended by the profession that attendance at a stocktaking was the best way of testing or checking the adequacy of the company's procedures. On the facts however, the Judge found that the plaintiff had failed to establish that the accounts for the year in question were misleading, and he therefore did not find it necessary to address the issue of reliance on the accounts.

The issue of accepting valuations of stock-in-trade or work-in-progress prepared by individual directors or by management has arisen frequently. It is far preferable for auditors to generate their own audit evidence directly, for example, by attendance at the stocktaking to establish the accuracy of the procedures employed. Sources of audit evidence include not only the accounting systems and underlying documentation of an enterprise, its tangible assets and management/employees, but also customers, suppliers and other third parties having dealings with or knowledge of the enterprise or its business. It is a matter of professional judgment in the circumstances of each case whether there is an adequate amount of reliable audit evidence, sufficient to enable the auditors to draw reasonable conclusions therefrom. However, in certain circumstances it may be appropriate to seek evidence from reliable and independent third parties, such as, for example, where the stock requires specialist valuation.

It emerges, therefore, that adherence to professional standards or accepted procedures in the profession may afford some protection, and the courts will often use such standards to assess a standard of care as in *Kelly* v. *Boland T/A Haughey Boland & Co.* However, if such practice is, or has over time become, inherently defective, the courts will not refrain from overturning or at least questioning long accepted auditing practices. The American and Australian courts have taken this course of action in *Continental Vending* (CCA FED.SEC.L.REP. 1992, 511) and *Pacific Acceptance* v. *Forsyth* (1970) 92 (NSW) 29 respectively.

THE AUDITOR'S DUTY TO THIRD PARTIES

One of the most contentious areas of auditors' liabilities in recent years has been the classification of categories of person to whom auditors owe a duty of care in tort. It is instructive to address briefly the genesis of the expansion of the frontiers of liability and then the variety of mechanisms by which the courts have sought to contain those same frontiers.

It was formerly the prevailing judicial view that there was no liability for a negligent misrepresentation made by one person to another who had acted upon it to their detriment, in the absence of any contractual or fiduciary relationship between the parties or of fraud. This view reflected a fear that the extension of actionability to third parties upon negligent misstatements would result in "a liability in an indeterminate amount for an indeterminate time to an indeterminate class" in the words of Cardozo C.J. in *Ultramares Corporation* v. *Touche* (1931) 174 N.E. 441 at p. 444.

The first solid judicial support for the extension of the parameters of liability for negligent misrepresentation came in the dissenting speech of Denning L.J. in *Candler* v. *Crane Christmas & Co.* [1951] 2

K.B. 164. The breakthrough in recoverability for pure economic loss came in the decision of the House of Lords in *Hedley Byrne & Co. Limited* v. *Heller & Partners Limited* [1964] A.C. 465, in which, but for a sufficiently wide disclaimer, the defendant would have been held liable on foot of a certificate of creditworthiness relied upon by the plaintiff. Hedley Byrne is generally regarded as requiring a special relationship to exist for one person to owe another a duty of care in the giving of advice or information. Lord Morris (at page 503) stated that a duty of care would arise "if in a sphere in which a person is so placed, that others could reasonably rely on his judgment or his skill or upon his ability to make careful enquiry, that person takes it upon himself to give information or advice or allows his information or advice to be passed onto another person who, as he knows or should know, will place reliance upon it ...". This statement was approved by Carroll J. in *McSweeney* v. *Burke* (unreported High Court, 24 November 1980).

The Hedley Byrne principle has been recognised in Ireland, initially by Davitt P. in *Securities Trust Limited* v. *Hugh Moore and Alexander* [1964] I.R. 417, and subsequently in the context of auditors' liability in *John Sisk and Son Limited* v. *Donal Patrick Flinn & Others* (unreported 18 July 1984, Finlay P.).

In *Bank of Ireland* v. *Smith* [1966] I.R. 646, Kenny J. observed that liability for negligent misstatement was restricted to those exceptional situations where, but for the absence of consideration, there would be a contractual relationship. If Kenny J.'s interpretation of the Hedley Byrne principle were to be applied generally it would make it virtually impossible for third parties to recover damages in negligence against auditors except in the most unusual cases. But there are indications that Kenny J.'s interpretation of Hedley Byrne has been superseded and O'Hanlon J. acknowledged as much in *T.E. Potterton Limited* v. *Northern Bank Limited* [1993] ILRM 225, where he observed that significant developments had taken place in the law of negligence since Hedley Byrne was decided and its effect interpreted in *Bank of Ireland* v. *Smith*, particularly in the areas of negligent misrepresentation and negligent misstatement. Indeed, in the Sisk case, Finlay P. eschewed the special relationship restriction and approved of the words of Lord Reid in Hedley Byrne:

> ... I can see no logical stopping place short of all those relationships where it is plain that the party seeking information was trusting the other to exercise such a degree of care as the circumstances required, where it was reasonable for him to do that and where the

information or advice was given when the person knew or ought to have known that the enquirer was relying on him.

The range and number of persons who may suffer loss consequent upon negligent performance of certain engagements by auditors is potentially very large. In the case of a negligent report on a company's accounts by its auditors, the potential range may include shareholders, prospective investors, banks and trade creditors who may have relied upon the report. Inevitably, the question of liability will, to a large extent, turn on the facts of each particular case. Understandably, the Hedley Byrne principle has sown the seeds of uncertainty regarding to whom a duty of care is owed, and the courts have been seeking to identify the exact parameters of this principle ever since. In so far as it can be applied to auditors, the Hedley Byrne test basically turns on whether the plaintiff is a person or within a class of persons whom the auditors knew or ought to have known would rely upon their report or other statement for a purpose which they also knew or ought to have known and that the plaintiff did in fact rely upon that statement to his or her detriment.

In *JEB Fasteners v. Marks Bloom & Co.* [1981] 1 All E.R. 583, the plaintiffs had entered into negotiations to take over a manufacturing company that had recently started trading in the same products as the plaintiffs. The defendants (the target company's auditors), knew that the plaintiffs were negotiating to take over the company and produced audited accounts which were made available to the plaintiffs. The plaintiffs knew that the audited accounts were inaccurate but did not appreciate the full extent of the inaccuracies. In the subsequent action for breach of the auditors' duty of care to the prospective investors, the court found that the primary motivation for the takeover was to secure the services of two directors of the target company, and that while the accounts had been negligently prepared, the element of reliance was absent. It emerges from this case that a valid action requires breach of a duty of care causing loss or detriment to the plaintiffs and that the defendants might have reasonably foreseen at the time the accounts were prepared that a person such as the plaintiff would rely on the accuracy of those accounts in the circumstances then prevailing. In addition, the court added the requirement of actual reliance on the statements.

In the UK, a temporary hiatus occurred in the development of liability for negligence generally, in the form of the two-stage test for liability formulated by Lord Wilberforce in *Anns v. Merton London Borough Council* [1978] A.C. 728. This two stage test asks:

- Whether between the parties there is a sufficient relationship of proximity or neighbourhood in which case a prima facie duty of care arises; and if so

- Whether there are any considerations which ought to negate, or to reduce or limit, the scope of the duty or the class of persons to whom it is owed or the damages to which a breach of it may give rise.

This approach is based on the foreseeability of the damage and the proximity of relationship between parties. Proximity of relationship concerns the closeness and directness of the relationship between the parties. It is not a definable concept, but rather a collection of circumstances involving, *inter alia*, the purpose for which the statement was made and the knowledge of the maker and the reliance of the recipient. The British courts have also added a further requirement, namely whether it is just and reasonable in all the circumstances to impose a duty of care. It is difficult to see what, if anything, this adds to the public policy element of the Anns two-stage test.

However, in the UK there has been a steady movement away from the two-stage principle applicable to all cases, towards separate duties of care applicable to particular situations. The seminal case in this respect is *Caparo Industries plc* v. *Dickman* [1990] AC 605. This case involved an action against the directors and auditors of a company arising out of an unprofitable takeover by the plaintiff. The auditors' report on the company's accounts stated that they gave a true and fair view of the relevant matters, but they were in fact grossly inaccurate. The plaintiff argued that the auditors owed a duty of care at least in respect of its purchases of shares made subsequent to the dissemination of the audited accounts (although the plaintiff was not registered as a shareholder when the accounts were circulated to the shareholders and did not attend the Annual General Meeting before which the audited accounts were laid). The plaintiff contended that if it had known the true position it would not have purchased the shares at all, or at least not at the price actually paid. The plaintiff contended that the auditors knew or ought to have known of the target company's need for financial assistance and that it was vulnerable to a takeover and that prospective investors might rely on the accounts in assessing a bid and would suffer loss if the accounts were inaccurate.

The House of Lords held that the auditors did not owe a duty of care to the plaintiff, either in its capacity as a potential investor or as a shareholder. The audited statements were in general circulation and could foreseeably be relied upon by third parties for any one of a variety of purposes which the maker of the statement had no specific reason to anticipate. In the speeches in the House of Lords there was considerable concern over the danger of indeterminate liability and support for the imposition of a limit on liability towards persons who have suffered economic loss. In particular, the House of Lords rejected the imposition of a duty of care arising from the auditing provisions of the Companies Act, 1985 (UK). It observed that the purpose of the auditors' report is to equip the shareholders with sufficient knowledge to enable them to monitor the financial affairs of the company to ensure that these matters are being managed properly and to vote accordingly at shareholders' meetings, and this purpose did not extend to the provision of information to assist shareholders or others in the making of decisions concerning future investment in the company.

A different, more expansionist, conclusion was reached by the Court of Appeal in *Morgan Crucible Co. plc* v. *Hill Samuel Co. Limited* [1991] BCC 82, where the plaintiffs made a takeover bid on the basis of the audited accounts of the target company. Further statements were made by the company and its advisers in an attempt to defend the company against the takeover bid. The plaintiffs ultimately succeeded in the takeover bid but subsequently brought an action against the company and the auditors, alleging that the accounts and defence statements were misleading and that the company was worth much less than they had paid for it.

The Court of Appeal found in favour of the plaintiffs and distinguished the House of Lords decision in *Caparo* v. *Dickman* on the grounds that not only were the defendants aware that the plaintiffs would rely on their representations for the purpose of deciding whether or not to make an increased bid, but that they intended that they should. This was so notwithstanding the fact that the plaintiffs had their own independent advisers, as much of the information on which the accounts and profit forecast was based was available to the defendants alone. Glidewell L.J. in *Galoo Limited* v. *Bright Grahame Murray* [1994] BCC 319, in the course of a useful discussion of the relevant authority expressed the distinction thus (at p. 336):

> A mere foreseeability that a potential bidder may rely on the audited accounts does not impose on the auditor a duty of care to the bidder, but if the auditor is made expressly aware that a particular identified bidder will rely on the audited or other statements

approved by the auditor, and intends that the bidder should so rely, the auditor will be under a duty of care to the bidder for the breach of which he may be liable.

Although the Court of Appeal in Morgan Crucible was bound by the decision of the House of Lords in *Caparo* v. *Dickman*, there is a certain degree of divergence evident, the Court of Appeal taking a more expansionist view of liability albeit against a compelling factual background. It is likely that tension will continue between different courts in relation to the limits of auditors' liability in takeover situations and each case will to a large extent have to be judged on its own merits.

A further restriction on the range of potential plaintiffs came in *Al Saudi Banque and Others* v. *Clark Pixley*, a case decided more than six months before the House of Lords decision in *Caparo* v. *Dickman*. In *Al Saudi*, the plaintiffs were bankers who had made loans to a company, and the defendants were the company's auditors who had audited the company's accounts for three years before it was compulsorily wound up with an estimated deficiency of Stg£8.6 million. The plaintiffs argued that the defendants ought reasonably to have foreseen that the banks would rely on the accuracy of the auditors' reports in deciding whether to continue, renew or increase their loans, and that the defendants were in breach of their duty of care as the reports did not give a true and accurate account of the company's affairs.

Millet J. held that the bankers were not in the same position as shareholders to whom the auditors had a duty to report, and that since the defendants did not know that the company intended to supply the audited accounts to the banks, they owed no duty of care to the plaintiffs. The judges in the House of Lords in *Caparo* v. *Dickman* were of the opinion that *Al Saudi* was decided correctly.

In *James McNaughton Paper Group Limited* v. *Hicks Andersen & Co.* [1991] 2. Q.B. 113, Neill J. set out a list of factors relevant to determining whether a duty of care exists. They are as follows:

- The purpose for which the statement was made
- The purpose for which the statement was communicated
- The relationship between the adviser, the advisee and any third party
- The size of any class to which the advisee belongs
- The state of knowledge of the adviser

- The reliance by the advisee.

This case involved an agreed takeover in respect of which draft financial statements were prepared by the auditors and were made available to the plaintiff. The chairman of the company had disclosed to the investor the poor financial state of the company, but the plaintiff proceeded with the takeover anyway. The court, in finding that no duty of care arose on the facts, emphasised the fact that the accounts were in draft form and the disclosure made by the chairman. In addition, the plaintiff had its own accountancy advisers and the court would not attribute any knowledge of the plaintiff's reliance on the defendant.

More recently in the Galoo case, the intermediate and ultimate parent companies of a subsidiary commenced proceedings against the auditors of the subsidiary when it went into liquidation. The plaintiffs claimed that the accounts for the years 1985–89 and the draft audited accounts for 1990 contained substantial inaccuracies, and that the defendants were in breach of duties in contract and tort to the plaintiffs as a result of which they had suffered loss. The Court of Appeal upheld the High Court's ruling that no reasonable cause of action was disclosed by the plaintiff's claim.

The court set out a test for determining reasonable cause in such action: firstly whether the alleged negligent act gave rise to an occasion for damage; and then to apply common sense to determine whether the act was in fact the effective or dominant cause of the damage. On the facts, the court found that the losses incurred by the subsidiary after the issue of the inaccurate audit report were not caused by the report. The court found that the losses flowed from trading rather than the audit reports.

There are few reported Irish cases on auditors' negligence, and there is some doubt as to whether the Irish courts will follow the approach taken in *Caparo* v. *Dickman*. The out-of-court settlement of the case brought against accountants Ernst & Whinney by AIB plc and Icarom has ruled out the short-term possibility of an authoritative exposition of the Irish law in this area.

In *Kelly* v. *Boland T/A Haughey Boland & Co.* [1989] ILRM 373, Lardner J. adopted as a statement of the appropriate test of liability the words of Woolf J. in *JEB Fasteners* v. *Marks Bloom & Co.* [1981] 3 AER 289 (which was later disapproved of by the House of Lords in *Caparo* v. *Dickman*) when he said:

> ...the appropriate test for establishing whether a duty of care exists appears in this case to be whether the defendants knew or reasonably should have foreseen at the time the accounts were audited that a person might rely on those accounts for the purpose of deciding whether or not to take over the company and therefore could suffer loss if the accounts were inaccurate.

However, *Kelly* v. *Boland* was decided before *Caparo* v. *Dickman* and cannot therefore be said to represent a divergence from British or Commonwealth law as it stood then, and indeed Lardner J. thought that he was applying principles identical to those applied in Great Britain and New Zealand. It is a strong case in favour of the existence of a duty of care by auditors to third parties but does not give any guidance as to the imposition of a duty of care in more extended situations, such as the purchase of shares in a publicly quoted company and reliance on the published accounts.

Further, McCarthy J. in *Ward* v. *McMaster* [1989] ILRM 400 (a case unconnected with auditors' negligence) preferred to express the duty of care as arising from the proximity of the parties, the foreseeability of the damage and the absence of any compelling exemption based on public policy, and he saw no reason to dilute the two stage principle set out in *Anns* v. *Merton London Borough Council*.

There has been subsequent Irish High Court authority which confirms continued Irish adherence to the principles expounded in *Anns* v. *Merton London Borough Council* and *Ward* v. *McMaster*. In *Sweeney* v. *Duggan* [1991] (Vol. 1) I.R. 274, Barron J., in a case unconnected with auditors' negligence, followed *Ward* v. *McMaster*. Barron J. observed that certain British cases concerning the recoverability of economic loss in tort decided since *Caparo* v. *Dickman* were of very limited authority.

Although there are very few cases in which anything approaching a comprehensive formulation of the law relating to negligent misstatement has been attempted by Irish judges, there are some indications that Irish courts may not follow the lead given by the House of Lords in *Caparo* v. *Dickman* and might adopt a more conceptual approach. Indeed, the two-stage principle has much to commend itself in the context of third-party claims against auditors. The second stage of the test expressly permits policy considerations to be taken into account in reducing the class of persons to whom a duty is owed and the damages to which a breach of the duty of care may give rise. There is a possibility that the two-stage principle might be used to circumvent the type of ad hoc restrictions that are built up on a case-by-case basis in British jurisprudence. However, it can be seen that neither approach contributes greatly to the reduction of the uncertainty inherent in this area. Some British commentators are of the view that in the light of numerous large claims against auditors at present before the courts, legislative intervention is unlikely, and that the courts are the most likely forum for development of the law in this area as evidenced by their restrictive interpretation of auditors' liability.

INSURING AUDIT LIABILITY EXPOSURE

The legal uncertainties in the area of audit liability mean that insurance is critically important for the audit practitioner. The recent difficulty of obtaining Professional Indemnity Insurance (PII) for accountants is accentuated by the publicity surrounding recent large claims and settlements and by the shifting sands of the legal liability of auditors in terms of the precise nature of the duty owed and the classes of persons to whom it is owed. The PII market for accountants is controlled by a small number of players and is heavily dependent on the reinsurance market, whereby a large proportion of potential risks are passed on at premium rates. The PII market has hardened in line with the trends of the insurance market generally, but the shortage of capacity for PII has been proportionally greater than the general market as the insurance market prefers to deal with more predictable risks.

This hardening of the PII market has made itself felt most acutely amongst small accountancy practices where many do not have any PII cover or are substantially underinsured or are not covered for certain risks such as incoming partners' previous business risks. Some of the larger accountancy firms now operate mutual insurance schemes for claims up to a certain amount, although they still have recourse to the international market to insure larger risks.

A further serious development in the insurance sector has been the move to an annual aggregate basis in many insurance policies and the increase of self-insured deductibles. In effect, this means that accountancy firms' insurance cover could be exhausted during the course of a year and the individual partners could be exposed to personal liability and bankruptcy in the event of a large claim.

The special vulnerability of accountants acting as auditors stems from their statutory function. Under Section 200 of the Companies Act, 1963, auditors of a company are not at liberty to negotiate a limit on their liability to, or a reimbursement in the form of an indemnity with, their client. Further, accountancy firms do not have the benefit of limited liability. There has been considerable pressure for reform and the matter has been studied by the Department of Trade and Industry in the UK (which invited submissions from the Institute of Chartered Accountants in Ireland) and its findings have been set out in the Likierman Report published in 1989. It is proposed to address briefly a number of the areas covered in that report.

1) The Likierman Report noted that there was considerable pressure for reform of Section 310 of the Companies Act, 1985 (UK) [which was amended by Section 137(ii) of the Companies Act 1989 (UK) — the Irish equivalent is Section 200, Companies Act 1963] and in particular, to allow auditors and their clients to negotiate agreed liability limits and also to allow companies to procure insurance for their directors and other officers. It was noted that this latter proposal would reduce the exposure of auditors by affording company directors sufficient resources to meet their potential liability. The Likierman Report supported a request for clarification or amendment of Section 310 to allow developments in these areas. It was considered that such a development would put audit services on the same footing as other accountancy and professional services where it is open to negotiate a limit on liability and indemnity. The report observed that the degree of limitation or level of indemnity would be set by market forces rather than by any outside intervention.

2) The Likierman Report rejected the idea of imposing a ceiling on claims which could be brought against auditors as it would prevent plaintiffs from recovering the full loss suffered by them and could also bring the profession into disrepute.

3) The report considered at length the nature of the principle of joint and several liability imposed on auditors. It was the feeling of many in the accountancy profession that, because of the perceived availability of professional indemnity insurance, auditors were seen as a "deep pocket" and had to carry an unfair burden of liability. Co-defendants such as company directors would frequently be uninsured and/or would not have sufficient personal resources to meet claims against them. The defendant auditors' right of contribution from co-defendants would, in such circumstances, be practically useless and the auditors would end up bearing the entire burden. The report examined proposals that liability should be

several and not joint, meaning that only a fair proportion of the loss should be borne by the auditor. The report considered that a change in the principle of joint and several liability would not be effective of itself to redress the imbalance that had developed, but recommended that the United Kingdom Law Reform Commission should examine the question of joint and several liability in the wider context of auditors' liability.

4) The report examined a proposal to allow the courts a discretionary power to reduce awards by whatever proportion appeared fair, taking into account the degree of negligence, the auditors' insurance cover and the comparative ability of each party to bear the loss. However, the report concluded that this type of proposal would merely add to the uncertainty already inherent in this area.

5) The report did not support the imposition of compulsory directors' insurance but did observe that if such insurance were to be allowed as a deductible expense for taxation purposes, then it might be encouraged and could contribute towards reducing the exposure of auditors as co-defendants in negligence claims.

CONCLUSION

The spiralling costs of insurance cover, the restriction in the nature of the risks covered, as well as the uncertainty as to the legal principles applied by the courts in determining liability, are creating great difficulties for accountancy firms generally and, in particular, in the carrying out of their audit functions. This has resulted in many firms being uninsured or substantially underinsured, thus posing the risk of personal liability and ultimately possible bankruptcy for the individual partners. This problem needs to be tackled on a number of fronts. Clearly, as the Likierman Report shows, there is scope for reform in the insurance sector. It would appear that some of the problems in this area can be accounted for by the turbulent nature of the insurance market reacting to high-profile claims by raising premiums and by withdrawing certain types of insurance product without reference to the individual client's record or standard of management.

It would not be fair to attribute the entire blame for rising insurance costs on the current legal régime. The perceived availability of insurance makes auditors a prime target for plaintiffs, whatever the merits of the claim. Insurance companies have shown themselves to be prepared to make substantial pre-trial settlements in order to avoid prolonged court battles, giving a further currency to the "deep pocket" theory.

It is possibly too early to determine whether the restrictive approach heralded in *Caparo* v. *Dickman*, and some but not all subsequent British cases, will ameliorate the situation or cause further confusion. It is far from clear whether Irish courts will in any event adopt this restrictive approach. Indeed, if the Irish courts continue to adhere to the two-stage principle approved by McCarthy J. in *Ward* v. *McMaster*, it may afford an opportunity to restrict liability and/or damages expressly by reference to compelling public-policy factors, rather than by seeking to manufacture a ground for distinguishing a case from previous authority, the occurrence of which can be seen in some recent British cases.

6
Directors and the Law

Michael Forde
Barrister-at-Law

INTRODUCTION
The question of directors and the law is a vast one and it would be impossible in this short chapter to give a comprehensive account of the present situation. That, however, is probably unnecessary: the existing books on Company Law have lengthy chapters on the subject, and there are books on directors' duties and liabilities, as well as several on the topic of insider trading. Accordingly, in this chapter, the discussion is confined mainly to the general conceptual framework within which the directors' liability system operates. The chapter begins with a review of the sources and goes on to examine these specific dimensions of the directors' duties.

SOURCES OF LAW
For registered companies, obviously the principal sources of the relevant law are the Companies Acts, 1963–1990. There are now so many Companies Acts and so many amendments by one or more acts that a consolidation of the law is badly needed in one single Act, as was attempted in Britain in 1985. At least in this regard, private enterprise has come to the rescue with two unofficial consolidations, which have proven invaluable to practitioners.

Ideally, the relevant law — indeed, the entirety of Company Law — should be codified. If that were done, then all of the main principles and rules would be contained in the one enactment and case law would play only a subsidiary part in the scheme of things — whereas, at present, there are several vitally important areas covered entirely by case law and without any pertinent statutory provision. The explanation, it would seem, is that in England the entire process of codification has been regarded as some kind of alien Continental aberration and, therefore, anathema. It is thought, mistakenly, that codes would deprive lawyers and judges of their creative role in keeping the law in touch with changing commercial and social circumstances. And, since they do not codify in England, why should we do so here? At times we strike European postures, but seem to shun that very sensible and European technique for making the law relatively simple and coherent, and rendering its content easily accessible to any intelligent person who wants to know what the law is on any particular point. Even in New Zealand, the Government has decided to codify one of the most difficult aspects of the subject — that of the duties of company directors.

At present, in Ireland, directors' rights and duties are governed principally by case law — the common law and equity. Many of the leading cases are decisions of the English courts, which the courts here tend to follow. However, there are divergences in the treatment by the cases of certain matters. Also, the position in the companies Acts on several matters differs between the jurisdictions — most obviously, perhaps, with regard to "insider trading". Although membership of the European Union is resulting in greater uniformity between the position in Ireland and that in Britain, even in areas that are covered by EU Directives there remain divergences of detail.

WHO IS A DIRECTOR?

Normally, a director will have been duly elected to the office at a previous annual general meeting of the company. Occasionally, the company's articles will lay down another method for selecting one or more of the directors. Problems arise with persons who have been acting as directors but were never properly appointed to the office. So far as the company's dealings with third parties are concerned, s178 of the 1963 Act provides a reasonable safeguard against outsiders being unfairly disadvantaged.

De Facto Directors

Is a de facto director a director for the purposes of the Companies Acts? According to s. 2(i) of the 1963 Act, the definition section, a director "includes any person occupying the position of a director by whatever name called". What this probably means is that a person can be a director even if, in the company, that person has been given some other title or description; although this definition could be construed as answering the question posed above in the affirmative. Where the articles of association lay down a procedure for appointing a director, it seems wrong to treat as a director a person who has not been duly appointed to the office, except where all the members have acquiesced in the de facto position. Some of the directors' liabilities under the Companies Acts apply to de facto directors too.

Shadow Directors

The concept of a "shadow director" existed prior to 1990 but was rendered far more significant by the Companies Act of that year. A "shadow director" is the person "in accordance with whose directions or instructions the directors of the company are accustomed to act".[1] Whether a person fits this description depends on the circumstance of the particular case.

Families of Directors

For several purposes, members of a director's immediate family are treated by legislation as if they also were directors of the company. Thus, they are ineligible to be appointed as the company's auditor, or as its examiner or liquidator. The restrictions against making loans to directors, and on substantial property transactions with directors equally apply to members of their families.[2]

RIGHTS AND DUTIES GENERALLY

A few basic points call to be made about directors' rights and duties generally, which are elaborated on in all of the standard textbooks.

Collective Rights and Duties

As a body or group, the directors' function is to manage the company's business; management is both their right and their duty. In companies with articles along the lines of article 80 of Table A, this means that even a majority of the shareholders have no legal right to dictate to the directors on matters of management; except where the articles provide otherwise, the board of directors is legally autonomous. However, most boards will be very attentive to the wishes of a majority of the shareholders, if for no reason other than that a simple majority vote is enough to remove any or all of the directors. The Companies Acts require many things to be done by the entire board of directors or by several directors chosen by the board for the purpose.

Individual Rights

Every director has two rights by virtue of their office, which have been the subject of two carefully reasoned decisions of the Irish courts. One is to be given notice of and be permitted to attend all board meetings.[3] The other is to be permitted to inspect all of the company's books and records.[4] In addition to these, the articles of association and also any service agreements may confer other additional rights.

Individual Duties

In a recent decision, involving a claim against one of Robert Maxwell's sons for the indifferent way in which he attended to the affairs of one of the Maxwell companies, Chadwick J. stressed the responsibilities of all persons who become company directors, in these terms:

> No one is obliged to accept office as a director of a company incorporated under the Companies Acts. Those who do so undertake duties imposed by the company's memorandum and articles of association, the provisions of the Companies Acts and the general law. In particular, they must be taken to accept those duties which are ancillary to the exercise of the powers conferred on directors by the articles of association. Those are fiduciary powers and, as such, are subject to the provisions of the general law relating to the exercise of fiduciary powers.[5]

In other words, every director, as well as being bound by the now very detailed provisions of the Companies Acts, is in much the same position as a trustee for the shareholders. Accordingly, they are bound by much the same obligations as the law imposes on trustees — known as fiduciary duties. These are duties which have been developed by the Chancery courts over time in order to protect persons whose property or affairs have been entrusted to the management of others. Thus, the standard of prudence and probity required of directors is a comparatively high one.

The vast body of cases on directors' duties can be reduced to three very general propositions, viz.

1) In managing the company's business, the directors must exercise reasonable care and should not act negligently. If the company suffers loss in consequence of any of their negligence, then it is entitled to claim compensation for that loss.

2) In exercising their powers, especially those conferred by the articles of association, the directors must use that power for a

proper purpose and not for some extraneous objective. Many of the cases under this heading concern alleged wrongful allotments of new shares or vetoing requests to approve transfers of shares.

3) The directors must avoid undue conflict of interests, and especially, not enrich themselves or any of them at the company's expense, or indeed gain from any commercial opportunity that came their way in consequence of their being directors of the company. Several of the commonest cases under this heading are now the subject of detailed statutory regulations, for instance :

- 1963 Act s.194: disclosing financial interest in contract
- id.s.196: shareholder approval for golden handshakes
- 1990 Act s.29: substantial property transactions with a company
- id.pt.III: loans to directors
- id.pt.V: insider dealing.

Regarding the category 3) duty, there is a surprising dearth of Irish case law on how demanding the law will be in potential conflict-of-interest situations. On several occasions, the English courts have condemned transactions in which a director gains financially, although it could be said that the director did not profit at the company's expense or act in a morally reprehensible manner.[6] The tendency is to lay down a very strict standard, in order to deter even contemplation of possible conflicts of interest. At times, courts in the Commonwealth have not been quite as demanding. Because of the dearth of cases, it is hard to predict the approach of the Irish courts; the various text books take it almost for granted that the strict English approach would be followed here.

Section 391 of the 1963 Act lends support to this view. This enables any company officer, who has acted unlawfully, to apply to the court to be exonerated from the consequences of the illegality. If in the circumstances the court is satisfied that directors acted honestly and reasonably, and if in all fairness they should be excused in whole or partly, the court will direct that they be relieved from the consequences of their actions. In one instance, where action was taken on the strength of Counsel's opinion, which proved to be erroneous, it was held that the directors had acted normally.[7] In another case, where the directors approved a somewhat complex transaction without having the benefit of Counsel's opinion, it was held that they had acted unreasonably.[8]

DIRECTORS' DUTIES IN SPECIAL CONTEXTS

Most of the reported cases on directors' fiduciary duties concern small to medium-sized private companies operating commercial undertakings. Often, the defendant director is also the majority shareholder in the company, so that often the actual plaintiff is not the company itself but an aggrieved minority shareholder. At times, the plaintiff is neither the company nor a shareholder but the liquidator seeking compensation for the losses that the alleged errant director inflicted on the company. In the case of public companies, especially those with shares quoted on the stock exchange, it is likely that the directors would be more professional, and less inclined to breach their duties; and, where there are allegations of abuse, the matter tends to be settled out of court.

Because this collection of essays is principally concerned with the auditor, some reference to directors' duties to auditors is called for. Some of the more atypical directors' duty situations then call for consideration.

Duty to Auditors

The duty of auditors to companies and their shareholders is a most controversial matter, engendering a spate of litigation, often involving claims of millions of pounds or dollars. A matter that seems to have escaped attention, however, is almost the other side of this coin, viz. the duty of the company and its directors to the auditors. There appears to be no reported case law on the point.

All that the Companies Acts say on the question is that the auditor is "entitled to require from the officers of the company such information and explanations that are within their knowledge or can be procured by them as he thinks necessary for the performance of the duties of auditors" (s.193(3) of the 1990 Act). Failure of a director to provide relevant information, when requested by the auditors, is a criminal offence, except where it was not reasonably possible to do so within the time specified. It therefore would seem that each director's statutory duty is to provide such information as the auditors request and no more than that; it is not a duty to bring to the attention of the auditors matters which one might reasonably expect to be drawn to their attention.

It is possible, however, that in certain circumstances the common law will impose some duty to inform or to warn auditors of matters of that nature. Against such a duty being imposed, it could be argued that the courts should not add to the requirement set out in s.193(3) of the 1990 Act, and, furthermore, the auditors could easily have got the directors to sign undertakings that they will disclose all relevant information, as a condition of conducting the audit.

Duties to Employees

It makes good practical sense for directors to take account of the interests of company employees: most successful companies have good employee relations. So far as legal obligations are concerned, however, formerly directors were not permitted to put the interests of employees before those of the company and its members: employee interests could be accommodated only insofar as doing so was also in the company's interests.

In 1990 the position was changed for registered and "unregistered" companies, although the extent of the change is debatable. Under s.52(1) of the 1990 Act, there is an affirmative duty to take account of the interests of the employees; directors who disregard those interests contravene the Act. It would seem that, on occasion, employees' interest can be put before the immediate narrow interests of the company and its members; if this were not so, s.52 would be an entirely redundant provision. However, once directors give due attention to the employees' interests, the law leaves it to them to strike the appropriate balance.

From the employees' point of view, the main weakness in s.52 is that the duty there is declared to be owed only to the company and, by inference, not to the employees. And that duty is "enforceable in the same way as any other fiduciary duty owed to the company", that is, by the company itself. This qualification makes a virtual nonsense of s.52 because, although it imposes a duty on the directors, only those directors (who control the company) have a right to enforce that duty! One can envisage most exceptional situations where a new board of directors authorises proceedings against the previous board for disregarding this duty. Even then, as it is the employees, not the company, who would have suffered the loss, can the plaintiff company recover compensation on behalf of those employees, who have a right under s.52 but are patently deprived of any remedy for it?

Duties to Creditors

While it also makes good practical sense for directors to have some regard for the interest of their company's creditors, generally they have no legal obligation in this matter. This principle was affirmed recently by the Privy Council in the Kuwait Asia Bank case, that as a "general principle ... a director does not by reason of his position as a director owe any duty to creditors or to trustees for creditors of the company".[9] Nor, generally, do a company's auditors owe any duty of care to its creditors.[10] Where creditors lose substantial sums in dealing with a company, ordinarily they have no legal redress — unless they have taken out bad debts insurance.

But there are exceptions to this principle, which may be summarised as follows:

- **Contract**: If the creditor has entered into a separate contract with a director, then the latter may in the circumstances be liable under that contract. The commonest example is a guarantee.

- **Fraud**: If a director deliberately misleads a creditor, to the latter's detriment, then the director will be liable for the tort of deceit. Active misrepresentation is required for liability under this head; as was explained in the Court of Appeal, "subject to certain exceptions, the mere passive non-disclosure of the truth, however deceptive, does not amount to deceit in law".[11]

- **Negligent Misrepresentation**: Circumstances can arise where directors give creditors information which is false; the directors were culpably careless in not knowing that that information was untrue and should have realised that the creditors would act, to their detriment, on that information. In those circumstances, the directors might be held liable in negligence, unless they had a defence, e.g. contributory negligence.

- **Liquidation**: Where the company is insolvent and is being wound up, then the liquidator may be able to pursue claims against one or more of the directors, most notably for "misfeasance", for "reckless trading", for "fraudulent trading" or for not keeping adequate books and records. Instead of the liquidator any creditor may bring proceedings on those grounds — under ss.298 and 297a of the 1963 Act and s.204 of the 1990 Act.

- **Defunct Companies**: Since 1990, where the company is insolvent but is not being wound up because it has insufficient assets to attract a liquidator, any creditor can sue a director under the above sections, i.e. ss.298 and 297a of the 1963 Act and s.204 of the 1990 Act. A creditor can also apply to interrogate a director on oath, under s.245 of the 1963 Act, regarding the company's affairs and property.

In the United States, once a company becomes insolvent, directors are regarded to some extent as trustees of the company's assets for creditors, and thereby owe some duties to the creditors. Although at times judges in this country and in Britain have expressed views broadly along the same lines, those have mainly been *obiter dicta* in "misfeasance" actions being brought by liquidators.[12] While there are certain attractions in the US doctrine, it generally seems preferable, where the company is insolvent, to have its affairs resolved through the normal collective liquidation procedures, which should be adequate to cater for most creditors' concerns. Yet in *Re Frederick Inns Ltd.*,[13] decided in November 1993, the Supreme Court opted for the US approach and set aside an across-the-group settlement made with the Revenue on the grounds that the group was insolvent at the time, and, accordingly, group resources should have been kept for the benefit of the creditors generally. If the logic underlying its decision is given full rein, it will have enormous implications for companies in financial difficulties, and for their creditors.

UNLIMITED LIABILITY — RECKLESS TRADING

One of the fundamental principles of company law is that, in limited companies, shareholders are not liable for their company's unpaid debts beyond any amount that remains unpaid on their shares. Once the shares are fully paid up, the creditors have no right of redress against the shareholders. This principle has been qualified to some extent, especially where there has been fraud by the shareholder in question.

As far as the directors are concerned, they are simply appointed to manage the company's business and, by virtue of their office, are only accountable to the company for any wrongdoing on their part. Sections 197 and 198 of the 1963 Act enable companies, by their memorandum of association, to impose unlimited liability on their directors or managing director, but these provisions are rarely used, if ever. Apparently there is a tradition in Germany whereby directors of private banks always undertake unlimited liability for the duration of their tenure. In companies with stipulations of this nature in their memoranda, it must be made plain to persons being nominated for appointment to the board that they will be personally liable for all of the company's unpaid debts.

Where a company is being wound up, proceedings can be brought under s.298 of the 1963 Act against directors for "misfeasance". But any damages awarded under this heading are restricted to the loss caused by the actual wrongdoing in question.

One of the most significant of innovations introduced in 1990 was unlimited liability of present and former company officers for "reckless trading", in s.297a of the 1963 Act (inserted by s.138 of the 1990 Act). Because a company, for the purpose of s.297a, is defined therein as "any body which may be wound up under the Companies Acts", it would seem that s.297a reaches a wide category of companies; not alone registered companies and so-called "unregistered companies", but also some foreign-registered companies and building societies and industrial and provident societies. Shadow directors can be caught by s.297a and so too perhaps are de facto directors.

Reckless trading is considered to occur where:

> any person [who] was, while an officer of the company, knowingly a party to the carrying on of any business of the company in a reckless manner....
>
> Without prejudice to the generality of [this definition] an officer of the company shall be deemed to have been knowingly a party to the carrying on of any business of the company in a reckless manner if:
>
> 1) he was a party to the carrying on of such business, and having regard to the general knowledge, skill and experience that may reasonably be expected of a person in his position, he ought to have known that his actions or those of the company would cause loss to the creditors of the company or any of them, or;
>
> 2) he was a party to the contracting of a debt by the company and did not honestly believe on reasonable grounds that the company would be able to pay the debt when it fell due for payment as well as all its other debts (taking into account the contingent and prospective liabilities).

Many directors of companies experiencing financial difficulties are very apprehensive about potential liability for reckless trading. Yet the thrust of s.297a may have been over-exaggerated by some commentators, as the leading case on the point, *Re Hefferon Kearns Ltd.* (No. 2)[14] would suggest. This case concerned a firm of heating and plumbing contractors which ran into difficulties in the severe recession of 1990, the year after it had been incorporated. When the management accounts showed that there was a substantial deficiency, the directors met and agreed on an informal compromise with the company's principal creditors, involving disposal of most of its existing projects, each of which was in the ownership of separate related companies. Attempts were made to secure the creditors' consent and eventually a creditors' meeting was called which approved proposals to have an examiner appointed. Allegations were made that the company's directors had profited personally from several transactions involving the company, but those claims were rejected by the court. Because several of the directors had given personal guarantees to the company's bank, the entire enterprise had been a financial disaster for them as much as for the unsecured creditors. In concluding that the directors were not liable for reckless trading, Lynch J., made the following general observations about this new head of liability:

> At the outset s.297a does not impose a collective responsibility on a board of directors as such in respect of the manner in which a company has been run. [I]t operates individually and personally against the officers (which includes the directors) of a company and the onus rests on the plaintiffs to prove in relation to each of the defendants ... that his conduct falls within the ambit of the conduct prohibited or liable to be penalised by s.297a ... The meaning of the expression 'reckless' has been considered under different branches of the law, including the criminal law and the law of tort ... [T]he best and most realistic test of recklessness which has yet been propounded in cases of torts [is]: ... Recklessness is gross carelessness — the doing of something which in fact involves risk whether the doer realizes it or not: and the risk being such having regard to all the circumstances that the taking of that risk would be described in ordinary parlance as reckless. The likelihood or otherwise that damage will follow is one element to be considered, not whether the doer of the act actually realised the likelihood. The extent of the damage which is likely to follow is another element, not the extent which the doer of the act in his wisdom or folly happens to foresee. If the risk is slight and the damage which will follow if things go wrong is small it may not be reckless, however unjustified the doing of the act may be. If the risk is great and the probable damage great, recklessness may readily be a fair description, however much the doer may regard the action as justified and reasonable. Each case has to be viewed on its own particular facts and not by reference to any formula. The only test in my view is an objective one. Would a reasonable man knowing all the facts and circumstances which the doer of the act knew or ought to have known describe the act as reckless in the ordinary meaning of the word in ordinary speech? ... [T]he ordinary meaning of that word is a high degree of carelessness.

The inclusion of the word 'knowingly' in s.297a requires that the [defendant] is a party to carrying on the business in a manner which [he] knows very well involves an obvious and serious risk of loss or damage to others and yet ignores that risk because he does not really care whether such others suffer loss or damage or because his selfish desire to keep his own company alive overrides any concern which he ought to have for others.

EXTENT OF LIABILITY

A declaration of personal liability will not be made if the company is solvent. If the court finds that the respondent had indeed traded recklessly, it may declare that person personally responsible, in whole or in part for the company's debts. Presumably, in most cases the court would not impose personal liability beyond the amount which was lost as a result of the respondent's activities. No doubt, in time, criteria will be adopted for determining the extent to which personal liability should be imposed.

EXONERATION

When declaring someone personally liable under this heading, the court may make various ancillary orders. It is provided that if in all the circumstances the respondent acted honestly and responsibly in relation to the actions being complained of, the court may relieve the respondent, either wholly or in part, from personal liability for the company's debts.

As Lynch J. pointed out in *Re Hefferon Kearns Ltd.* (No.2), because the definition of reckless trading, and especially para. b (i.e. contracting an unpayable debt) is so wide-ranging, the power of exoneration was incorporated into s.297a. The scope of the court's power here is somewhat more extensive than under corresponding provisions of the English Act: the court may relieve a defendant from any personal liability whatsoever. Since one defendant in that case had been a party to the company contracting a debt when it was insolvent and when there were no real prospect of repayment, his actions were caught by para. b. However, because in all the circumstances he had acted honestly and responsibly, he was relieved from all personal liability without imposing any terms.

CONCLUSION

In the case of companies which are solvent, perhaps the principal focus for the law on directors' duties is preventing undue conflicts of interest and personal profit-taking at the expense of the shareholders. In the case of insolvent companies, the focus is very much on protecting the creditors' interests, especially the general unsecured creditors. When the 1990 Act was passed a view gained some currency that its reckless-trading rules would impose stringent and almost excessive standards on directors. Happily, as the decision of Lynch J. illustrates, the courts have not imposed unrealistically onerous standards on directors whose companies have been forced into liquidation or examinership. Indeed, the courts seem to have been reasonably lenient on directors.

Commentary

Alex Spain
National Irish Bank

Michael Forde has performed a valuable service in directing us to the heart of directors' legal status — that of a trustee responsible for the property of others. The standards required of a director are those long established for trustees. Whatever statutory provisions are in place, at the end of the day the test will be one of probity, prudence and care.

Forde directs us to the comments of Chadwick J. in a claim against one of the Maxwell sons:

> Directors undertake duties imposed by the company's Memorandum and Articles of Association, the provisions of the Companies Act and the general law. In particular, they must be taken to accept those duties which are ancillary to the exercise of the powers conferred on directors by the Articles of Association. Those are fiduciary powers and as such are subject to the provisions of the general law relating to the exercise of fiduciary powers.

Forde comments that, in other words, every director, as well as being bound by the Companies Acts, is a trustee for shareholders. Accordingly, every director is bound by much the same obligations as the law on trustees, known as fiduciary duties. These are duties which have been developed by the courts over time in order to protect persons whose property or affairs have been entrusted to the management of others. The standard of prudence and probity required of directors is a comparatively high one, based on extensive precedent for trustees.

The bottom line for directors is probity, prudence and care. If these are present the courts are unlikely to hold directors responsible or will use the relieving provisions available to them to lift from directors a specific responsibility imposed by statute.

Statute law imposes frightening and sometimes unreasonable responsibilities on directors, particularly the Companies Act, 1990. In *Re Hefferon Kearns*, Judge Lynch describes the 1990 provisions as "draconian". However, Forde makes it clear that the courts will interpret the statutes in a reasonable fashion and that directors should not be too alarmed. That is, of course, not too alarmed about specific detailed legal provisions provided that directors act properly and in good faith.

The legal position of directors must be considered in the light of directors' wider responsibilities. The responsibilities of directors broadly comprise:

1) The overall commercial and financial success of the enterprise
2) The integrity, ethics, philosophy and operating style of the entity
3) The setting of objectives and policies for the entity and communicating those objectives internally and externally
4) The establishment of management and organisational structures and financial and operating controls
5) The appointment, remuneration, evaluation of and, where necessary, replacement of the chief executive
6) Compliance with applicable laws and regulations.

Excessive focus on directors' legal obligations and on corporate governance generally has tended to cloud directors' primary responsibility — the commercial and financial success of the enterprise. The late Desmond Traynor, in his last annual statement as Chairman of CRH, in a caustic comment on the trend, observed:

> We have had a proliferation of reports, guidelines and recommendations on corporate governance. I must say that personally I feel that the overall emphasis appears to be on control and monitoring rather than on what should be the main responsibility of directors, to ensure profitability, adequate return on investment and increased value for shareholders. Nothing proposed will improve commercial judgment or increase productive drive.

Chairman Traynor's impatience with the mass of documentation on corporate governance and directors' legal status published in Ireland, the UK, and the United States is understandable. It mirrors the views put forward in the UK by the "100 Group" — chief financial officers of major UK quoted companies. The "100 Group" has been instrumental in slowing down implementation of the Cadbury Guidelines, on the grounds of overload in the area of corporate governance.

It is reasonable that directors should be focused on their primary responsibility — the commercial success of the enterprise. However, exclusive focus on commercial success is dangerous. We are all aware of the many well-publicised collapses of companies which have operated in this mode. Directors should consider carefully each of the six headings set out above. If they are satisfied on each of the six counts they are unlikely to be at risk. If they have a material reservation in respect of any of those matters they should consider their position.

Integrity, ethics, philosophy and operating style of a company are rarely discussed at the board table. They are crucial to assessment of risk for directors. The Cadbury Guidance on internal control should be helpful in this area. Internal controls conjure up for most of us a somewhat mundane picture of financial controls, division of responsibility and so forth. However, the Cadbury Guidance places internal control in a very different context. The Guidance requires that prior to considering specific controls the board address the overall control environment. Features listed for consideration include:

- Commitment to truth and fair dealing
- Commitment to quality and competence
- Leadership in control by example
- Communication of ethical values
- An appropriate organisational structure
- Independence, integrity and openness at board level
- Appropriate delegation of authority with accountability
- A professional approach to financial reporting.

It will be a novel experience for most directors to address these issues in a formal way so as to comply with the Cadbury requirement to confirm the effectiveness of internal controls. Nevertheless, the process will assist directors in ensuring that they act with probity, prudence and care.

QUALITIES OF A DIRECTOR

The basic qualities of a good director are common sense and experience. Common sense speaks for itself — very difficult to define but you know it when you see it. There is no substitute for experience. Balance, judgment, wisdom and patience flow from experience. Experience both of successful companies and of problem companies is valuable. It is useful to have some board members who have learnt the hard way.

RELIANCE ON EXECUTIVES

A difficult area for non-executive directors is the extent to which they are entitled to rely on the knowledge and expertise of the executive directors and the information flowing from "trusted and senior staff". There can be no absolute answer. Directors again must fall back on common sense and experience. Where directors have good reason over time to trust the executives and, in particular, the chief executive, then it is reasonable that they should rely on them. However, the decision is subjective and a question of judgment, and reliance on executives carries an element of risk. To reduce that risk, non-executive directors may wish to have access to independent professional advisors selected and hired by them and charged with providing them with independent assurance on the integrity of the financial information.

Such an arrangement would be unusual. Indeed, there may not be a precedent. However, it is probably the only arrangement which might satisfactorily answer questions such as that posed by Cadbury. "What ensures that the chief internal auditor is independent of operational management?" What indeed!?

The Cadbury Code envisages independent professional advice being available to the non-executive directors. Directors also need to be mindful of the catalogue of scandals and collapses that have occurred in situations where non-executive directors placed too much trust and reliance on their executive colleagues and, in particular, the chief executive. When things go badly wrong it is usual to find that the chief executive is involved and probably also the chief financial officer.

There are no easy answers. It is a tough call. However, directors should generally live with the risk of reliance on their executive colleagues where their judgment indicates that it is right to do so. Not to do so may create conditions of mistrust between non-executives and the chief executive. Such an environment is unsuitable for achieving the primary aims of commercial and financial success. To achieve success, the board must be cohesive with a high degree of mutual confidence and trust among all concerned.

Perhaps chief executives should give some thought to this issue and help to take non-executives off the hook by taking the initiative in proposing mechanisms that provide non-executive directors with independent assurance on the integrity of financial information. Perceptive chief executives may judge that such an initiative can only strengthen their own position. Such a process might be regarded as best practice but it is unlikely to be a standard which could reasonably be required by the courts at this time.

RECKLESS TRADING

Directors are understandably concerned at their possible exposure to personal unlimited liability as a result of the stringent and unrealistic provisions of the 1990 Companies Act. Michael Forde sets out in some detail the conditions in which a director can be held personally liable for "Reckless Trading". However, he directs us to the only reported case on the subject since the provisions became law. In *Re Hefferon Kearns Limited*, Lynch J. has adopted a pragmatic and sensible approach to the interpretation of these draconian provisions. He has effectively unwound the minutiae of the sections and restored the test to the basic issues of probity, prudence and care of a reasonable director. We cannot be sure that subsequent cases will follow this pattern — but it is a good start.

CONCLUSION

Michael Forde's paper is helpful. It directs us clearly to the central core of directors' responsibilities as trustees. Common sense and integrity will continue to protect directors despite the frightening array of statutory liabilities and case law. So, directors should get on with their primary task of creating an environment where chief executives and their colleagues can ensure the long-term commercial and financial success of the entities with which they have been entrusted.

7
Auditors and Directors

Denis O'Hogan
Ernst & Young

INTRODUCTION

One could hardly expect the relationship between auditors and company directors to be other than fraught. Legislation gives shareholders in every company the legal right to appoint independent auditors to perform whatever tests they consider necessary in order to form an opinion on the truth and fairness of the financial statements prepared by a company's directors. Auditors are given a statutory freedom of access to a company's books, records and management that no other individual or group is given as a right. In theory, it sounds like a recipe for internal conflict.

Yet, by and large, the relationship between directors and auditors is not one that, in the past at least, has been particularly controversial. If conflict has arisen, it has rarely been made public and, except for instances of high-profile litigation, auditors and company directors usually present a united front at gatherings such as Annual General Meetings. More recent developments in auditing standards and the momentum of what has been called "the corporate governance roadshow" look like upsetting this cosy relationship.

In the first part of this chapter, the rather curious relationship between the auditor and the company director is explored with specific reference to the Irish environment. The focus is not legal or regulatory, but rather from the perspective of the practising auditor. The chapter focuses primarily on the working relationship between the director as agent of the shareholders, and the auditor as watchdog for the shareholders. It considers the nature of the working relationship, the sources of difficulty and conflict in the relationship, and ways in which these might be minimised and/or accommodated. Finally, it examines the forces that currently threaten to upset the delicate balance that has been maintained up until now.

THE WORKING RELATIONSHIP

Company law entitles shareholders to appoint, or to continue the appointment of, auditors to serve from one annual general meeting to the next. It does give the directors the right to appoint the first auditors to a company but such auditors automatically retire at the first annual general meeting (AGM), and so the shareholders can change the auditors very simply if they are not satisfied with their performance or independence. Prior to the Companies Act, 1990, there was considerable doubt in auditors' circles as to whether auditors could legally resign in between AGMs, as they were appointed to hold office from one AGM to the next. In practice, however, many did do so and were replaced by other members of their profession who regarded themselves as in good standing with their Institute, its rules and the law. Eventually, the Companies Act, 1990, introduced explicit provisions for the resignation of auditors other than at AGMs but required them to state both to the secretary of the company and to the Registrar of Companies whether there were any circumstances relating to their resignation which should be brought to the attention of shareholders or creditors of the company concerned.

The classical structure, therefore, envisaged by the Companies Acts is of shareholders who appoint, reappoint or remove independent external auditors, who also have the power to fix the auditors' remuneration and to whom the auditors report once a year on the accounts prepared by the directors. Auditors can therefore expect the directors to provide them with properly presented financial statements which they can audit. They are entitled by law to require from the officers of their audit clients such information and explanations as are within their knowledge or can be procured by them, as they think necessary for the performance of their duties. They have a right of access at all reasonable times to the books, accounts and vouchers of a company. The law supports auditors by giving them strong, perhaps one might even say draconian, powers.

In theory, therefore, the shareholders have a watchdog with a reasonable degree of security of tenure. Like any good watchdog, they expect auditors, in return for their remuneration, to keep the shareholders' best interests firmly in mind and to challenge the actions of the directors that might not be in their best interests. It might be expected, therefore, that there would be significant matters on which the directors and auditors could conflict. Areas of potential conflict might include directors' remuneration, transactions with directors, risky business strategies, weaknesses in internal control, choices of accounting principles, disclosures about uncertainties or contingencies, and many others.

Such then is the theoretical relationship. In practice, and in the Irish environment particularly, things are very different. Three of the main reasons for this are:

1) The widespread confusion and ignorance concerning the respective responsibilities of directors and auditors

2) The ease with which directors in practice can influence the appointment or removal of auditors

3) The structure of Irish business.

We deal with each of these in turn.

THE RESPECTIVE RESPONSIBILITIES OF DIRECTORS AND AUDITORS

It is clear from technical literature and media comment that the respective responsibilities of directors and auditors are not well understood. The respective responsibilities envisaged in the Companies Acts are for the directors to keep proper books of account, and to ensure that accounts giving a true and fair view are prepared from those books, and for the appointed auditors to audit those accounts and report to the shareholders. Yet in developing the suggestions put forward in "Future Developments of Auditing", the Auditing Practices Board (APB), in 1992, invited a number of individuals with interest in the audit to give a critical appraisal of the state of auditing. Some of the concerns perceived by those commentators at that time included:

- A gap between the role expected of the auditors and that performed by them. A demand for auditors to recognise the interests of a wider group than shareholders alone. Perceived gaps in the scope of the audit, particularly regarding directors' stewardship, future prospects and risks, fraud, internal control and interim reporting.

- A perception that auditors are not sufficiently independent of the companies they audit, with the result that they have not taken a tough enough stand on the appropriateness of accounting policies used in some instances. Related to this — a lack of shareholder involvement in the audit.

- A demand for greater disclosure by auditors, which stemmed in part from inadequate disclosure by directors in financial statements. Auditors' reports were seen as uninformative, failing to disclose material findings, issues and concerns arising from the audit.
- The lack of warning by auditors of the imminent collapse of certain public companies.

The APB commented that it was clear that action was needed to resolve the issues giving rise to concern, to build public confidence in auditors and to provide a more solid foundation for the future development of the auditing profession.

However, in this aspiration the APB appears to be proposing to change the respective responsibilities of directors and auditors as set out in law, and to impose on the auditor new responsibilities to fulfil the expectations of the public even where those expectations may not be well informed. That there is significant misunderstanding about the respective responsibilities of directors and auditors, even among senior management and directors of companies, can perhaps be illustrated at the micro level in relation to the effects of fraud and error in financial statements.

In *Statement of Auditing Standards (SAS110): "Fraud and Error"*, fraud is defined as referring "both to the use of deception to obtain an unjust or illegal financial advantage, and to intentional misrepresentations affecting the financial statements, by one or more individuals among management, employees, or third parties. Fraud may involve:

- manipulation, falsification or alteration of records or documents;
- misappropriation of assets or theft;
- suppression or omission of the effects of transactions from records or documents;
- recording of transactions without substance; or
- intentional misapplication of accounting policies."

The Statement's explanatory notes clearly state that the responsibility for the prevention and detection of fraud and error rests with the directors through the implementation and continued operation of adequate accounting and internal control systems. Such a system reduces but does not eliminate the possibility of fraud and error. Moreover, it confirms that it is not the auditor's function to prevent fraud and error although the fact that an annual audit is carried out may act as a deterrent.

The auditing standard states that, "when planning the audit, the auditors should assess the risk that fraud or error may cause the financial statements to contain material misstatements" (SAS110.2); and "based on their risk assessment the auditors should design other procedures so as to have a reasonable expectation of detecting the misstatements arising from fraud or error which are material to the financial statements" (SAS110.3).

The explanatory text goes on to state that the likelihood of detecting errors is ordinarily higher than the likelihood of detecting fraud, since fraud is usually accompanied by acts specifically designed to conceal its existence, such as collusion between employees or falsification of accounting records. Because of the inherent limitations of an audit, there is unavoidable risk that material misstatements in the financial statements resulting from fraud may not be detected. A subsequent discovery of material misstatements of the financial affairs resulting from fraud during the period covered by the auditors' report does not, in itself, indicate that the auditors have failed to adhere to the basic principles and essential procedures of an audit.

From the auditors' point of view, this is a reasonable and acceptable allocation of responsibilities to them. In practice, however, a major expectation gap exists. As shown by various surveys, a very large element of management and directors either are not aware of, or do not take adequate (or in some cases any!) steps to fulfil, their primary responsibility for the prevention and detection of fraud, and furthermore erroneously consider that it is the external auditors' responsibility to detect not only material fraud but also a much wider class of substantial fraud which may be significantly less in amount than that which would be considered material.

It is the experience of many auditors that when any fraud, even though it may not be material to the financial statements, is discovered in a client organisation, one of the first questions raised by management or the directors is "Why didn't the auditors discover this?" or "Why didn't the auditors warn us this could happen?" The fact is that in many such cases the auditors will have warned of some weakness in internal controls that may have facilitated the fraud, or will have been hoodwinked by collusion between employees who hold key positions in the segregation-of-duties masterplan. Even a 100 per cent check of all transactions for fraud (and really this is not feasible in any audit), will not necessarily reveal the presence of fraud where concealment through collusion has occurred. Most systems of internal control are designed around the premise that, provided that no individual has control over the initiation, execution and recording of transactions and custody of the related assets, then barring collusion, the system will be robust against defalcations. In general, it would be impractical or prohibitively expensive to have a system that would be proof against all possible collusion because of the costs of employing sufficient personnel to double-check everything.

Insufficient effort has been made in the past to ensure that the respective responsibilities of directors and auditors are widely publicised and understood. This is partly a result of the structure of much of Irish business, which is considered in more detail later, and partly because of a lack of appreciation of the importance of good communications to audit reporting. There may even have been a slight élitist attitude that assumed that anybody holding shares in a company and reading the audit report would automatically be aware of the context in which the report was given and the responsibilities undertaken by the auditor. Developments in these areas are discussed later in this chapter.

DIRECTORS' INFLUENCE ON THE APPOINTMENT AND REMOVAL OF AUDITORS

Whereas in theory the directors only appoint the first auditors to hold office until the first AGM, (when they must be either reappointed or replaced), in practice they have far more influence over the appointment and removal of auditors. The agendas and notices for Annual General Meetings are sent out well in advance and, by law, extended notice has to be given if the auditor is to be removed at other than the first Annual General Meeting. In practice, it is the company secretary, working with the directors, who prepares the papers for the Annual General Meeting, and so, any attempt to remove the auditors or appoint alternatives in their stead at the Annual General Meeting will inevitably begin with the secretary or directors. It cannot be a spontaneous move from the floor by unhappy shareholders. In practice, therefore, incumbent auditors are largely dependent on the goodwill of the directors for the continuation of their appointment. Likewise, any potential new appointees as auditors will be dependent on the directors recommending their appointment in the notice for the Annual General Meeting. Thus, shareholders only ever have a choice between the incumbent auditors and a potential replacement selected and proposed by the directors.

While in law the incumbent auditors can make a reasoned argument for their retention and have this circulated to shareholders, and/or make a statement at the AGM as to why they should be retained, in practice the battle is already lost when the directors propose a change. Auditors know that if the directors recommend their removal and do not succeed, then their working relationship will have been irretrievably damaged such that the effective exercise of their duties will be almost impossible, making resignation the most suitable course of action. Of course, if there is a major issue of principle involved, the auditors have a duty to bring that to the attention of the shareholders and would normally do so; but even then, unless the directors themselves are changed, the auditors' position is effectively untenable.

Furthermore, it is almost universal practice in companies to authorise the directors to fix the remuneration of the auditors. While it is clearly impractical for the auditors to try to negotiate fees direct with a large body of shareholders, the delegating of this task to the directors by the shareholders results in a clear conflict situation where the auditors have to try to reach agreement on fees with the very people whose actions and stewardship they are supposed to be monitoring and challenging. It is really too much to expect that a director who, having had a contentious and difficult relationship with the company's auditors, would not be tempted to be just a little unreasonable in relation to the quantum of the audit fee.

THE STRUCTURE OF IRISH BUSINESS

The vast majority of companies incorporated in Ireland are private domestically-owned companies, individually of modest economic importance, in which, as a general rule, there is some overlap between directors and shareholders. Another major class of companies comprises those which are majority-owned subsidiaries of foreign or multinational businesses. A third category includes the public companies and, perhaps, some of the larger private companies where the directors are the top management and are also largely distinct from the majority body of shareholders. In the Irish context, this third category is by far the smallest in numerical terms but is the one that most closely fits the classical image of the relationship between directors, auditors and shareholders as envisaged in the Companies Acts.

The Owner/Director-Managed Business

To the auditor, the coincidence of ownership and management in such businesses in effect eliminates the difficulty of having a direct relationship with the directors while trying to report in an independent manner to the shareholders. This is not to say that there will not be tensions in the relationship, or disagreement about the figures, the presentation of information and the accounting policies used, but all the discussions and debates between the audit team and the directors in such instances are also, in effect, with the shareholders to whom the auditor will ultimately report, and so the existence of the difficulty will not come as any surprise news to the shareholder; nor does it result in a three-cornered stand-off between directors, auditors and shareholders.

In many owner/director managed businesses, the professional relationship between owners/directors and the auditors usually extends well beyond the statutory reporting role. The auditor is required by law and by professional standards to be independent, and most auditors vehemently assert that they can maintain their independence in undertaking the audit role, while providing other services to their clients. Auditors frequently act as close business advisers to owners/directors, and in the case of many smaller businesses, they, or their staff, may often draft the statutory accounts from the underlying books and records. It is not uncommon to hear management and/or directors refer to "the auditors' accounts", nor indeed to hear staff of audit firms refer to "our accounts" in such circumstances. In the past, auditors seldom appeared to be unduly concerned about this transfer of ownership of the preparation of accounts. Frequently it was seen as an integral part of the client service, as that service was seen as more of an assistance to management in complying with statutory requirements than the pure "audit" role of rendering an independent opinion on the truth and fairness of a set of financial statements. Yet in reality this service extension represents a very significant transfer of respective responsibilities between directors and auditors.

The Majority-Owned Subsidiaries

In these circumstances, the working relationship between auditors and directors generally has two separate aspects. On the one hand, the directors want to comply with statutory (compliance) requirements properly but minimally and at minimum cost or disruption to operations. The parent company, usually the 100 per cent shareholder, has minimal interest in the statutory reports or audit, except to ensure compliance with local regulations. The directors typically give the audit a low priority but will co-operate with the auditor to get the audit completed. In some circumstances, there may be relatively little interaction with the statutory auditor. Moreover, given the choice, many foreign-owned businesses operating in Ireland would choose not to have a statutory audit if that were possible.

On the other hand, it may be vital from the consolidated reporting viewpoint that certain audit work is carried out on such a subsidiary. The working relationship in these circumstances generally reflects much greater concern on the part of management and/or directors to avoid serious management letter matters or material adjustments being relayed to the holding company by the auditors (who need not necessarily be the same as the auditors of the holding company). Indeed, the focus of management/directors' concerns will be on controls and the suitability of figures for inclusion in the consolidation. Group reporting packages do not generally present information in such a way as to be capable of giving "a true and fair view" of any individual subsidiary, and so presentation and disclosure has lower priority in these cases. The relationship between directors and auditors in such companies is not of any great interest in the context of this chapter and will not be considered further.

The Public and Large Private Company

Although very much in the minority of cases when measured either by number or by fee income to auditors practising in Ireland, the case of the public company or large private company where there is a clear distinction between shareholders and directors is probably the most interesting case in terms of the relationship between the directors and auditors, and the one in which the influence and impact of new developments is most clearly seen.

To the outsider, there is little evidence from the past of severe tensions in the director/auditor relationship in this sector. Changes in audit appointments have been relatively infrequent in the past. Auditors have many "war stories" about frank and somewhat heated debates with directors on choices of accounting policies or the treatment of particular major transactions, but such debates nearly always have been concluded with a treatment in financial statements, acceptable to both parties and which is supported by a united front against challenges by shareholders or the media. Instances of audit reports of such companies qualified on the grounds of disagreement with the amount, treatment or disclosure of a transaction in the financial statements are so rare as to be from all practical points of view non-existent. The auditors' general experience with directors of companies in this sector of Irish business is that directors take their responsibilities seriously and appreciate and try to achieve consensus with auditors on all important issues. In general, attempts to bully auditors by threatening to have them replaced are, thankfully, rare. Unfortunately, there are notorious incidents where, on the face of it, it appears that auditors may have failed to stand up to domineering directors or chief executives; but, on the other hand, there are some notable occasions when the auditors stood their ground strongly and publicly and reaped the rewards for so doing. And on a practical level, the negotiation and agreement of audit fees has not in the past proven to be fraught with major problems, as both parties have tended to approach this task just like any other one involving the purchase and sale of a service.

NEW INFLUENCES ON THE RELATIONSHIP BETWEEN AUDITORS AND DIRECTORS

In the past few years, developments or trends in four areas have influenced and continue to influence the relationship between directors and auditors. Those four areas are:

- Corporate governance
- Litigation against auditors
- Economic pressures on business margins
- The Auditing Practices Board's programme of work.

Corporate Governance Developments

A series of spectacular corporate failures and frauds in the late 1980s, including BCCI and Maxwell, heightened concerns in the United Kingdom about the standard of financial reporting and accountability. A significant aspect of the concerns was the quality of corporate governance exercised by company boards, and the so-called "expectations gap" in relation to the auditor's role. Controversy also arose over accountability for directors' remuneration, particularly in the light of certain well-publicised large compensation payments for loss of office. In response to the concerns, the Committee on the Financial Aspects of Corporate Governance ("The Cadbury Committee") was set up. The purpose of The Cadbury Committee, as its title indicates, was to consider financial aspects of corporate governance and make recommendations for improvement. The Committee's approach was to provide a framework for establishing good corporate governance and accountability. This was done through The Committee's Code of Best

Practice ("the Cadbury Code") which it put forward as a benchmark against which companies can be assessed. The Code embodies underlying principles of openness, integrity and accountability. It is aimed at listed companies, but other companies may also benefit from applying it. The London Stock Exchange has adopted the recommendations as part of its listing requirements, requiring companies to report whether they have complied with it. This is supplemented by the requirement to report details of, and reasons for, any non-compliance and to have the Directors' Report reviewed by the auditors insofar as it relates to objectively verifiable matters in the Code.

In Ireland, the Financial Reporting Commission (Ryan Commission) reported in January 1992. Its recommendations went even further than those of Cadbury, and in September of 1992 the Institute of Chartered Accountants in Ireland issued its response to the report of the Financial Reporting Commission in the form of two statements of best practice entitled "Companies Reporting in the Republic of Ireland" and "The Audit of Companies Reporting in the Republic of Ireland". The exact status of these statements is somewhat uncertain although they have been described as "aspirational". In practical terms, and because of the support of the Stock Exchange for its recommendations, the Cadbury Code is having a daily impact on listed companies, while the Ryan report has been pretty much left on the shelf.

The Cadbury Code includes recommendations that the board should ensure that an objective and professional relationship is maintained with the auditors and that it should establish an audit committee of at least three non-executive directors with written terms of reference which deal clearly with its authority and duties. As envisaged by the Code, the Audit Committee gives the non-executive directors the opportunity to consider, in more detail than is generally possible at board meetings, the important financial aspects of the approach and system of corporate governance. A specific step in the process is for the audit committee to hold a separate meeting with the auditors at least once a year, without executive board members present. This allows discussion to ensure that there are no unresolved issues of concern.

Such a structure could be of considerable help to auditors where the client has a very domineering chief executive, but it also results in a rather peculiar situation where the auditors find themselves reporting in considerable detail to a sub-committee of non-executive directors, but in far less detail (simply through the text of their formal audit report) to the shareholders to whom they have an obligation in law to report.

Nonetheless, from the auditors' viewpoint, there is no doubt that such structures provide them with additional means to ensure that significant audit issues are fully dealt with. It is somewhat ironic that this should be achieved by detailed reporting to a subset of directors rather than to some representatives of the shareholders not directly involved in the management and control of the company.

For the auditors to a company which takes corporate governance seriously, the development and promulgation of corporate governance standards such as the Cadbury Code enhances their ability to maintain an independent line. It is less likely that the agreement of fees will be used to put pressure on the auditors, where there is disagreement about the treatment or presentation of a transaction. The requirement for the board to meet regularly and to retain full and effective control over the company and monitor the executive management can, if carried out effectively, assist the auditors in establishing that the tone at top levels of management is good, resulting in a reduction in the risk level of the audit.

The Code has not of course been greeted with open arms in all of its recommendations. In Ireland, there was significant opposition to the greater disclosure of directors' remuneration information, particularly as Irish company law has significantly less onerous disclosure requirements than UK law. Indeed, this opposition quickly resulted in an agreement by the Stock Exchange, which watered down the requirements in this area for Irish companies. The requirement for auditors to report on the directors' statement of compliance with the Code has strained their respective relationship in some cases where directors have wanted to be perhaps less than frank about certain matters, and the auditors have expected a full-blown commitment to both the letter and the spirit of the Code. Auditors have also suffered from a lack of definitive guidance in certain areas, particularly for accounting periods that included the transition date of 1 July 1993. Also, problems have arisen for some auditors who have been expected to associate themselves with the positive statements of the directors on the appropriateness of the going-concern basis, and on the effectiveness of internal controls. Unwillingness to be so associated, pending the issue of guidance on the independent valuation of such statements, has caused considerable displeasure.

Litigation Against Auditors

The initiation of major litigation against auditors has spread to the UK and Ireland. As a result of the system of joint and several liability enshrined in our legal system, auditors have been identified as having deep pockets because of their professional indemnity insurance cover. They are therefore a much better source of compensation in the event of corporate collapse than the directors, who may have been directly responsible for the collapse, but who will generally not have had insurance cover; and where the litigant faces the uncertain outcome of a case on directors' negligence where there is relatively little case law or precedent. Awards or settlements in negligence cases against auditors, particularly when costs are taken into account, have been thousands, maybe even hundreds of thousands, of times the fee earned by the auditors for the particular assignment giving rise to the claim. Professional indemnity cover has become increasingly more difficult to get, with continuing premium increases and ever-increasing deductibles. Against this background, particularly that of ever-increasing deductibles, it becomes vital for the auditor to avoid getting into a situation where a claim is likely to arise. It has become abundantly clear that it is far better to forego the fees of a lucrative appointment, than to act for a client where involvement in a lawsuit is regarded as a possibility.

The implications of this for the relationship between directors and auditors is that, whereas previously directors looked to the reputation of the audit firm when making an appointment, the tables are now turned in a rather ironic manner. In considering whether to continue with or take on an audit engagement nowadays, the auditor assesses very carefully the integrity of the directors, their competence and general business reputation and the nature of the business. Auditors want to deal with directors with whom they can have an open and frank relationship and where they believe that all relevant matters will be disclosed to them whether or not they specifically ask about them. The trend nowadays is to evaluate what might be called the "control consciousness" of directors and executive management. In the present environment a positive evaluation of control consciousness is increasingly regarded as a prerequisite to acting as auditor. Auditors generally obtain representations from the directors at the end of the audit that they have been provided with access to all relevant books and documents, including those relating to meetings, and to information on procedures for handling disputes, claims, law-suits, violations of laws or regulations, and so on. Any indications to the auditors that the directors were being less than frank in relation to any of these areas would certainly cause the auditors to question whether the relationship was on the right basis, and whether they should continue to act.

A further aspect of control consciousness which is of significant concern to auditors is whether or not an effective system of internal control is in place in the client organisation and whether directors' and management attitudes to such a system are supportive. Again, this is an indication of the overall tone set by top management in the organisation; and reaction to management letter recommendations provides a further indicator of the tone being set. The Cadbury Code will, once guidance is available, require directors of listed companies to comment on the effectiveness of their internal controls, but auditors already consider a responsible and supportive attitude to continuing improvement in internal controls as an essential feature when they are considering the risk of continuing to be associated with a particular client.

Economic Pressures on Business Margins

Economic pressures on business margins have resulted in businesses carrying out "down-sizing" or "right-sizing" restructurings and have caused most businesses to look carefully at their costs and introduce programmes of cost reduction. Audit fees have come under the same intense pressure for reduction as the other cost streams in businesses. "Value-added" has become something of a catch phrase in business circles, and auditors are told that their services must contribute added value in order to justify the fees being charged. The fulfilment of the statutory compliance role by rendering an audit opinion is generally not perceived by directors as a value-added service. Accordingly, auditors have come under pressure to provide solid business advice or other services perceived by directors to add real value to their businesses, but which may inevitably impinge on the auditor's independence.

The strains involved in the relationship between the auditors and directors by the emphasis on adding value from the audit service have caused some auditors to look at re-engineering the whole audit process. This is an exceptionally difficult task because the trend in auditing standards and audit regulation is for ever increasingly prescriptive statements on procedures to be followed, tests to be carried out and documentation to be obtained. Meanwhile, the thrust of re-engineering is towards greater emphasis on risk assessment and on knowing the business and industry, more frequent interaction with executive management of audit clients and eliminating the "ticking and bashing" type of auditing. Experience in auditing firms suggests that the clients perceive themselves as receiving relatively little value from junior audit staff, but often significant value from interaction with the experienced partners and managers. To achieve greater interaction across the board without devastating the economics of an auditing practice will require the auditors to be able to convince the directors that they are adding significant value in the process and thereby should earn increased fees. The auditors will also have to convince directors that there is value-added in the fulfilling of the compliance role, and the increased emphasis on corporate governance is certainly a help in this area.

Auditing Practices Board's Programme of Work

The Auditing Practices Board's (APB) Statement of Objectives sets out its commitment to leading the development of auditing practice in the UK and Ireland so as to:

- Establish high standards of auditing

- Meet the developing needs of users of financial information

- Ensure public confidence in the auditing process.

To achieve this, it states its intention, *inter alia*, to advance the wider public's understanding of the roles and responsibilities of auditors. In February 1993, it published a paper "Audit and Related Services — an Explanation for Users", which could have gone some way towards achieving this intention. However, there was no blaze of publicity, no extensive media comment, no attempt to ensure wide dissemination of the paper or even of the knowledge of its existence that might have resulted in the wider public's education.

The majority of the APB's work in the last two years, valuable though it is, has been concentrated on the auditors who are on the other side of the so-called "expectations gap". The promulgation of standards certainly contributes to establishing high quality in auditing and better communication by auditors to users, but unless the users are educated as to what they can reasonably expect from an audit, the audit expectation gap will only be narrowed rather than bridged, and the desired public confidence in the auditing process will not be achieved.

Statement of Auditing Standards 600 on audit reports has resulted in significant changes in communications between auditors and the general public. The previous fashion of a very short audit report, which simply stated that the accounts gave a true and fair view and complied with various statutory requirements, has been superseded and replaced by a longer more informative audit report with a logical structure and appropriate headings for the paragraphs. SAS 600 now requires an explicit statement in the financial statements or documents attached thereto, or failing this, in the auditors' report, of the directors' responsibilities for the preparation of the financial statements, for keeping proper books of account and for the prevention and detection of fraud and other irregularities such as might have a material effect on the financial statements.

For very many businesses, but particularly for the smaller or owner-managed business, the requirements of SAS 600 may well have come as something of a shock. Although the representation letters which auditors normally request of directors generally refer to the directors' responsibility for the accounts, it has not been the general practice to hammer home this responsibility, principally because auditors and their staff were really the ones undertaking the preparation of statutory financials and ensuring that these complied with the appropriate disclosure requirements and gave a true and fair view. The suggested wording for directors' responsibilities is so substantial and the re-formatting of the audit report, including reference to the statement of directors' responsibilities, or the recital of those responsibilities by the auditors if the directors fail to provide such a statement, is so far reaching as effectively to force the auditor to address the respective roles and responsibilities of directors and auditors with their clients. It will surely cause many auditors to stand back from the relationship and consider whether they have inadvertently over the years lapsed into a practice of taking responsibility for matters, such as the preparation of statutory financial statements, which are really not their responsibility, and whereby they may, at least in appearance, compromise their independence.

In the case of public companies and bigger businesses, the explicit introduction of a statement of directors' responsibilities has resulted in directors becoming ever more keenly aware of the considerable responsibilities they undertake when acting as directors. Combined with the changes in corporate governance, it has caused many to re-evaluate their relationships with their auditors. The recital of their respective responsibilities in the SAS-600-style audit reports has been helpful in clarifying what the relationship should be. In particular, the abolition of "subject-to"-type qualifications, which were qualifications where the auditors said that the outcome of a future uncertain event could have a major impact on the position shown by the financial statements, and its replacement by a reference in the audit report drawing attention to where the matter is discussed and disclosed in the financial statements and stating that the opinion is not qualified in respect of such a matter, has been helpful in emphasising to directors their responsibility for proper and adequate disclosure in financial statements.

CONCLUSION

The relationship between auditors and directors across the whole spectrum of Irish businesses is in a period of significant change. From the auditors' side, the advent of audit regulation and the APB's programme of work on new and revised auditing standards requires reconsideration of independence issues and a revisiting of the question as to whether the respective responsibilities of directors and auditors are clearly understood and actually fulfilled in that same division. Litigation against auditors has meant that the auditors must consider carefully the engagements they accept so as to manage the risks of current-day practice, and the integrity, reputation and attitude to good corporate governance of the directors of potential clients is of great concern to them in this context.

For directors, the developments in corporate governance and the explicit recital of the respective responsibilities of directors and auditors for financial statements has heightened the awareness of the significant responsibilities they undertake and also of how maintaining an objective and professional relationship with the auditors is an essential element in fulfilling their role. Undue dependence on auditors must be avoided, but getting the balance right, so that maximum benefit and added-value is obtained from the audit service without compromising its independence, is a task which both directors and auditors are having to relearn and refine in the changing regulatory and business environment of today.

Commentary

Sir Desmond Lorimer
Lamont Holdings plc

In responding to Denis O'Hogan, this author intends to limit his comments to the conduct of public companies. In private companies, the relationship between directors who are frequently also substantial owners, and auditors, differs radically from that pertaining to public companies, and requires extensive consideration by somebody more familiar with the field.

Denis O'Hogan has fairly assessed the relationships between directors, auditors and shareholders, as they exist today. He has been somewhat cautious as to whether he regards the present position as a satisfactory one. In this writer's view, however, despite the positive and constructive impact of the Cadbury Code and of Statement of Auditing Standards 600, leading towards greater transparency, and a more precise definition of the respective roles of directors and auditors, further changes are necessary, and, it is hoped, inevitable.

Whilst the title of this chapter refers to auditors and directors, and deals with the relationship between them, such a relationship cannot be adequately considered without including in the discussion their respective relationships with the shareholders. Indeed, that factor is pivotal, and should determine and colour all transactions between the directors and the auditors themselves.

This author's intention, therefore, is to consider first the position of shareholders, and to proceed from there to some thoughts on the independence of auditors, on the question of competitive tendering, and on fraud prevention and detection.

SHAREHOLDERS: HOW THEY ARE SERVED

O'Hogan refers to the "cosy relationship" between management and auditors, which in his view may be upset by recent developments in auditing standards and the momentum of the "'corporate governance roadshow". Indeed, while recent developments are likely to affect the too cosy relationships of the past, very much more radical measures are needed.

At present, the only effective channel of communication between the auditors and the shareholders (whose interests they are appointed to serve) is through the brief and formal audit report. Since the wording of this report is standardised, and is repeated in form from year to year, it is improbable that many shareholders actually bother to read it unless it is very clear that major reservations are being expressed — a situation which does not arise except in the most extreme circumstances. Consequently, the shareholders are never made aware of the less than drastic concerns which the auditors may have on the quality of internal controls, on the adequacy of financial-statement presentation and disclosure, on the quality of management, on the morale of the management team and the staff — indeed on almost anything which might enable them to form judgments relating to the inner health of the company. Lengthy discussions on these matters may take place between the directors and the auditors, but to the almost entire exclusion of the shareholders.

Shareholders deserve, and indeed should have, the right to better access to the auditors, and such access could give the auditors greater strength and independence. This access could be achieved in a number of ways, and if the principle itself is accepted then the detailed application of it is undoubtedly a matter for careful consideration. The suggestions herein are not intended to be final, but to indicate the direction in which we ought to be going.

AN EXTENDED AUDITOR'S REPORT

It is suggested here that on completion of the audit the auditors should submit to the directors a report commenting on a number of matters dealt with at greater length in the following paragraphs. This report should be attached to, or incorporated in, the directors' report to the shareholders, and the directors themselves should respond thereto, if they so wish.

The auditors should be present at the Annual General Meeting, and should be available to be questioned on the report, or indeed on any matter relating to the audit, the accounts and the "true and fair view" — not through the chairperson, but directly — since the auditors are there to protect the interests of the shareholders, and, in theory at least, are appointed by them for that purpose.

The report should comment on the state of health of the company — a form of "health certificate" which would highlight, without going into finite detail, satisfaction or otherwise with management, a general view of the adequacy of systems, the existence (or absence) and the quality of long-term strategies, comparisons of achievement with pre-stated objectives, morale, succession planning and other relevant matters. Comment should be made only where the auditors wished to express concern. Such a report would place additional responsibilities on the non-executive directors, and would enable the shareholders to take an active and informed role, resulting possibly in action being taken much earlier than might otherwise be the case.

O'Hogan mentions, as one of the continuing criticisms of auditors, the lack of warning given of the imminent collapse of certain public companies. Usually, unless the matter is observed during an interim audit, the opportunity for such "whistle-blowing" does not occur until the final audit has been completed — perhaps some months after the end of the year. Nevertheless, the report which is proposed here would be the ideal opportunity for "whistle-blowing", and indeed not only an opportunity, but virtually an unavoidable necessity.

The additional work involved in the preparation of a report such as that envisaged above is likely to increase audit costs But, whereas the statutory audit is not perceived by many managements as adding value to a company, the provision of the additional service would certainly add value for the shareholders, thereby justifying the additional fees. It is readily acknowledged that some managements might not share this view!

Auditors may have two concerns with the above proposal: first, that the auditing profession has not the competence or training to carry out the additional functions; and second, that the extension of their role to expressing opinions on management, strategy etc. may expose the profession to greater liability.

It cannot be denied that the extension of the auditors' reporting function can provide opportunities to those intent on litigation for negligence. However, this extension would seem to be vital if the auditing profession is to give a full service to shareholders, and the risks must be accepted, and possibly mitigated eventually by some method such as the limitation of liability.

In regard to competence and training, the profession itself can provide such additional instruction as may be necessary to enable its members to deal with the new responsibilities. In this connection, we will now elaborate more fully on the kinds of issues envisaged in such a report.

- **An appraisal of management.** Speaking generally, it is doubtful whether auditors are capable, arising out of a purely statutory audit, of expressing a view on commercial decisions or on many aspects of stewardship, unless that stewardship is blatantly corrupt — but even then such comment would be extremely valuable. They should, however, be capable of examining control mechanisms and risks, and the basis on which directors have planned for the future of their enterprises. They should be aware of the nature and adequacy of budgetary control, of the control of inventories, of ordering procedures, of credit control and debt-collection methods, of the structure of financing, and many other aspects which reflect on management competence.

- **A general view of the adequacy of systems**. All auditing today is based on the assessment of control systems and the degree of risk. This is an area at present entirely within the competence of any properly equipped auditor.

- **The existence and quality of long-term strategies**. It is not difficult to determine whether such strategies exist. Quality is another matter. Except in gross terms, it may not be possible for an auditor to assess the quality of strategies. But if they are deemed to be grossly deficient, there seems no reason not to say so.

- **Comparison of achievement with pre-stated objectives**. In the first instance such a comparison should be with the objectives stated in a prospectus. Thereafter it must be assumed that management each year, in the directors' report, provides an adequate statement of prospects and plans. The auditor can comment only on measurable aspects, and cannot be expected to give an opinion on all commercial judgments. Assessment against budgets should be reasonably straightforward and easily measured — failure to achieve the budgets may, however, be more difficult to comment upon.

- **Morale**. Any auditor, intimately in touch with the company in the course of an audit, will be aware of the state of morale. However, it is a very much an area of judgment, and comment should probably be restricted to observable facts — numbers of days lost through strikes, rate of staff turnover, level of changes in management personnel, and similar indicators.

- **Management succession planning**. Here again it is a matter of fact whether there has been adequate planning in this area.

SHAREHOLDERS' NOMINEE ON AUDIT COMMITTEE

In a sizeable company, and one that is not shareholder-managed, audit committees of non-executive directors are necessary and serve a useful purpose. The committee is probably the only opportunity that the auditor has to present to directors who are not involved in the operational activities a view on the management of the affairs of the company. On the basis that the non-executive directors are effective and independent (so often the non-executive directors are mere cyphers), the audit committee provides a forum for discussion and appraisal of executive directors' performance.

Since in theory the non-executive directors are appointed by the shareholders, it seems unnecessary to suggest that a shareholders' nominee should be appointed to the audit committee. In practice, however, the non-executive directors are normally proposed by the existing board, or by the management, and therefore represent the choice of the "establishment" rather than the shareholders. Ideally, at least one of the non-executive directors should be chosen and proposed by a small selection committee elected by the shareholders for that purpose, and that director should be specifically one of those appointed to the audit committee. Designing rules to achieve this end may be difficult, but certainly not insurmountable.

In such a structure, the audit committee should be responsible, inter alia, for the appointment and discharge of auditors, for defining the scope of their duties, and for the fixing of their remuneration. Through their nominee or nominees on the committee the shareholders would then have a less remote involvement in these matters.

REDUCING SHAREHOLDER APATHY

Generally shareholders are concerned with little more than that they receive their dividends on a fairly regular basis, and the tiny proportionate representation of shareholders at Annual General Meetings reflects an almost complete lack of interest in anything else to do with the company.

So, it is a circular process. Shareholders' apathy permits auditor/director privacy and exclusivity. Auditors' and directors' defensiveness, lack of transparency, and failure to communicate, inhibit shareholder participation.

At least one part of this process can be opened up through the proposals herein. Nobody can predict how the shareholders would respond, but at least they would have the opportunity and the information now denied them.

AUDITORS' INDEPENDENCE

Because of their dependence on fee income and their reluctance to lose it, auditors can never be regarded as truly independent, and in many cases allow themselves to be talked into acquiescence where their better judgment would dictate that they should "blow the whistle". This arises very often in the grey areas surrounding accounting standards and the treatment of controversial items in the financial statements.

If the above proposals in regard to extended reporting to shareholders, and in regard to the appointment of shareholders' nominees as non-executive directors, were adopted, then the independence of auditors would be greatly enhanced.

It is recommended, however, to go further. Frequently auditing firms regard their auditing practices as providing opportunity for developing more remunerative, and possibly more interesting, work in the provision of services other than audit — management consultancy, liquidations and receiverships, tax, investment, acquisitions and finance advice, and so on. Apart from the potential for consultancy or management advice conflicting with audit considerations, the fact that a firm derives perhaps the greater part of its fees from work other than audit creates an even greater fee dependence. To lose the audit can mean the loss also of a large amount of highly remunerative other work.

It is suggested that a firm carrying out an audit function for a company should not undertake any other work for that company. This author has little faith in the "Chinese wall". A firm is an integrated entity, the partners sharing the profits of all the divisions of the firm. A nominal independence may be established between the audit section and the management consultancy section, but there is no true and absolute independence. If, for example, an audit partner is asked to advise on the selection of a suitable organisation for the provision of consultancy services, it is hardly likely that that person would, or could, give objective and independent advice, if another section of their own firm could carry out the work.

It has been argued that a firm carrying out no functions other than audit will become stylised and bureaucratic, and will lose the dynamic awareness of business life; and since the audit, as a purely statutory function, offers little opportunity for development and innovation, the staff attracted to it may be of lower calibre than that involved in the other, more creative services. However, the total division of the audit function from all other services for a particular client company does not imply that a firm will become exclusively an audit firm. Rather, it is envisaged that firms will act in a variety of capacities for enterprises that are not their audit clients. Adjustments would probably be traumatic; but in the end a firm would probably wind up by having one set of audit clients, and another completely different set of consultancy clients.

ECONOMIC PRESSURES AND AUDIT TENDERING

O'Hogan worries that "audit fees have come under the same intense pressure for reduced costs as any other cost stream in business. "Value-added" has become something of a catch phrase in business circles, and auditors are told that their services must contribute value-added in order to justify the fees being charged." Related to this is the growing tendency amongst the larger companies to seek tenders from competing audit firms. There appears to be some fear that these pressures may impact on quality, and lead to the cutting of corners.

However, we live in a competitive world, and tendering is an acceptable process, provided that a proper specification is prepared by the company — another function of the audit committee. It is not easy to see how the pure statutory audit can be regarded as "adding value", as has been said above, since it refers to a ratification process. However, value can, and should, be added arising out of the audit process, through the communication structure outlined above. And within that structure there could be strong influences, flowing from shareholder involvement, on the maintenance of quality.

THE PREVENTION AND DISCOVERY OF FRAUD

It is quite wrong for auditors to attempt to disclaim responsibility for fraud discovery. Having said that, one cannot fault the provisions of *Statement of Auditing Standards 110* as outlined by O'Hogan (p. 113), and the allocation therein of responsibility between the directors and the auditors. It is certainly a primary responsibility of the directors to ensure that systems are in place that have a reasonable chance of preventing fraud, and of detecting it if it occurs. This is a further area where the audit committee has an important role to play in examining, with the auditors, the systems in place, and both being satisfied that they are as adequate as may be, within ordinary economic constraints.

Thereafter, during the audit, the auditor must assess the risks and design the audit accordingly. However, where collusion at the higher level occurs, it may be difficult, if not almost impossible, for ordinary audit methods to detect well-designed fraud.

CONCLUSION

As things stand at present, the auditor is looked upon by management as a necessary evil imposed by statute, providing little or no value to the company. The imposition of accounting standard after accounting standard, which may not have been necessary if the auditor were truly independent, has led to more complex and voluminous accounts within which vital information is buried to be extracted only by those with expertise or a familiarity with the process. The end result is that the small shareholder is generally apathetic about attendance at Annual General Meetings, completion of proxies, election of auditors, election of non-executive directors, or indeed in making a keen perusal of the published accounts other than to determine the level of profit and the increase in dividend.

If greater shareholder involvement is to be a precursor to improved standards in both management and auditor, and a removal of the "cosy" system at present evident, then institutional shareholders must play a greater part than hitherto, and exercise their responsibilities as shareholders by attendance at general meetings, and by setting an example to the smaller individual shareholder. After all, institutions own upwards of 70 per cent of our quoted companies.

Finally, a question: if auditors are statutorily required to be elected on an annual basis, why not executive directors? It could be salutary for many if they were required to account for their stewardship on, say, a triennial basis.

8
Audit Failure

Edward Cahill
University College Cork

INTRODUCTION

The practice of auditing is coming under increasing scrutiny by the accounting profession and the public generally. Over the past 20 years, problems and responses have multiplied. More recently, the situation has been exacerbated by the scale of business collapses. These have been caused by poor management, changed economic conditions, fraudulent activities, or a combination of these. However, it has been frequently suggested that the auditors should have recognised the problems earlier than they did. Thus, fairly or unfairly, these business failures have often, in the public's eyes, become audit failures, and an audit expectations gap has thereby developed.

In this chapter, we discuss the nature of audit failure, its impact on the financial reporting process, and the wider aspect of corporate governance. Determinants of audit failure are discussed and examples provided. Actual evidence on the extent of audit failure in Ireland is limited. Thus, we do not know how serious a problem it may or may not be, or the extent to which it is associated with corporate collapse and management fraud, as is often the experience in other developed countries. Although Ireland has endured an unusually large number of corporate failures in the past decade, unlike many other countries, the state has not considered it desirable to inquire into the reasons for these collapses. Arising from inquiries of this nature, many other countries have found it necessary to modify and strengthen their systems of corporate regulation.

First, however, it is necessary to consider the objectives of financial reporting, the nature of the audit, and its authority. With this background, we go on to define audit failure, examine its root causes and explore the extent of the problem in Ireland. We conclude by arguing for a wider definition of the scope of the audit.

THE OBJECTIVES OF FINANCIAL REPORTING

The annual financial statements are one of the primary sources of information about the performance of an enterprise. Obviously, financial statements do not adequately capture and reflect the richness and complexity of the underlying activities which make an enterprise a living and self-sustaining system. The weaving together of scientific and engineering expertise, the application of computer-driven technology, product and personnel development, marketing and pricing policies, and a suitable organisational climate, are elements of the enterprise which are not explicitly captured in the financial statements — though they may be crucial to an enterprise's self-sustaining ability.

A dominant objective of financial statements is to provide useful information about financial position, performance and sustainability of an enterprise to a wide range of users making economic decisions. The economic decisions for which financial statements may be useful encompass a range of aspects about the company's affairs including: decisions relating to expansion, divestment, capital structure, comparative economy of capital use, profitability, dividend policy, and reward through profit participation schemes.

Of course, financial statements have a role that is wider than the purely economic. From an accountability perspective, financial statements provide shareholders with some assurance concerning the stewardship by management of the resources entrusted to it. In a wider social sense, financial statements are central to the tax-collection system, and they also touch on employer–employee relationships in terms of employment risk and the firm's ability to pay certain wage rates.

However, financial statements are not a seamless and objective representation of business activity. Modern business firms and their economic relationships are often complex and changing. Selectivity and judgment can play a significant role in financial reporting in certain types of firms: consider a building or engineering contractor and the time-scale of a large contract, or an insurance company and the nature of claims. Thus, financial statements may appear to present a precise and real corporate snapshot of economic phenomena when, in fact, it (or part of it at least) is somewhat imprecise, messy and subjectively evaluated.

THE AUDIT

The need for an independent auditor to form a view on the representational faithfulness of financial statements can be readily appreciated in view of the different interests referred to in the previous section. The audit is perhaps even more important in larger "public concern" firms where there is a variety of stakeholders. A comprehensive definition of audit is provided by Woolf:

> In its modern sense an audit is a process (carried out by suitably qualified "auditors") whereby the accounts of business entities, including limited companies, charities and professional firms, are subjected to scrutiny in such detail as will enable the auditors to form an opinion as to their truth and fairness. This opinion is then embodied in an "audit report", addressed to those parties who commissioned the audit, or to whom the auditors are responsible under statute.[1]

We observe the two elements of the audit process: scrutiny and opinion. It should also be noted that the auditor is seen as possessing specialist expertise — "suitably qualified". Underlying the objectives of company auditing are four main concepts, proposed by Lee:[2]

1) Auditor independence

2) Auditor responsibility

3) Truth and fairness

4) Audit evidence.

These may be summarised as stating that auditors must have complete independence to be objective; they should be legally and professionally responsible for the conduct and quality of their work and opinions; the financial position of the company should be truly and fairly described based on generally accepted accounting principles and statutory requirements; and auditors should investigate and collect sufficient competent evidence to support the audit opinion provided.

The right to audit certain types of companies is restricted to members of certain designated professional bodies under the Companies Acts, 1963–90.[3] In turn, these bodies operate their own internal registration arrangements following a prescribed training and educational process leading to certification. It is relevant to note that the formalisation and strengthening of these professional registration and supervision requirements for auditors in Ireland (i.e. Sections 188–

192 of the Companies Act, 1990) and other European countries was stimulated by the implementation of the Seventh EC Directive.

AUTHORITY FOR AUDIT

The history of accountability and audit in our society is a long one. Bird (1974) provides examples of the audit of large estates in ancient Babylon and in Mediaeval England. And, long before financial reporting and audit were made compulsory by Gladstone's first Companies Act of 1844, audits were often negotiated between parties engaged in trade. Incidentally, the compulsory financial reporting and audit provisions of the 1844 Act were repealed 11 years later and only reintroduced following public outcry over large-scale fraud and deception; the losses suffered by stockholders in City of Glasgow Bank in 1878 were catastrophic and led to the 1879 Companies Act which required banking companies to have an annual audit.

Later, the Company Law Amendment Committee of 1894 (with the support of leading accountants of the day, such as Waterhouse and Whinney, who were among the vanguard of the fledgling profession) recommended compulsory audit for all limited companies — enacted in the Companies Act of 1900. It was, perhaps, one of the earliest instances of a successful lobby by the accountancy profession influencing company law and financial reporting. This mandatory audit requirement for all companies (which remains to this day) was in stark contrast to public policy in the US and other developed countries. It became the basis of the enormous growth of the auditing profession.

It is difficult to say whether fraud was ever conquered as a corporate illness and whether all independent auditors zealously toiled in its pursuit and disclosure. Whereas the detection of fraud and error was seen to be one of the primary objectives of the auditor up to the early 1930s, and was accepted by the auditors as part of the contract of professionalism, a major change in emphasis has been brought about by the accountancy firms. Lee indicated that the move from fraud detection to providing an opinion on the credibility of accounting information took place in the early 1930s. He suggests that the reasons were the increasing size of enterprises, and the views of leading accountants in London, such as Sir Nicholas Waterhouse who advocated the view that the suppression and detection of fraud was an internal administrative responsibility. Accounting and disclosure compliance became the new governing aim of the audit. Interestingly, the public perception of the role of an audit has not accepted this more narrowly defined responsibility, and it is not surprising that "an expectations gap" between auditors, users and the general public has, in the course of time, become such a controversial issue.

Today, the Companies Acts, 1963–90, and the European Communities (Credit Institutions: Accounts) Regulations, 1992, govern audit matters. The Acts are remarkably silent on the objectives and nature of the audit other than to say that the auditors "... shall make a report to all the members on the accounts examined by them..." relating to the adequacy of information received for their purposes, on whether proper books of account were kept, as well as branch returns, and whether the balance sheet and profit and loss account are in agreement with the books of account (Section 193; CA 1990). The Act also requires the auditor to express an opinion as to whether the balance sheet and profit and loss account have been properly prepared in accordance with the provisions of the Companies Acts and whether they give a true and fair view. The auditors are also required to report whether the company's net assets amount to more than half of the called-up share capital at the balance-sheet date. If net assets fall below this level, the auditors must report that fact and state that an extraordinary general meeting is required to be convened under Section 40 of the Companies (Amendment) Act, 1983.

Probably the most noteworthy aspect of recent companies legislation (and, at the time of writing, proposed taxation legislation) is the state's attempt to widen the responsibility of auditors. Under Section 194 of the 1990 Companies Act, auditors are required to advise the Registrar of Companies if proper books of account have not been kept, having first served a notice on the company. In addition, Section 46 of the Act sets out new duties in respect to disclosure of a wide variety of transactions between directors, and other connected parties, and the company. To a degree, these new duties have brought the auditor into a quasi-policing role from a regulatory perspective. This stems from the many corporate abuses and irregularities observed by receivers and liquidators in the past. It should also be noted that auditors have certain additional responsibilities relating to insurance companies, banking concerns and building societies in respect of returns to their regulatory authorities (i.e. the Central Bank and the Department of Trade, Industry and Tourism).

Apart from statutory prescription, auditing is also affected by professional pronouncements and the common law. Auditing standards were first introduced by the accountancy profession in the UK (and Ireland) in 1980, following a series of very critical commentaries regarding the quality of audit practice by UK Department of Trade inspectors.[4] These auditing standards (which were extremely short in comparison with their US counterparts) were expected to provide a basis for improved practice which would, in turn, enhance audit quality. Criticisms, however, continued right through the 1980s, and in 1990 the earlier professional accountancy body dominated Auditing Practices Committee was superseded by the more independent and broadly based Auditing Practices Board (APB). In setting out its brief, the new APB commented:

> Against a background of widespread criticism of auditors, and a growing public scepticism about the value of the audit function ... CCAB recognised the need for a standard-setting body which could be seen to be more independent and authoritative than the APC....[5]

The courts play their part in auditing through decided case law. A revealing illustration[6] of the link between case law and the courts' expectation that auditors observe changing professional practices and standards was provided by the decision and comments of the judge in the case of *Kelly and others* v. *Haughey Boland & Co.* (1985). It concerned the alleged negligence of the defendant in not attending stock-taking. The judge made reference to the recommendations and professional standards of the Institute of Chartered Accountants in Ireland in operation at the time.

AUDIT FAILURE AND ITS CONSEQUENCES
What Does "Audit Failure" Mean?

It may now be useful to define the term "audit failure". Audit failure refers to the non-performance by the auditor in achieving the objectives of the audit role. If the purpose of the audit is "... to conduct an independent examination of, and express an opinion on the financial statements of an enterprise...",[7] this non-performance may occur in one or both elements of the audit role. In other words, the examination of the affairs of an enterprise may be ineffective, or the communication by the auditors of their opinion may be inadequate.

The Consequences of Audit Failure

The consequences can be far reaching resulting in the following:

- Bias in the financial statements
- Difficulty in assessing risk

- Loss of organisational control
- Exposure to litigation
- Weakened corporate governance.

Bias in Financial Statements

A consequence of audit failure may be that the financial statements do not represent faithfully what they claim to represent because they contain a degree of bias which makes them misleading for accountability and decision-making purposes. The bias may be caused by defects in the nature of the measurements of economic events adopted, or the misapplication of measurement methods, judgments or accounting-information presentation principles. This may be a result of a lack of skill, or integrity, or both, and it may be intentional or inadvertent.

The complications can be far-reaching, since financial statements are used widely in both the private and public arenas. To gain some sense of their significance, we need only recall the recent critical public roles of accounting information in the controversial negotiations between employers and trade unions in the reorganisation of TEAM/Aer Lingus and Irish Steel, and in the earlier, long-running saga at Waterford Crystal.

Difficulty in Assessing Risk

Risk assessment is inevitably affected by audit failure: shareholders, stockbroker analysts and fund managers use accounting information to judge a firm's equity share value and the risk profile of future returns. The market shows its reaction, in share price terms, when a firm issues an earnings announcement. Bankers also use clients' financial statements in assessing the risk associated with lending.

Loss of Organisational Control

A breakdown in audit quality can lead to distorted feedback, which undermines the "triggers" for controlling or taking corrective action at board level. In turn, resulting managerial actions may weaken the performance of the enterprise and its financial position. After all, creative accounting and misleading accounting information are often associated with corporate failure. One writer put it very well when he observed:

> The top managers know, probably before they admit it to themselves and long before anyone else knows, that their company is not doing well. They also know that if this becomes generally recognized the bank will tighten its credit terms, customers will sidle away, suppliers will begin to demand cash on or before delivery. But worse than this the managers themselves will be seen to have failed....
>
> ...they cannot further revalue the stocks or exaggerate the value of buildings and they now have to resort to some of the more intricate devices.... Later on things become worse still and the managers may then have to step over that ill-defined boundary between optimism and fraud. Whether they do so depends partly, I believe, upon the inner psychological make-up of the boss....[8]

In such cases the role of the independent auditor in ensuring that financial statements faithfully represent an objectively "true and fair" view of the enterprise is critical.

Exposure to Litigation

It is not surprising, bearing in mind the above comments, that there have been many (successful) lawsuits against leading audit firms. Indeed, many academics (and a US government agency) have argued that poor accounting standards and spineless auditing contributed to what is sometimes referred to as our present era of "deals" and "excesses".[9] In Ireland, perhaps the legal proceedings against audit firms in the cases of Icarom (ICI), Primor (PMPA), Aer Lingus Holidays and the De Lorean motor car manufacturing firm might represent the equivalent response.

In the case of Insurance Corporation of Ireland (ICI), which collapsed in March 1985, and which was placed in administration, Allied Irish Banks (AIB plc) and the administrator, Mr W. McCann of Price Waterhouse, sued ICI's auditors, Ernst & Whinney for over £500 million alleging negligence and breach of duty.[10] AIB plc had to write-off a loss of almost £90 million at the time, being the investment cost of ICI, quite apart from the subsequent contributions it made towards funding ICI's deficit of over £260 million. The ICI case was finalised in 1993 in an out-of-court settlement, with Ernst & Whinney agreeing to pay IR£77 million, without admission of liability. In the case of PMPA, which collapsed in 1983, the administrator, Mr K. Kelly of Coopers & Lybrand, took an action against the auditors of PMPA, Oliver Freaney & Co. and Stokes Kennedy Crowley & Co., for £175 million damages for negligence.[11] However, in 1995, the auditors were successful in an application to the Irish Supreme Court to have the case dismissed because of the inordinate delay in bringing the action against them to court.

Weakened Corporate Governance

Audit failure also affects the very foundation of our system of corporate governance. The state has created a legal control framework (including audit), to support and enable a limited liability company to play a vital economic and social role in our society. When the control system breaks down, the consequences reverberate through the system, particularly when the company is large. The recent restructuring of the state concerns, Aer Lingus, TEAM/Aer Lingus, B&I, Irish Steel, and the private companies such as Goodman International, Kentz Corporation or the GPA Group, and some of their subsidiaries, illustrate how individual enterprises have important economic and social interactions with local economies and specific stakeholder groups. Consider the possible consequences for Clonmel or Cobh if Kentz or Irish Steel were to close down.

THE DETERMINANTS OF AUDIT FAILURE

Given the regulatory structure surrounding audit, comprising statute, professional pronouncements and the extensive training and education associated with accountancy and auditing as professional activities, it might be difficult (for some) to understand how audit failure can occur. We need to look to the US and the UK for explanations.[12] In a research analysis of 472 litigation cases against auditors in the USA in the period 1960–85, Palmrose disclosed some interesting and extremely relevant findings.[13] In 44 per cent of the cases, management fraud — involving the intentional misrepresentation by upper-level executives — had occurred. Litigation in respect of errors directly relating to business failures accounted for 18 per cent of the sample. A surprisingly large 30 per cent of cases, in a category described as "other", was dominated by litigation associated with acquisitions and initial public offerings. Palmrose concluded:

> Nearly half the cases alleging audit failure involve business failures or clients with severe financial difficulties. However, a large portion of failed companies are not involved in auditor litigation.
>
> A majority of lawsuits involving bankrupt clients also involve management fraud.[14]

In the US, the Securities and Exchange Commission, as an ultimate supervisory body in accounting and auditing matters, has a powerful influence on auditing practices. Specific cases heard before the SEC have highlighted problem areas and have motivated the auditing profession to correct deficiencies in auditing standards and procedures.[15] Also, of course, the SEC prosecutes and disciplines auditors where there is evidence of poor work in public-interest cases. The regulatory philosophy of the SEC as regards investigations for "enforcement actions" and "sanctions" has been cogently articulated by Burton, a former senior official:

> In deciding whether to institute an enforcement action, the Commission considers the case in the light of several factors, including the seriousness of the professional deficiency and the extent to which the auditor had knowledge of what was happening. The Commission also considers the degree to which the auditor appeared to be an active participant in a scheme to mislead the public through artful or incomplete disclosure or through creative selection of accounting principles designed to present a picture inconsistent with reality....[16]

Burton also disclosed that where the SEC has been uneasy with the auditor's performance, but where formal action was not warranted, the SEC will invite the senior management of the auditing firm to a meeting, where policies as regards remedial action and improved procedures in the auditing firm will be discussed. An illustration of enforcement actions in the USA is provided from the SEC 1990 Annual Report where it stated:

> In the Spring of 1990, the Commission organized a new group within its office of General Counsel to focus primarily on the litigation of administrative disciplinary cases against professionals....

In *Re Ernst & Whinney*, Administrative Law Judge Jerome Soffer found that Ernst & Whinney (now Ernst & Young) and one of its partners had engaged in improper professional conduct by violating generally accepted auditing standards during the audit of US Surgical Corporation's 1980 and 1981 financial statements. Judge Soffer found that audit partners "all the way up to the top level including the co-chairman" participated in the outcome of the audit, and that the auditors unduly relied upon representations of Surgical Corporation's management, even after serious questions concerning management's integrity had been raised during the audit. Based on his findings, Judge Soffer suspended the New York region of the firm from undertaking any new Commission engagement for a period of 45 days. No appeal to the Commission was taken from the ruling.[17]

Reliance on management assertions, rather than independent and objective documentary or other corroboration of material facts or judgments relating to the financial statements, has often been shown to be an aspect of audit failure. In terms of the four concepts underlying auditing, the Surgical Corporation case appears to be an example of insufficient audit evidence and, perhaps, insufficient independence.

In the UK, many illustrations of accounting and audit deficiencies have been highlighted in the published reports of investigations undertaken by inspectors appointed by the Department of Trade and Industry (DTI). These DTI reports stimulated the development of accounting standards and auditing standards[18] in the 1970s and later the establishment of a new disciplinary scheme in the UK, effective from 1980.[19&20]

In the case of Milbury plc and Westminster Property Group Ltd., the inspectors were critical of a domineering and unscrupulous director, Stock Exchange listing practices, certain internal management, and the auditors — Arthur Young. The inspectors concluded that the 1984 Milbury group accounts should have been qualified by the auditors, because they did not show a true and fair view of the group's trading and financial position. It was felt that the profits had been materially overstated by at least £1 million, and possibly by as much as £2 million. There were serious doubts about valuations of building developments, work-in-progress and properties.

As a result of these findings, the Joint Disciplinary Committee of the three "public practice" accountancy bodies investigated the matter and concluded publicly against Arthur Young as follows:

> ... the professional conduct and competence of Arthur Young, as composed of the partners in that firm on 17th July 1984, fell below the standard which should have been displayed by, and which may reasonably be expected of, a firm of chartered accountants, serving as auditors of a public company in that they gave an unqualified audit opinion on the accounts of Milbury for the year ended 31st March 1984, when they knew or should have known, that the accounts did not give a true and fair view and were seriously misleading.

The Committee ordered that Arthur Young be fined £100,000 and pay the sum of £40,000 towards the cost of the inquiry.[21]

In the case of Rotaprint plc, the inspectors criticised the auditors for their failure to qualify the 1987 financial statements on "going-concern" grounds.[22] The inspectors were critical of audit working papers, and they concluded that the auditors were aware of Rotaprint's financial difficulties, certain weaknesses in its accounting and control systems, the level of bank facilities available, and the fact that there were production problems. It was felt that the auditors' review of Rotaprint's cash-flow projections was inadequate as there was insufficient margin for contingencies, and that the basis of the projections deserved much more caution in view of the accounting-system problems and the heavy reliance on a new product. At the time of the completion of the audit, it was known that there was a shortfall in targeted production, and there was insufficient evidence that the problems had been overcome.

The recent report of the inspectors relating to one of the largest collapses in the UK in recent years, Atlantic Computers plc (which in turn triggered the failure of British & Commonwealth Holdings plc), concluded that there were many serious accounting and auditing problems in this computer-leasing company.[23] Imprudent accounting policies led to excessive front-loading in profit recognition and insufficient provisions against potential losses. There was the matter of placing a residual interest valuation on computers and taking such valuation into profit at the inception of the lease. There was also a failure to apply the requirements of applicable Accounting Standards (SSAP 18 and SSAP 21). The inspectors were critical of the work of Spicer & Oppenheim (the auditor) on many fronts — from their assessment of audit risk, audit planning, working papers, testing of internal controls, audit of stocks, audit of debtors, accounting policies adopted and disclosures of potential liabilities, audit manager review and many other matters. Atlantic was seen as a difficult client with a domineering chief executive. Interestingly, the inspectors felt that the fundamental cause of the audit problems originated in Spicer's insufficient understanding of the complexities of Atlantic's business as it expanded rapidly. The inspectors indicated that they thought that Spicer acted in good faith throughout their audits, but they appeared to imply insufficient professional expertise for the nature of the task.

Finally, a recent Australian example of audit failure relating to AWA Ltd. and its court action against Deloitte Haskins & Sells, reported by O'Leary in *Accountancy Ireland,*[24] revealed audit failure on a number of fronts — auditor independence, competent staffing of an audit, reporting of serious internal-control deficiencies and proper audit evidence on matters relating to foreign exchange transactions.

Audit Failure

Many examples from UK negligence court cases are provided by Gwilliam.[25] In the UK, there is a body of evidence from the findings of the Joint Disciplinary Scheme which included a number of instances of audit failure.[26] In the Milbury case, referred to earlier (and the many others investigated by this disciplinary scheme in the UK), the accountancy firms are being reviewed by their peers. Consequently, there would be quite a clear understanding about norms of behaviour expected of auditors when the alleged "audit failure" occurred.

Thus, audit failure appears to result from incompetence on the part of the auditor or a dilution of independence. Regarding the independence issue, evidence from the US suggests that conflicts between client management and the audit firm over accounting principles, the adequacy of disclosure and the need to make adjustments to the financial statements are the most common causes of difficulty. No doubt, where such difficulties arise, company management is often in a powerful position economically to press for its preferences on the auditor. However, it will not always be straightforward. Audit firms are supported in their attitudes by their good name, by the authority of professional auditing and accounting standards, and by their own internal procedures; and those who bow to such pressures risk a great deal in any subsequent public exposure. It is a risk trade-off.

From the foregoing examples, the determinants of audit failure may be summarised as follows:

- Undue reliance on the representations of management
- Lack of independence: collusion of the auditor in the use of "artful or incomplete disclosure, or through creative selection of accounting principles"
- Insufficient understanding of the entity being audited
- Lack of adequately trained or competent staff
- Inadequate audit procedures, and faulty supervision.

HAS THERE BEEN AUDIT FAILURE IN IRELAND?

We have little independent research information on auditing quality in Ireland. Like many "professional" occupations, it is difficult to observe externally the quality of the work. In contrast to the UK, New Zealand, Australia or Canada, Ireland has only recently appointed inspectors (after a gap of almost 20 years), to investigate companies in connection with alleged irregularities or insufficient or inaccurate disclosure of information.

In other countries, there has been a much more active regulatory response (involving sanctions and disciplinary actions), where investigations have revealed instances of irregular conduct by management and/or poor professional work by accountants and auditors. Remarkably, there were no inspectors' investigations or tribunals of inquiry into the ICI, PMPA or Irish Shipping collapses — despite the fact that these were very definite "public-concern" affairs. This writer is not aware of any professional disciplinary inquiries in these or many other cases where there was a question mark over accounting and audit issues.

Again, unlike many other countries, there have been very few Irish court cases from which to derive evidence on the quality of auditing practice. Many Irish cases have been settled on the steps of the court. However, the fact that legal proceedings were initiated against the auditors to Primor plc (formerly PMPA Insurance) by the Administrator, and against the auditors of Aer Lingus Holidays Ltd. by its parent, Aer Lingus, is some indication that audit failure is being alleged. Some years ago, it was reported that a settlement had been reached between the auditors to the collapsed Merchant Banking Ltd. and that company's liquidator. It is relevant to note also that there was a change of audit firm associated with the restructuring of Goodman International, following its spectacular financial crisis when the first Examiner in the state was appointed under hurriedly approved Oireachtas legislation in late August 1990.

In his judgment in *Re Superwood*, Justice O'Hanlon was reported as being critical of certain accounting matters and the nature of the trading record of the group as reported in the prospectus.[27] Both the Stock Exchange and the Institute of Chartered Accountants in Ireland were reported to be reviewing the case.

The revelations of the inspectors in the Greencore investigation[28] indicated that conflicts of interest can arise between management and the company, which have important consequences for shareholders and creditors. It should be stressed that there was no allegation of audit failure. There were several management resignations — including the Secretary/Financial Director of the company who was a chartered accountant. The foregoing, when taken together with other recent Departmental inspections into behaviour in matters relating to Telecom and Countyglen, suggests that in some instances, Irish corporate behaviour may not be much different from that revealed in other countries. If this is the case, then the area of audit quality may not be materially different from UK or US experience as regards public-concern companies.

It should be pointed out that there is some evidence that auditors do not necessarily bend to managements' wishes when there is a difference of opinion on material financial reporting issues. A public example occurred in the mid-1980s, when Memory Computer plc issued a misleading preliminary profit announcement before the completion of the audit. The audit firm involved did not approve certain of the transactions and basis of profit recognition underlying the figure announced. When the financial statements were recast, there was a very material reduction in profit (to near break-even) which had implications for its financial position and its share price on the stock market. This case illustrates the very different views on economic events which can be taken by management and auditors.

Perhaps we are seeing just the "tip of the iceberg" in terms of audit failure in Ireland. After all, the "Big 6" accountancy firms are linked with their worldwide counterparts not only in name but also in audit methodologies, systems, procedures, and internal quality control. These six accountancy firms dominate public-concern audits in Ireland, generating a combined turnover of over £140 million in Ireland in 1993.[29] We in Ireland would expect from these larger accountancy firms standards of audit quality similar to those in the UK or the US. In turn, could we not speculate that similar levels of audit failure might be experienced in Ireland?

The fact that the Institute of Chartered Accountants (to its credit) established the Financial Reporting Commission in 1991 under the chairmanship of Professor Louden Ryan, to examine, among other issues, the "audit expectations gap", was a kind of public acknowledgement that there were problems with regard to the quality of accounting and auditing. The Commission's report clearly identified the weaknesses in Ireland's regulatory, monitoring and enforcement structures — as compared to the UK and many other countries in the European Union, as well as the US.

On the self-regulatory side, the accountancy profession has a practice review process (conducted by the Institute of Chartered Accountants in Ireland) and there are professional standards investigation and disciplinary committees. Other "recognised" accountancy and audit bodies appeared to lag behind the ICA arrangements. However, compared to the UK, Ireland stands out in terms of a lack of transparency and reporting of disciplinary actions and initiatives into accounting and auditing matters — particularly in relation to public-concern cases. This is all the more critical here because Ireland lacks a Financial Reporting Review Panel (which in the UK monitors the truth and fairness of company accounts). The UK is somewhat unique in the EU in its financial reporting and corporate regulatory framework and mechanisms. Ireland is associated with part of the self-regulatory framework, in terms of settings standards, but it has not brought in the corresponding monitoring and enforcement structures. With such a "one-leg" approach, the effectiveness of financial reporting regulation in Ireland must be questioned.

In many other developed countries there is a Securities Commission, modelled somewhat on the lines of the SEC in the US, with a wide range of statutory powers. Examples can be taken from France, Canada, Australia and New Zealand. As regards active or transparent regulation, Ireland, in comparison, seems to operate in a vacuum.

TOWARDS A WIDER DEFINITION OF THE SCOPE OF AUDIT

In Ireland, we have tended to accept the objectives and nature of an audit, together with the auditor's responsibilities as developed in the UK. Much of our company law, particularly relating to financial reporting matters, has been heavily influenced by UK philosophy and practice. Even the mandatory audit for all limited companies (including small companies) has been part of Ireland's historical baggage — although this requirement is not mandatory in the US. Obviously, with the extensive trading and financial links, there have been good reasons for this level of co-operation in the past.

However, as European integration continues apace with its quite different business structures, financial reporting and regulatory philosophies, we might consider whether our economic development might not be better served by alternative financial reporting and regulatory models. One possibility could be the German approach. Just as easily, we could consider approaches developed in Canada (i.e. Toronto) or New Zealand.

At present, the role of the audit has been primarily left to the accountancy profession to specify. It might be argued that the profession has defined the objectives and nature of an audit in too narrow a frame — possibly for a variety of reasons. However, if we adopt a public-interest perspective, viewing the audit as an important element in securing our economic development and the effective operation of our financial markets, perhaps other criteria and objectives could be considered. For example, it would be relevant to a variety of stakeholders for the auditors to comment not only on the representational faithfulness of the financial statements, but also on the discovery of management, or other, fraud, and on whether the internal control and management planning and control systems were appropriate to the nature and scale of the organisation. This auditors' review could also cover administrative and capital structures. The auditors could comment on the general efficiency trends in the firm and how its performance and financial condition had progressed and how it compared with others in the sector. Finally, issues such as the extent of arrears of debt and taxes might be included. It is this writer's contention that the needs of external and internal users are much greater than the current restricted definition of an audit and that this wider "economic-efficiency-needs gap" should constitute a basis of defining an alternative view of audit failure in Ireland.

Commentary

Brian Conroy
Bastow Charleton

The business scandals highlighted by Edward Cahill typically involve inappropriate business decisions, based in part on inaccurate "audited" financial statements, followed by corporate failure. In many cases of this kind, the culpability of the auditor has been neither proven nor even alleged. However, the scandals reflect poorly on the audit profession and the audit process.

These corporate failures have created a perception of failure of the regulatory process, of which the audit process is a key part. Therefore, a more generalised conclusion is drawn. That is, audit reports on financial statements are perceived as having been inappropriate or misleading.

USERS'/STAKEHOLDERS' REACTION

From the perspective of the professional auditor, public reaction to these scandals has been surprising. Rather than undermining the status of the audit, it would appear that the reaction is quite the opposite. Ironically, audit failure has highlighted the importance of the audit process. The corollary of attributing "corporate failure" to a failure in the "audit process" must be to attribute an exceptional importance to that audit process.

Stakeholders in corporate viability (employees, government, creditors, shareholders etc.) are taking an increasing interest in the audit process. The instances of corporate failure appear to have chastened stakeholders. Those with a special interest in corporate viability have a need for scrutiny and information beyond that provided by the statutory audit alone. Therefore, additional reports are requested from auditors. Examples include: regulatory agencies requiring validation of grant-aided expenditure, banks requiring confirmation of preferential creditors, management requiring "due diligence" confirmation of prospective investments. Such reports are primarily provided

Audit Failure

by statutory auditors in addition to their statutory responsibilities. In other situations, business scrutiny is pursued by the stakeholders themselves. Revenue Audit Procedures and Independent Accountants' Reports for trade unions are typical examples.

With regard to the statutory audit process, the level of interaction between client and auditor is growing. Our larger companies have set up Audit Committees. There is an increasing incidence of fixed-term appointments of auditors, as well as rotation of the appointment through competitive tender. The increasing priority given to audit quality would appear to reflect the increasing sophistication of the business community in a rapidly changing and increasingly complex business environment. The taxation authorities have increased surveillance and increased their demands for information and controls. Banks and other creditors are concerned at potential legal and taxation exposures. Trade credit surveillance has increased the demand for information, and, with it, a demand for independent verification of business transactions.

THE AUDIT PROFESSION'S FAILURE

The response of the profession in the UK and Ireland to audit failure has been low key. Audit practices and standards have not been altered significantly. On the contrary, the promulgations of the profession over the past 10 years have seen a codification of existing procedures and standards, rather than the introduction of anything new. There appears to be little demand (from the regulatory authorities or from the profession) for more (or even better) auditing. Pressure for the abolition of the statutory audit for small companies underlines the trend in this regard. Those "audit failures" that have become the subject of public scrutiny have been failures in application of established auditing standards, rather than failures of the audit process.

Therefore, the profession is presented with two problems. Firstly, there is a widespread public perception that auditors (as distinct from directors) are responsible for "inaccurate financial statements followed by corporate failure". Secondly, instances of "failure in application" by a self-regulating profession reflect poorly on the "policing" of that profession. Both of these problems are considered below.

The Public Perception of the Auditor's Role

Undoubtedly, the profession has a difficulty in communicating effectively. The wording of standard audit reports was revised in 1993 in an attempt to clarify (perhaps even to minimise) the auditors' responsibility for the reliability of financial statements. The new audit report includes the following statements:

> An audit includes .... an assessment of the significant estimates and judgements made by directors.
>
> .... the directors are responsible for the preparation of the financial statements ....

In addition, further disclosure is now required in the directors' or auditors' report as follows:

> The directors are responsible for keeping proper accounting records which disclose with reasonable accuracy at any time the financial position.

These statements reflect the profession's attempt to deal with what is called the "expectations gap". The Report of the Commission of Enquiry into the Expectations of Users of Published Financial Statements (the Ryan Commission), which reported in 1992, had recommended essentially that more "disclosure" could help to alleviate the "expectations-gap" problem.

As part of the audit process, the Ryan Commission proposed specific disclosures dealing with:

- Financial statements
- Audit report
- Special reports to client audit committees and boards of directors
- Engagement letters.

These disclosures dealt with:

- Responsibility for financial statements
- Going concern/solvency
- Independence
- Fraud/illegal acts
- Efficiency of records and controls
- Auditor independence, details of fees paid to auditors for non-audit work.

Outside the disclosure aspect, the Commission came down firmly on the side of the status quo. It recommended:

- Continuation of self-regulation
- Preservation of auditors' "freedom to tender"
- No compulsory rotation of auditors.

However, to enhance auditor independence, it recommended that auditors should not have greater than 5 per cent of fees arising from a single client or group.

Interestingly, the submission to the Ryan Commission from Ireland's largest audit practice, KPMG Stokes Kennedy Crowley, made a quite vigorous distinction between two groups of financial-statements users:

> It is our experience that the users of financial statements are reasonably aware of the main advantages and limitations of an audit. The expectations gap is concentrated mainly in those users who are infrequent users or who are not financially expert. This would appear to include the media as well as the "general public", including private shareholders.

These observations drive at the heart of the statutory audit process. If audits are perceived to fail, the perception arises because financial-statements users rely too heavily on the audit process and the audit report. They do not adequately recognise that the entire financial reporting and "financial intermediation" process is part of society's attempt to facilitate the allocation of its economic resources. The statutory audit has a small, but important, part in that process.

The developments in financial reporting of the past 20 years are designed to make financial statements more meaningful and more comparable. This is done not only for the financially astute but also to communicate to a wider and better-informed society. The KPMG Stokes Kennedy Crowley submission emphasised the educational nature of the problem. However, the process by which society allocates its economic resources is directed, primarily, by the marketplace. Edward Cahill emphasises this broader role: "... financial statements have a role wider than the perspective of decision-makers such as shareholders and bankers...."

Society's attitudes to taxation, pension planning, wage negotiations, price increases etc. are influenced by the full financial reporting and auditing process. Thus, whilst society may be ignorant of the implications of the statutory audit, it is nonetheless reliant on it to regulate and protect its economic aspects. Audit failure undermines credibility, ultimately affecting economic-resource allocation. Business corruption, as is seen for instance in many parts of the Third World, undermines economic development. In our country, the banks' customers will not save, and investors will not invest if the regulatory framework is not understood and relied upon. Therefore, it seems important that the financial reporting and audit process should be well understood and respected throughout society.

Policing Audit Performance

Three possible instances of audit failure in Ireland are referred to by Professor Cahill:

- Icarom (formerly Insurance Corporation of Ireland)
- PMPA Insurance
- Aer Lingus Holidays.

In each case, litigation was initiated alleging auditor negligence. Implicit in such litigation is the assertion that financial statements were misleading (leading to inappropriate financial decisions and consequent financial loss). The primary responsibility for the reliability of financial statements rests with the directors. However, the regulation of the performance and behaviour of directors appears to escape the censure and soul-searching that is the lot of the audit profession. These "one-sided" inquests are unhelpful. Where the independence or performance of the auditor is questioned, appropriate disciplinary action should be taken.

There is little doubt that, in the three cases mentioned above, the general public was disappointed with the regulatory process (including appointment and performance of directors, board meetings, annual reports and audit). Both sophisticated analysts and the general public developed a consensus view: the regulatory and audit process should have prevented misleading information being relied upon.

It seems fair to conclude that (irrespective of legal liability), the regulatory and audit process failed, and that public confidence was undermined. From a policing point of view, the difficulty is associating this failure with blame and liability. How can the blame be shared between directors, auditors, the Stock Exchange and other regulatory agencies?

Both the Irish and UK accounting bodies independently examine the work of practising firms though *Practice Review*. Furthermore, complaints and criticisms of the auditors' work are subject to quite vigorous disciplinary procedures. Unfortunately, the general public is unaware of the extent of these self-regulation and policing procedures. Likewise, the improvements in disclosure introduced, in part, as a consequence of the debate within the profession about the expectations gap, have received little media interest. Even sophisticated users of financial statements may not be aware of the quality of the "policing" procedures. It is argued here that the audit profession has failed to communicate the developments that have taken place through the Joint Monitoring Unit in the UK and the Practice Review procedures developed by the Irish Institute. This author is unaware of equivalent "self-regulatory" policing by other professions.

STRUCTURE OF FINANCIAL REPORTING

In Ireland, the accounting profession and the country's financial reporting structures (e.g. Stock Exchange, company law, accounting standards etc.) are integrated comprehensively with those of the UK. It is difficult to envisage an independent structure for Ireland alone.

Perhaps for this reason, the Ryan Commission's proposals were somewhat modest. In contrast, the Canadian profession's 1988 Commission (Study of the Public's Expectation of Audits) identified these fundamental potential changes in the structure of financial reporting:

> First ... a change in the method of audit appointment (so that) the power to appoint the auditor and negotiate fees be removed from anyone associated with the enterprise (whether shareholders, directors or officers).
>
> Second ... the auditor be given responsibility for preparing financial statements.
>
> Third ... the auditor's right and obligation to include in the audit report explanations about the content of financial statements, together with inclusion of supplementary information.

Each of these changes is designed to enhance auditors' independence. The Canadian Commission eventually took the view that the above proposals were impractical, perhaps even counterproductive. However, the proposals highlight two key issues, in terms of user expectations. First, reliance on the audit process is founded on the principle that the auditor is seen to be independent. Second, audit failure arises because users perceive that the auditor may not have been independent.

CONCLUSION

Ireland has a well-developed, competitive audit profession. At a practical level, attempts to develop financial reporting and policing structures so as to protect against audit failure can only be developed within the context of our close relationship with the UK (as well as the growing integration with the European Union). For practical reasons, any changes must be incremental, building on existing professional and legal structures, not creating new ones. The objective of improved procedures and structures will be to strengthen auditor independence, which is of paramount importance. Three proposals seem possible (each discussed in the Ryan Commission's Report):

1) Statutory auditors should have fixed-term appointments, not to exceed five years. This is proposed, despite the Ryan Commission's opposition to compulsory rotation of auditors, because of the perceived or actual danger of a too close or cosy relationship developing between auditor and client. It will, quite naturally, be resisted by many in the profession.

2) Statutory auditors should be precluded from providing non-audit services for clients. The perceived or actual risk of a link between the audit practice, and the benefit of fees from other work for the same client, must be addressed. In addition, there must be a fear that consultative advice in matters relating to management, even though given by a separate section of the same firm, may tend to bias audit judgment.

3) Statutory auditors should be required to report to their professional body all litigation, claims and out-of-court settlements with audit clients.

From society's point of view, the great advantage of these proposals is that they are "cost-free". The first two proposals are administered and controlled by clients and their auditors. The third is little more than a filing obligation, which can be supervised within existing disciplinary structures. Whatever effect these changes may have on the incidence of audit failure, certainly auditor independence would be enhanced.

9
The Audit of Small Companies

Cecil W. Donovan
Deloitte & Touche

INTRODUCTION

Few issues have so divided opinion among practising auditors, business people and other interested parties as the statutory audit requirement for the small company in Britain and Ireland. To speak of a statutory audit requirement for the small company is not, strictly speaking, accurate. The requirement in these islands can be traced back to the UK Companies Act, 1900, reinforced in the UK by the 1948 Companies Act and in Ireland by the 1963 Act. These statutes imposed a requirement on all companies to appoint an auditor who would report annually to the shareholders in a prescribed form. The legislation made no distinction between companies on the basis of size. It must be remembered that no other basis was distinguished. Quite simply, an audit was required in the case of all companies.

Until recently, that is how things have remained. At various times over the years, accountants, lawyers and business people have questioned the sense and necessity of the audit requirement for the general class of small companies whose shareholders are few in number. Some have argued for outright abolition of the statutory requirement — leaving it to shareholders to decide whether they wish to have an audit conducted. Others have proposed a range of alternatives to audit, including:

- Limited review
- Modified small-company audit
- Review leading to a compilation report.

Whatever the view that one might have on this matter, there is no doubt but that it represents one of the most important public policy issues facing the auditing profession today, and it is fair to say that there is as little agreement now as there was 20 years ago, before the arguments for and against were crystallised.

In this chapter, we examine the modern form of this debate. The chapter sets out and identifies three important periods during which the debate has taken place; the early period (1979–81), the mid-1980s (1985–88) and the present period of debate (1992–95). Before examining these in greater detail, some preliminary remarks about the small company and its definition are appropriate.

THE SMALL COMPANY

Definitions always cause trouble, particularly where the terms are themselves relative: to be small in the United States is to be large in Ireland. To a number of debaters on the question of the retention or abolition of the audit requirement for the small company, "size" of itself has never been the appropriate issue around which the debate should be conducted. "Control", in particular the number of shareholders and their direct involvement in the business, has been considered more important than size.

The first attempt to distinguish companies on the basis of size was provided by a Green Paper published by the UK Government in 1979 in response to the EEC Fourth Directive produced a year previously.[1] Following the Fourth Directive, the Green Paper classified companies in three tiers:

- A top tier, comprising all companies listed on the Stock Exchange and all other companies which exceed two of the following three criteria:

    ◊ A turnover of £5 million

    ◊ A balance-sheet total of £2.5 million

    ◊ An average number of employees of 250

- A middle tier, comprising all public companies not included in the top tier and all private companies not falling within either the top tier or the bottom tier

- A bottom tier, comprising small private companies which did not exceed two of the following three criteria:

    ◊ A turnover of £1.3 million

    ◊ A balance sheet total of £650,000

    ◊ An average number of employees of 50.

A proposal at that time was that bottom-tier companies might be exempted from the audit requirement — though in the case of Ireland and the UK, this option was not adopted in the national legislation giving effect to the Directive. In fact, when the UK finally legislated to exempt certain companies in 1994, it chose quite a different classification. For companies with annual turnover of less than £90,000, the audit requirement was abolished altogether. For companies with annual turnover between £90,000 and £350,000, the audit requirement was replaced by the less onerous requirement to receive an independent accountant's assurance that the company's accounts correctly reflect its books.

THE EARLY DEBATE, 1979–81

The EEC's Fourth Directive was a landmark document. Published in 1978, that Directive permitted member states to exempt small companies from the audit requirement, an exemption that was already available in a number of European countries. The UK Green Paper on company law, referred to above, expressed the desire to promote a wider debate and presented the following choice for discussion:

- To continue with the statutory audit requirement for all companies, however small; or

- To dispense with the statutory audit requirement for certain small companies, to be defined.

In response to the Green Paper, the Auditing Practices Committee (APC) of the Consultative Committee of Accountancy Bodies (CCAB) issued a discussion paper entitled *Small Companies — The Need for Audit?*[2] The intent of this paper was to stimulate discussion on what was clearly a subject of immediate concern to accountants, to shareholders in small companies and to other users of their financial statements. The paper was circulated widely and the APC received a lot of responses. The APC was eager to ensure that any specific legislative proposals, arising from the EEC Fourth Directive, would be based on properly considered views. It recognised that those who argued for and against relaxing the audit requirement for small companies held strong views as to the merits of their respective cases. In the discussion paper, the APC set out those arguments neutrally and without prejudice. At the time, most of the comment had come from practising auditors and it was important to get a wider airing of views. Comment was therefore particularly invited from directors of small companies, bankers, the Inland Revenue, trade associations and other users of accounts.

From those who favoured abolition, through those who favoured some modification of the scope of the statutory audit and right through to those who preferred the status quo, a whole host of arguments was mounted, claims made and lobbies mobilised. However, although the arguments were often technical in nature, in essence two baseline positions can be discerned — the "abolitionist" and the "retentionist".

Abolitionist

The essence of the argument presented by those who favoured changing the law (whether to abolish the requirement or to modify it in some way) was based on the premise that, if one was starting from a greenfield site, the statutory audit would not be the kind of legislation one would design in the present day. In order to support this contention, they presented a whole host of arguments centring around the increasing cost of the audit, the inherent "unauditability" of small companies and the questionable "usefulness" of the audit to those whom it was supposed to serve. The following are some of the detailed points made:

- The EEC Fourth Directive contained provisions whereby small companies, as defined in the Directive, would be exempted from the audit. Therefore, to abolish the audit requirement for the small company would merely be following the EEC Directive. It would mean that commercial life in the UK and Ireland was keeping in step with the norm established within the EEC.

- The accountancy profession, through the APC, already recognised that a large number of small companies were, and always had been, unauditable. In this regard, to be auditable a transaction must be capable of independent and objective verification. In many small companies the only form of verification frequently available to the auditor was the word of the shareholder/ proprietor, which, although reliable in a great majority of instances, could not be termed independent or objective.

- If one agreed with the "unauditable" argument, then it followed that many audit reports should contain "qualified opinions" — or even disclaimers of opinion. This would dilute the value of the audit and its end product, the audit report.

The Audit of Small Companies

- A number of other countries — France, Germany, The Netherlands, Canada, New Zealand and the United States, for example — did not have an audit requirement for small companies. They either never had a statutory requirement for the audit of small companies or had subsequently exempted them through legislation. This did not mean that small companies in those countries were never audited. What it did mean was that audits were carried out because of the specific requirements of banks, creditors, all or some shareholders, etc. They were conducted for a definite business purpose and not in response to a statutory requirement, as was the case in the UK and Ireland.

- Auditors' independence might be threatened where they acted as accountants, tax and financial advisers, etc. in addition to being auditors. If the small company was exempted from the audit requirement, the directors and shareholders could then use the accountant's talents in a more constructive way and the latter would be freed from the ethical problems of independence.

- A proposed alternative to an audit report was an Accountant's Report, based on a review which would not impose the same exacting requirements on the accountant as an audit does.

- The imposition of the same Auditing Standards on both large and small companies was likely to result in a substantial increase in fees to smaller clients and this would not be acceptable to the public and to the directors and shareholders of small companies.

- It might be impossible to formulate a single set of Auditing Standards which would be appropriate for the audits of both large and small companies. If this proved to be the case, then we would have tiers of classification of companies which might defeat the whole legal concept of company law and limitation of liability.

- It was contended that an audit report was not needed by banks. It was pointed out that, in the typical small company, personal guarantees were demanded from the main shareholders and the directors, and consequently, although there was limited liability in theory, the main shareholder or shareholders had unlimited liability where the bank was concerned.

- Even allowing for the then imminent public filing of accounts at the Companies Office in Ireland (it was an ongoing requirement in the UK), it was argued that suppliers did not place any value on publicly filed financial statements and, therefore, that the value of these accounts being audited was doubtful.

- Conscientious application of the Auditing Standards was likely to produce disclaimers of opinion in instances where clean opinions had previously been given. Companies receiving such disclaimers might find that the credibility of their accounts had diminished with the Revenue Authorities.
- In view of the auditing and reporting requirements incident to the expression of a clean audit opinion, coupled with the Fourth Directive requirements for reporting and disclosure, it was questionable whether corporate status was not now too high a price for such companies to pay for the benefit that it conferred.
- There was no evidence to suggest that the Inland Revenue in the UK or the Revenue Commissioners in Ireland placed greater reliance on audited financial statements of companies than on the unaudited statements received from sole traders and partnerships.

Retentionist

Those who favoured retention of the statutory audit requirement rejected all of the arguments presented by the abolitionists, with varying strength of conviction. In summary, it might be said that the strongest view coming through may have been the impossibility of predicting the unintended consequences of relaxing a regulation that seemed to be working well and had proven itself in the testing world of commercial life right through the twentieth century. Setting out the discussion in the same order as for abolitionists, the following is a summary of the points made:

- The UK Green Paper on company accounts observed that the exemption provision proposed in the Fourth Directive was largely intended to help those member states that had too few qualified accountants to undertake the audits of all small companies. These circumstances were not present in the UK or Ireland; therefore, the "ideal" of audit should remain.
- In relation to the abolitionist claim that small companies are unauditable, the following points were made:
    ◊ Retentionists argued that the absence of internal control did not necessarily make a company unauditable. Rather,

it simply meant that more substantive audit testing needed to be performed.

◊ It was acknowledged that evidence obtained by close questioning of management fell into the less reliable category but it might, nevertheless, be reliable in a great majority of instances. It was the prime task of the auditor to make searching enquiry and to assess the consistency of such evidence, and thus to gain confidence in its reliability. The auditor was forming and expressing an *opinion* on the accounts, not *certifying* their accuracy.

◊ By its very nature, the small company carried less documentary evidence of transactions. But, inspection of documentation is only one of five principal methods of obtaining audit evidence. In auditing small clients, there had to be a greater concentration on the other techniques of observation, enquiry, computation and analysis.

- It was argued that a qualified audit report might not necessarily be a bad thing, particularly if the qualification were constructive and if it set out the true position. Industry would prefer an audit report which told the story as it was, rather than, by comparison, an Accountant's Review Certificate weakly written.

- It was pointed out that in only one major instance, namely, Canada, had the audit requirement for the smaller company been removed in recent years. In other major instances — and in particular the US and various EEC countries — there never had been an audit requirement for the small company.

- The aim of the EEC Directive was to set *minimum* standards. The minimum standard in some EEC countries was that there was no requirement for an audit of a small company. If the UK and Ireland followed this practice, they were doing nothing more or less than reducing their own standards.

- It was acknowledged that the close relationship between auditors and their small-company clients could pose problems of independence, which required careful handling. However, it was pointed out that, in practical terms, the close relationship itself made available to conscientious auditors information that enabled them to formulate a clean audit opinion or, alternatively, a qualified one. Put another way, the close relationship of itself was an aid to conscientious auditors.

- It was further argued by some industrial accountants that they valued the independent view of the good professional auditor. Those who were conscientious and independent in performing their audit inevitably knew more about the company than virtually anyone else. They were in a sound position to cope with potential acquirers or potential investors in the company and could supply them with knowledge and reliable information in connection not alone with the books and records of the company, but with the far wider aspect of the company's business affairs.

- It was pointed out that no satisfactory form of "Accountant's Review" had yet been developed. An alternative to the audit had been discussed in the APC paper but there was no consensus as to the form which the review might take, nor indeed as to the wording or detail of an "Accountant's Report".

- It was claimed that abolitionists were misled if they believed that the abolition of the audit requirement would mean a reduction in accounting/audit overhead costs. It was argued that, in fact, in the absence of systematic audit over an extended time, a costly exercise could ensue if the company concerned was required by its bankers to have an audit conducted in support of a financing application or for some other reason. It was also pointed out that, if there was an erosion in financial record-keeping resulting from the lesser constraint of the Accountant's Review, then there would be an inevitable proliferation of qualifications in audit reports where an audit was subsequently required.

- The claim that lenders did not find the audit useful was rejected. Indeed, at the time, representatives of a major Irish bank had stated quite categorically that it was not in favour of the abolition of audit, bearing in mind its reliance on the report in considering the validity of their clients' financial statements. In general, financial institutions regarded the preparation of audited accounts as a starting point from which they could critically and constructively view budgets, forecasts, cash-flow projections, etc.

- It was argued that the removal of the audit requirement would remove the protection available to the creditors of small limited-liability companies. At the time, legislation was pending in Ireland which would require all private companies to file accounts at the Companies Office. In view of the fact that the authorities recognised the necessity of such a step, it was wrong to dilute this development by removing the audit requirement from small companies.

- Where disclaimers of opinion in audit reports were concerned, it was accepted that these could cause problems with the Revenue. The Revenue Commissioners at the time, however, had advised representatives of the various accountancy institutes that the *qualified* report proposed for small companies, as set out in the Auditing Guidelines, should not cause problems. It was also pointed out that Counsel's opinion, given at the time, had emphasised that a disclaimer of opinion should only be given as a last resort. Thus, it was argued that disclaimers of opinion would not, in fact, be numerous.

- It was difficult, and possibly fallacious, to depart from the position that one of the costs of limited liability must be the audit. It had to be appreciated that to an outside creditor there was a substantial difference between a sole trader trading under the protection of limited liability and the unincorporated sole trader. There was little protection for the creditor of the first-named and, subject to the law of bankruptcy, a far greater degree of protection to the creditor of the individual. In years gone by, our forebears, both legal and accounting, had seen it in their wisdom, in drafting successive Companies Acts, to insert the audit requirement for a limited liability company. Any proposal to remove the audit requirement for small companies should only be done against the much wider canvas of a serious review of company law and, even more particularly, of the entire area of bankruptcy law.

- The need for the audit in a small company was the same as with a large company — primarily for the protection of shareholders and creditors. Removing the audit requirement would remove the protection which should be available to shareholders, and particularly those with minor holdings.

- Proposers of the abolition of the audit requirement had stated that some formula could be reached whereby minority shareholders could require an audit. However, there was a fear that some minority shareholders might not be aware of their rights and indeed might have this right concealed from them by manipulative directors. Shareholders accepted an audit as a matter of course and, if the onus was on the shareholder in the future to require the audit and, therefore, to take a positive step to ensure that the audit was carried out, the danger would be that shareholders might overlook the positive step or, alternatively, might not even be aware of it. There was, therefore, a serious danger that an existing defensive bulwark made available to a minority shareholder might be removed.

The debate continued in the accountancy press and national media during 1980. Opinions were sharply divided on the issues raised. Broadly speaking, no substantial majority position emerged. Quite apart from the responses to the discussion paper issued by APC, the British Government itself received direct submissions on its Green Paper. It must be presumed that the conclusion was reached by Government that no consensus had emerged for change. Thus, when the Companies Act, 1981 was enacted, it did not alter the status quo as regards the statutory audit of the small company.

In the following four years some discussion ensued and public comment was made from time to time by interested parties. It could be said that there was a fairly continuous debate on the subject without it exciting active discussion or argument.

LIFTING BURDENS, 1985–88

In April 1985, The UK Government issued its report, *Burdens on Business*,[3] containing a number of proposals intended to reduce the burden on small businesses. The report suggested, *inter alia*, the abolition of the statutory audit for shareholder-managed small companies. Shortly afterwards, the Department of Trade and Industry (DTI) issued a consultative document, *Accounting and Audit Requirements for Small Firms*.[4]

The thrust of the debate about the audit of small companies seemed now to be inspired from a different direction. In 1979 it was driven as a response to EEC legislation. Now the debate was driven by an apparent concern to help small business to grow and to reduce the regulatory and accounting burdens on small companies. Thus, the audit issue had re-emerged in the context of a Conservative Government's desire to promote economic growth by encouraging entrepreneurship. The audit requirement came to be interpreted as a burden on small business, and the question of its abolition seemed to turn on cost.

The argument suggested that professional accountants might be used in the more constructive role of the providers of useful financial information and advice, rather than as auditors of accounts recording past financial achievement. Owner-managers seemed to be indicating that the production of management accounts and budgets and cash-flow projections for the future might be a more constructive use of accountants' expertise. Such an argument made sense where it was clear that management retained a commitment to maintaining discipline in the keeping of proper financial records and information which might be required by banks, Revenue Authorities, etc. What had to be of concern was the temptation for owner/managers of small companies to reduce essential record-keeping where this omission would have been detected and reported on as a result of the statutory audit required by the Companies Acts.

During this phase of the debate, more consideration and thought were given to alternatives to audit. The options of a statutory "review" with an accountant's report or a compilation report were considered in some detail, although opinion differed on the alternatives.

The most important single factor in favour of retaining the small-company audit was seen to be the integrity and independence that an external accountant brought to the year-end accounting procedures. Therefore, in the event of a review replacing an audit, consideration would have to be given to the form of report on the underlying financial records.

More detailed thought was also given to the question as to whether the abolition of the audit requirement should:

1) Require the actual consent of *all* the shareholders, or

2) Be automatic unless at least one shareholder required an audit to be carried out.

Another matter more deeply considered at this time was whether the abolition should be restricted to shareholder-managed small companies as suggested in the initial Government report or extended to all small companies as defined. The views of the various accounting institutes differed.

The Institute of Chartered Accountants in England and Wales (ICAEW) favoured abolition. While recognising the value of the audit, it could see no justification in imposing an audit upon those small companies whose investors agreed that they would prefer to dispense with it. Therefore, it recommended that small companies, which fulfilled two of the criteria mentioned below, should be allowed to dispense with the requirement provided that the shareholders unanimously agreed every year. The criteria were any two of:

- Under £1.4 million turnover

- Under 50 employees
- Under £700,000 gross assets.

Where the shareholders consented, the directors should instead prepare and sign a public statement affirming that they had fulfilled their statutory duties in relation to the accounts.

The ICAEW also recommended that small companies should only be required to prepare one set of statements for the members and for Companies Office filing and, furthermore, that the amount of disclosure required by law should be reduced. This was a sensible suggestion.

The Institute of Chartered Accountants of Scotland (ICAS) recommended that small owner-managed companies should be released from the audit requirement if the shareholders, who attended the general meeting or who voted by proxy, agreed unanimously, As an alternative, it favoured the company appointing a reporting accountant who would be involved in the preparation of accounts and would append a "preparation report". The ICAS went on to recommend that these financial statements should be prepared in a format which was useful and comprehensible to the owner/manager. Under its recommendations, the accountant would not be expressing an opinion on the "truth and fairness" of the accounts — that is, in accordance with Section 228 of the Companies Act, 1985 — and, therefore, they would be taken out of the scope of the various Statements of Standard Accounting Practice (SSAPs).

The Institute of Chartered Accountants in Ireland (ICAI) voted to support retention of the audit requirement for the small company. It did, however, support a single set of modified accounts for both Companies Office filing and shareholders' use, provided that such dual purpose accounts satisfied the needs of users and that there was a worthwhile saving in the cost of preparation. In this latter respect, the ICAI was in agreement with the ICAEW.

The Chartered Association of Certified Accountants (ACCA) also favoured the retention of the requirement of the audit for the small company — for reasons similar to those advanced by ICAI.

In early 1986, the UK Government issued a second White Paper on reducing the administrative and regulatory requirements for small businesses. Two further years of debate then ensued.

At the beginning of March 1988, in a letter sent to interested parties, presumably in an effort to draw the debate to a conclusion, the DTI set out proposals for possible alternatives to small-company audits. The alternatives included:

- A statement from the directors or an assurance by a competent person that the accounts met the Companies Act requirements
- A statement by a competent person that the accounts had been properly prepared from information supplied by management and that their form and content complied with Companies Act specifications
- A similar statement to the preceding one but with an additional assurance that the company had kept proper accounting records
- A statement giving limited assurance on the validity of the accounts.

At this stage it was clear that the Chartered Institutes in England and Scotland differed on one particular fundamental matter. Both agreed with the abolition of the small-company audit requirement but not on what should replace it. The ICAEW continued to opt for a Directors' Declaration. The ICAS wanted to see the appointment of an independent reporting accountant to confirm that the company's accounts complied with the legal requirements and that accounting records had been maintained. After two years of debate, opinion was still firmly divided within the accountancy profession, and also within the business community, as to whether the small-company audit should be abolished.

Eventually, in November 1988, the UK Government announced its intention to retain the statutory audit for small companies. Apparently, Government had rejected the idea of abolishing the requirement because of strong representations made by the Inland Revenue. Pressure was also exerted by the Treasury, and it appeared that both wished that the audit be retained as an additional protection against malpractice.

In Ireland, there was little, if any, serious public debate about the status of the small-company audit. Neither the Irish Government nor the Civil Service issued any statement indicating a wish for the profession and business in Ireland to become involved in the matters being discussed in the UK. As no statement was issued by any relevant Government Department, it is difficult to know whether there was any discussion within Government to establish a position on one side or the other. It is likely that, if such a debate did take place, the Irish Revenue Authorities would have encouraged the retention of the audit requirement so as to ensure that financial discipline was maintained and that fiscal rectitude was exercised.

Again, the debate subsided. There were occasional references to the subject in the columns of professional journals and in some pronouncements, but the UK Government's decision to retain the audit effectively closed the discussion. It was known that during that period the ICAEW in particular continued to press the case for abolition to the DTI, but to no avail.

1992–95

Early in 1992, the DTI in the UK commenced a further review of the accounting and auditing requirements for small companies.[5] In response to this review, the ICAEW set up a working party to reconsider the question of the abolition of the small-company audit. The working group was to examine:

- The benefits of the small-company audit
- The alternatives to audit
- The costs of the audit, and
- The criteria for relaxation or exemption.

In August 1992, it issued its report and, once again, recommended abolition.[6] It recommended that the statutory requirement should no longer apply to a company of a size below the VAT turnover registration threshold of £36,600 and, additionally, those companies that met the VAT cash accounting limit requirements of £300,000 should be allowed to opt out of the audit, provided that there was unanimous agreement among the shareholders. The Working Party added that the abolition should not apply to public-interest companies such as those registered under the Financial Services Act.

As an alternative to the audit, the Working Party recommended that the financial statements should contain a "compilation report" on their preparation. Such a report would be signed off by an accountant suitably qualified but not necessarily independent of the company. It further recommended that the directors should be required to make a statement about their responsibilities in relation to the financial statements.

At this time within the profession a new and more forceful argument for abolition emerged. For a number of years, a form of audit report qualification had been available permitting auditors to draw attention to uncertainty arising from the necessary acceptance of management assurances in small businesses. Auditors were permitted to emphasise the dependence of the company's system of control upon the close involvement of the directors/managing director and to acknowledge their acceptance of assurances from the directors that all of the company's transactions had been reflected in the records.

The availability of this form of qualification was withdrawn in the late 1980s, leading some commentators to promote abolition of the small audit on the basis that the non-availability of the qualification made it impossible for auditors to report adequately and correctly on the financial statements of owner-managed small companies.

Between 1990 and 1994, substantial additional accounting and audit regulation came into force. The regulatory pressures on auditors were expanding all the time and practitioners were worried about the Joint Monitoring Unit (JMU). The paperwork required by the regulatory régime was becoming an unwarranted burden, and many practitioners formed the view that the burden of regulation might be reduced, or even avoided, if they could be relieved of the requirement to express a true and fair opinion on the accounts of small companies. In addition, it must be emphasised that a number of practitioners had always viewed the small-company audit as an expense for clients which outweighed the benefits. These sentiments gained support despite the issue of excellent guidance on the audit of small businesses from the APC in 1991.

Among those who continued to oppose abolition, a view was emerging that the burden on small business might best be relieved by a form of simplified financial reporting, involving reduced compliance with detailed accounting standards. In tandem with this, proposals were advanced to devise a fuller and more explanatory audit report.

Nevertheless, early in 1993, ICAS reiterated its view that it favoured abolition of the statutory audit in order to reduce the legislative burdens on small businesses. In addition, ICAS favoured legislation which would make it easier for small companies to disincorporate. It emphasised that it wanted to see the audit report replaced by an accountant's report.

In April 1993, a further consultative document was issued by the DTI on the options for relaxing the audit for very small companies. It emphasised that the options were being explored because of what it felt was a disproportionate cost of the statutory audit. The DTI stated that the alternative would only be permissible if all shareholders agreed. It suggested that the right of abolition would be available to small companies with a turnover threshold under £36,000 and a balance-sheet total not exceeding £100,000. It was suggested that a possible alternative was a compilation report produced by an accountant, confirming that the accounts had been prepared from the company's records in accordance with the Companies Act, 1985. This would differ from the statutory audit in that the accountant would not have to investigate the accounts and, therefore, the costs would be reduced.

The trend over the years is interesting. In the first phase, 1979–81, the debate was driven by Euro-legislation. At that time there was a genuine concern to discuss fundamental questions about the role and purpose of the audit. The discussion of the second period focused almost exclusively on the untested assertion that the audit was a significant burden on small business. In the final period, other factors gained momentum, such as the form of audit report and the deemed burden of regulation on the practising side of the profession. To a convinced retentionist, there seemed to be a determination to find any reason to abolish the audit requirement for the small company as fitted the circumstances of the particular time.

The debate terminated suddenly with the surprising announcement in the Budget Speech of the Chancellor of the Exchequer given in the House of Commons on 30 November 1993 that it was the intention of Government to introduce regulations which would have the effect of abolishing the audit requirement for small companies under a certain size.

Companies with a turnover between £90,000 and £350,000 a year in future would only require an independent Accountant's Report on whether the company's accounts correctly reflected its books. Companies with a turnover of less than £90,000 would have the audit requirement abolished altogether. In both cases, it would be a requirement that the balance-sheet total for the particular year was not more than £1.4 million. (The precise details were not announced in the Chancellor's speech but were subsequently framed in the regulations.)

Further debate, discussions and action took place over the following eight months. The detailed package of measures and the draft regulations were issued for public comment by the DTI in April and May 1994. The Auditing Practices Board (APB) was asked to prepare a "Standard" for reporting accountants on the subject of Compilation Reports, and this was produced in a timely fashion in June 1994. It was realised by the accounting institutes, the accountancy profession and business people generally that a major step was taking place which could have far-reaching effects on financial discipline, on the future work of practising accountants — particularly smaller firms — and on the rights of shareholders. In July 1994, the DTI laid before Parliament the required Regulations, which became The Companies Act, 1985 (Audit Exemption) Regulations, 1994. The Act came into force on 11 August 1994 and the new regulations were presented as a major step in the Government's drive to free business from regulatory burdens.

The audit exemption is not available to a company where any member or members holding not less in the aggregate than 10 per cent in nominal value of the company's issued share capital or any class of it advise by notice in writing that they require the company to obtain an audit of its accounts for a particular year. Such notice in writing must be deposited at the registered office of the company during a financial year, but not later than one month before the end of the particular financial year.

Companies with annual turnover between £90,000 and £350,000, which qualify for a Compilation Report, must have such report prepared by a reporting accountant confirming that the annual accounts have been prepared from the company's accounting records in accordance with the relevant format and disclosure requirements of the Companies Act, 1985. The reporting accountant must be a member of one of the bodies listed below, and eligible for appointment as a company auditor under the rules of the body. The bodies are:

- The Institute of Chartered Accountants in England and Wales
- The Institute of Chartered Accountants of Scotland
- The Institute of Chartered Accountants in Ireland
- The Chartered Association of Certified Accountants
- The Association of Authorised Public Accountants.

What of the Republic of Ireland? The country remained silent on the debate until early 1994 when the Task Force on Small Business produced a report which, amongst many other recommendations, suggested that the Government should remove the audit requirement for limited companies with turnover of less than £100,000 per annum.[7] Around that time, the Government established a Company Law Review Group to examine many aspects of company law, including the Task Forces' recommendation concerning the audit requirement for small companies. That Group reported in December

1994 and has recommended that the statutory audit requirement be removed for companies with turnover under £100,000.[8] The Review Group's recommendation is simple and unambiguous: only one exemption is proposed. If enacted, it means that Irish company law will not have that second category of company that in the UK may present an accountant's compilation report in place of an audit report.

At the time of writing, the proposals are with the Government and in the public domain. It remains to be seen whether the Revenue Authorities in Ireland, through the Department of Finance, will record reservations on the grounds of the necessity for financial accounting discipline as imposed by the statutory audit. If the annual audit requirement for small companies is abolished, the Revenue may create an alternative which could be Revenue-driven or, at least, Revenue-influenced — a sobering thought!

One hopes that Ireland will learn from the results of the introduction of the legislation in the UK. The following are some of the issues that will need to be considered by the legislative draftsmen in this country:

- Will shareholders be fully aware of their rights to require an audit? Who will be responsible for advising them of this right?
- What will be the attitude of banks and financial institutions, tax authorities and creditors? Will some or all of these institutions continue to require audited accounts?
- What provisions will be made to permit revision of thresholds over time? If a substantial number of companies opt for total exemption (under turnover £100,000), will there be significant lobbies in the future to remove further numbers of companies from the audit requirement?

Before concluding, it is timely to consider the effect on the practising accountancy profession in Ireland, and particularly on firms whose clients in the main fall into the small-company categories which might be exempted from audit. Opinion has been divided on this matter for years. Some firms believe that the availability of abolition will enable them to deregister for the purposes of audit regulation. This is debatable, particularly if, as one might expect, a substantial number of small companies will opt for an audit or, alternatively, if 10 per cent of their shareholders will require it. Some practising firms that specialise in auditing small companies believe that their services in future will be required for the more practical work of preparing management accounts, budgets and cash-flow projections where their small-company client is released from the cost of the statutory audit. This writer is inclined to doubt this, fearing that a release from the audit requirement might encourage small companies to dispense with accounting advice altogether or, alternatively, reduce this to an absolute minimum.

It is worthy of note that the most basic and commercial effects on practices did not become a major issue for debate on the occasions when the whole question of the audit of small companies was being considered and discussed, particularly over the past 15 years. It would have been a matter of regret if the subject had been reduced to the merits or demerits of the move from the aspect of commercial advantage or disadvantage to practising firms. Only time will tell whether the abolition of the audit requirement will cause a downturn in professional work for practising firms. On balance, one is inclined to believe that the effect will not be that serious.

CONCLUSION

In a debate of this nature, one inevitably takes a view on one side or the other. This writer must confess to serious disappointment at the UK legislation and the recommendations of the Company Law Review Group in Ireland.

Over the past 15 years, from 1979 onwards, the accountancy profession prepared excellent advice for practitioners, in particular in regard to matters relating to audit. The Auditing Standards and Guidelines produced 15 years ago and modified as necessary over the years have provided much needed advice and counsel to firms engaged in professional auditing work. The APC built on the platform of the Standards and Guidelines by adding excellent documentation on subjects of direct interest, such as the form and content of the audit report, going-concern concepts, the auditor's responsibility in relation to illegal acts and fraud, guidance on audits of small companies, etc. In addition, regulation for auditors was introduced, and this has been implemented through the recognition of the major professional institutes as supervisory bodies backed up by the operations of the JMU. The profession was conducting its own research on standards of auditing and the maintaining of financial discipline and it is ill-timed that such efforts should be offset by proposing the abolition of the audit requirement for small companies.

What should have been encouraged over the long period of debate was the undertaking of a substantial and comprehensive review of the present absurd amount of disclosure required in small companies. Such a review would enable a satisfactory restructuring of the annual accounts of such companies, so as to reduce greatly the volume of detailed information sought under the Companies Acts. This would be the best service to business and would enable the cost of the annual audit and preparation of accounts to be reduced. The cost of compiling, checking and auditing of the present volume of detail in annual accounts of small companies would have declined substantially. Such a step would have reduced the perceived burden on business and would have met the UK and Irish Governments' main aspiration.

At the time of writing, the accounting profession in the UK and Ireland is debating the proposals of the Wild Report.[9] This consultative document, entitled *Exemptions from Standards on Grounds of Size or Public Interest,* examines on a standard-by-standard basis, whether exemption from all or part of a standard should be provided for certain types of enterprise on the grounds of size or public interest, and recommends appropriate criteria for making such exemptions.

Finally, if the intention was to relieve business of the burden of audit, would it not have been more logical to assist in preventing the need to incorporate in the first instance? Government should have taken steps to remove the need for business to seek incorporated status. Thought could have been given to making the unlimited form of incorporation more attractive and removing the existing taxation disadvantages on the deregistration of small limited companies. At the time of writing, some of these steps are being researched.

In the UK, it seems that the opportunity has been lost. What has been produced by way of audit-abolition legislation satisfies very few people. Many questions remain unanswered and many doubts remain. It is not too late in Ireland to step back from the brink!

10

Substance over Form

Robert Kirk
University of Ulster

INTRODUCTION AND HISTORY

This chapter is concerned with the conflict that has emerged in recent years between the concept of "economic substance" — that is, reflecting the commercial reality of a transaction in financial statements — and the concept "legal form" — that is, reflecting the strict legal form of a transaction in financial statements.

Substance is defined in the *Oxford English Dictionary* as: "the essence or most important part of anything; the real meaning". The development of the idea that substance should prevail over legal form has not always met with universal approval. In financial reporting in these islands, the concept was first broached in the Corporate Report (1975) which was quite explicit on the point: (para. 3.14) "corporate reports ... should give recognition to economic substance in preference to legal and technical form".[1]

The 1970s and 1980s saw a period in which the financial directors of many public limited companies first came under severe scrutiny from investment analysts. This was primarily caused by the growth in the percentage of equity that was controlled by institutional shareholders, namely, the pension funds and insurance companies.

These institutions, because of pressure on themselves to show good performance, were primarily interested only in investing in those companies which could guarantee consistently rising levels of earnings per share and, preferably, also low gearing. Competition amongst providers of financial and banking services led to many of the so-called "off-balance-sheet schemes" emerging from this sector at that time. The main purpose of many of the schemes was to increase earnings by minimising costs in the profit and loss account whilst at the same time avoiding high gearing by ensuring that any related finance was not included on the balance sheet.

Various schemes were devised by the lawyers in the financial services sector, with the express intention of remaining within the "rule of the law", but at the same time providing the "best" economic effect in the financial statements. As a result, financial statements were being prepared which bore little resemblance to the underlying commercial reality.

In Ireland and the UK, this came to a head with the huge growth in leasing. Between 1980 and 1985 there was a 640 per cent increase in the adoption of leasing as a form of corporate finance. In August 1984, in *Statement of Standard Accounting Practice 21* (SSAP 21),[2] the accounting profession in these islands took what was regarded as a revolutionary step, by introducing the concept that economic substance should take precedence over legal form in the financial reporting of finance leases. The basis of this concept is best explained by the SSAP itself in paragraph 12:

> Conceptually, what is capitalised in the lessee's accounts is not the asset itself but his rights in the asset (together with his obligation to pay rentals). However, the definition of a finance lease is such that a lessee's rights are for practical purposes little different from those of an outright purchaser. Hence, it is appropriate that lessees should include these assets in their balance sheets.

Following the Argyll Foods case in 1981, however, it appeared that accounting for the substance of a transaction could lead to a conflict with company law. In that particular case, Argyll Foods had consolidated a retail grocery company, Morgan Edwards, in its audited group balance sheet for the year ended 31 December 1979, even though its offer to purchase the company did not become unconditional until 25 March 1980. It was held that this presentation in the group balance sheet did not give a true and fair view under the Companies Act. It therefore appeared that consolidating an entity which the directors considered to be *in substance* a subsidiary was contrary to law.

This view was endorsed by the Department of Trade at the time in its statement, *The True and Fair View and Group Accounts,* issued in 1982 after the Argyll case. There it stated that "only when [the provision of additional information] is impossible is departure from other requirements permitted, and required, to the extent necessary to provide a true and fair view".

The seriousness of this legal decision was not fully realised until Ian Brindle carried out an investigation into the extent to which off-balance-sheet finance schemes were being used in practice.[3] He concluded his study by commenting that:

> ... this dearth of information is deliberate; to borrow a response from the Australian secrets trial — the financial statements do not lie, they are just economical with the truth.

In an attempt to initiate the debate on how best to account for off-balance-sheet financing, in December 1985, the Technical Committee of the Institute of Chartered Accountants in England and Wales (ICAEW) issued a technical release, entitled TR 603 *Off Balance Sheet Finance and Window Dressing*,[4] which attempted to clarify some of the issues emerging from recent developments and from points arising out of the Argyll Foods case.

TR 603 recommended that in order to give a true and fair view of an enterprise's performance and financial position, the economic substance of transactions should be considered, rather than merely their legal form, when determining accounting treatment. The balance sheet should, therefore, be adjusted to reflect that substance. This was, however, issued as a discussion document, and it was not intended to give mandatory guidance. The ICAEW intended that it should be regarded as being persuasive in considering whether or not a company's financial statements were in fact giving a true and fair view. However, in order to appreciate fully the impact of recording substance over form, it is essential to understand what actually constitutes a true and fair view, and this is examined in the next section.

THE TRUE AND FAIR VIEW

Both the Companies (Northern Ireland) Order, 1986, and the Companies Act, 1963, require that a company's financial statements give a true and fair view, and this overrides the detailed rules on the legal form and content required by the Acts. However, where the "true and fair override" is used to depart from the provisions of the Acts, the financial statements must disclose particulars of that departure, the reasons for it, and its effect (Urgent Issues Task Force, Abstract 7).

The accounting profession has always felt uncomfortable with the term "true and fair view" and on two occasions it has tried to clarify in legal terms what is actually understood by it. Hoffman and Arden, in a legal opinion delivered in 1983,[5] expressed their belief that what would constitute a true and fair view would have to be determined by a judge, but that the courts would look for guidance on this question from the ordinary customs of professional accountants. The financial statements must be sufficient in both quantity and quality to satisfy the reasonable expectations of the readers to whom they were addressed. However, they argued that the expectations of readers would be moulded by the practices of accountants, because by and large they would expect to get what they ordinarily got and that in turn would depend upon the normal conventions of accountants. In other words, the true and fair view is what the profession says it is.

Under this interpretation, Parliament merely lays down broad guidelines and leaves the fine-tuning to the accountancy profession — the experts in the subject. The true and fair view may vary at different times, is subjective and avoids being caught in a possible straitjacket which might prohibit exceptions to the general rule.

Since the advent of the Accounting Standards Board (ASB) in 1990, the standard-setting operation has become more rigorous. That, together with the creation of an Urgent Issues Task Force to provide a temporary consensus on emerging accounting issues, and the new investigative powers awarded under statute to the Financial Reporting Review Panel, has dramatically improved the regulatory framework around which the accounting profession works.

In an opinion in April 1993,[6] Miss Arden QC (now Justice Arden) formed a view that the courts are now more likely than ever to rule that compliance with accounting standards is necessary to meet the true and fair requirement. The recent changes in the UK Companies Act have strengthened the status of accounting standards, and — together with the existence of a review procedure and the fact that due consultation and discussion must have taken place before the implementation of a standard — will, in her view, almost inevitably lead a court to conclude that compliance with it is essential to give a true and fair view. As Miss Arden's opinion concludes:

> Just as a custom which is upheld by the courts may properly be regarded as a source of law, so too, in my view, does an accounting standard which the court holds must be complied with to meet the true and fair requirement become, in cases where it is applicable, a source of law in itself in the widest sense of that term.

Thus, if the accounting profession wishes to produce an accounting standard based on the concept of economic substance taking precedence over legal form, and this finds broad acceptability within the profession, then it will become an essential part of the decision as to whether or not a company's financial statements show a true and fair view. This, of course, could change as the economic environment changes. Accounting standards represent best practice at a particular point in time and are not written in stone for all time. They are flexible and will be adaptable as times change.

THE DEVELOPMENT OF A STANDARD ON SUBSTANCE

Returning now to the substance over form debate, the International Accounting Standards Committee (IASC) recognised the problem as early as 1975 in *International Accounting Standard 1* (IAS 1)[7] and later in the section on the qualitative characteristics of financial statements of its *Framework for the Preparation and Presentation of Financial Statements*.[8]

Paragraph 35 of that framework states that:

> If information is to represent faithfully the transactions and other events that it purports to represent, it is necessary that they are accounted for and presented in accordance with their substance and economic reality and not merely their legal form. The substance of transactions or other events is not always consistent with that which is apparent from their legal or contrived form. For example, an enterprise may dispose of an asset to another party in such a way that the documentation purports to pass legal ownership to that party; nevertheless, agreements may exist that ensure that the enterprise continues to enjoy the future economic benefits embodied in the asset. In such circumstances, the reporting of a sale would not represent faithfully the transaction entered into (if indeed there was a transaction).

Unlike SSAP 2, this concept has been enshrined in the international accounting standards as one of three considerations that should govern the selection and application by management of the appropriate accounting policies and the preparation of financial statements (para. 17, IAS 1 *Disclosure of Accounting Policies*).

The development of a standard on substance in these islands has been a long and tedious operation. It has emerged in a somewhat piecemeal fashion, partly as a result of the negative reaction to the whole concept from within the legal profession.

The Law Society, in particular, was concerned about the possibility that the accounting profession was trying to replace objective legal criteria with its own subjective ideas on what might be construed as showing a true and fair view.[9] As a result, the accounting profession initially trod very carefully with the development of an accounting standard based on the concept of substance. The first attempt to initiate debate on the subject occurred in March 1988 with the release of ED 42, *Accounting for Special Purpose Transactions.*[10]

The notion behind the use of the term "special purpose" was to ameliorate the concerns of the Law Society, by emphasising that the proposals were only designed to deal with those unusual transactions in which their substance had deviated from their strict legal form. It would not be applicable to the vast majority of transactions in practice. A special-purpose transaction was therefore defined as:

> ... one which combines or divides up the benefits and obligations flowing from it in such a way that they fall to be accounted for differently or in different periods depending on whether the elements are taken step by step or whether the transaction is viewed as a whole.

The Exposure Draft attempted to adopt wide descriptions of assets and liabilities and to set out broad general concepts, instead of trying to identify and prescribe detailed accounting regulations for the vast array of schemes on the market. It was felt that, by adopting the tax analogy of *Furniss* v. *Dawson*, it was better to tackle the schemes globally as opposed to on an individual basis. Any other approach, it was felt, might have led to the creation of a new industry of professional advisors whose only function would be to search for loopholes in each scheme, in the manner in which tax-avoidance schemes emerged in the 1970s and 1980s. Thus, for the first time, assets were no longer defined as items that were owned by an entity, but rather as items that were controlled by it. Similarly, liabilities were now described in terms of present obligations entailing a possible sacrifice of benefits involving a transfer of assets or the provision of services to another party.

ED 42 was the most conceptually-based project undertaken by the Accounting Standards Committee (ASC) since the issue of SSAP 2 *Disclosure of Accounting Policies* in 1971. The exposure draft was intended to be part of the development of an overall conceptual framework for financial reporting.

Developments accelerated quickly after the publication of the Seventh European Directive on Group Accounts. In that document, the concept of substance was clearly enshrined in the extended definition given to a subsidiary undertaking. Subsequently, in paragraph 62 of FRS 2, *Accounting for Subsidiary Undertakings*, the ASB explained that the accounting concept that underlies the presentation of consolidated financial statements for a group as a single economic entity is summarised in the definition of control. Control is defined as:

> ... the ability of an undertaking to direct the financial and operating policies of another undertaking with a view to gaining economic benefits from its activities (paragraph 6, FRS 2).

The effect of FRS 2 and its related legislation, the Companies (NI) Orders 1990 and the European Communities (Companies: Group Accounts) Regulations 1992, was to widen the definition of a subsidiary undertaking by emphasising the control that a parent has over another entity. This ensured that many of the vehicles set up in the 1970s to avoid consolidation, were, in fact, captured in the net.

As a result of both the European legislative changes and the FRS, there was a clear signal to the profession that they had legislative clearance to tackle other off-balance-sheet transactions. The ASC quickly brought out ED 49 as a successor to ED 42 and was able to drop the word "special" from the title. ED 49 was now titled *Reflecting the Substance of Transactions in Assets and Liabilities*,[11] and this sent out a clear message that the recording of substance is vital to a clear understanding of the underlying financial statements.

Paragraph 1 of ED 49 required that the financial statements be presented in a condensed form so as to reveal the strength of the resources, the obligations and the performance of the reporting enterprise. In order to present the information in a useful manner, it was stated that it was essential that the "underlying classification and analysis are based on the substance of transactions and arrangements." Paragraph 3 states that what is meant by substance is that its accounting treatment should fairly reflect its commercial effect.

Both EDs 42 and 49 emphasised the fact that most transactions are fairly straightforward and embody several standard rights and obligations whose commercial effect is the same as their legal description. However there are a number of transactions that combine or divide up rights and obligations in such a way that the reporting of their strict legal effect could not give a true and fair view of the enterprise.

Some of the common features of these transactions are listed in both ED 49 and its successors, Financial Reporting Exposure Draft 4 (FRED 4) and Financial Reporting Standard 5 (FRS 5), both entitled *Reporting the Substance of Transactions:*[12&13]

- The severance of legal title from the ability to enjoy the principal benefits and exposure to the principal risks associated therewith.

Two examples are cited of this form of off-balance-sheet financing — finance leases and goods sold under reservation of title clauses. In both situations the legal title remains with the lessor/seller respectively but the established accounting practice has been to record where the commercial control of the asset lies. As a result, the asset has been recorded in the books of the lessee/buyer respectively under SSAP 21 and under a Consultative Committee of Accounting Bodies (CCAB) Technical Guidance Note.[14]

- The linkage of a transaction with one or more others in such a way that the commercial effect cannot be understood without reference to the series as a whole. Two examples of this type of arrangement are commonly cited — the sale and repurchase of stock (e.g. maturing whiskey stocks) and consignment stock (e.g. the sale of motor vehicles).

One of the major problems that emerges from the discussion about how to record the economic substance of a transaction is identifying where the control lies. This has been clarified in FRS 5 where control in the context of an asset is defined as:

> ... the ability to obtain the future economic benefits related to an asset and to restrict the access of others to those benefits.

Both FRED 4 and FRS 5 emphasise the importance of risk in determining which party to a transaction has, in substance, control over an asset. The allocation of risks amongst the parties to a transaction is regarded as a significant indicator as to which party controls that asset and therefore should record that asset on its balance sheet. The FRS only applies to those transactions which fall directly outside the scope of an existing accounting standard or statutory requirement. In those other specific situations, the standard/statute takes precedence over the general recognition rules of FRS 5.

FRS 5 requires an asset to be derecognised when there are no significant rights or access to material economic benefits retained in that asset and any risk retained is also immaterial. There are provisions, however, in special cases to ensure that a "partial" transfer of risks/benefits is recognised by being included in the form of a linked presentation of the balance sheet.

These issues have been recognised elsewhere and in Ireland: the Ryan Commission,[15] which reported in January 1992, recognised the importance of substance:

In some cases, the emphasis is placed on legal form rather than economic substance, as with guarantees for borrowings by non-group companies or other off balance sheet items. This can be misleading — for example, by giving too favourable a view of the company's gearing in the published balance sheet.

The standard developed in FRS 5 is therefore likely to obtain wide support from accountants and users throughout these islands.

THE APPLICATION OF THE CONCEPT OF SUBSTANCE OVER FORM IN PRACTICE

The application of the concept of substance has emerged in practice in recent years and a number of examples of its adoption are now investigated.

Accounting for Leases and Hire Purchase Contracts (SSAP 21)

During the 1970s, leasing developed as a popular alternative means of financing plant and machinery to outright purchase. Suddenly, assets which would normally have been capitalised in the books of the lessee company were being written off through the profit and loss account by way of rental charges.

The switch from outright purchase to leasing resulted in an understatement of the assets employed in those businesses, and also an overstatement of the return on capital employed. It was argued by the ASC that this resulted in a loss of comparability between those companies which were asset-acquiring and those which were leasing, and that the true gearing effects were distorted, as substantial liabilities were now hidden off balance sheet.

SSAP 21 was therefore the first accounting standard that expressly applied the notion that the economic substance of a transaction be recorded in preference to its legal form. As a result, those leases which are termed finance must be capitalised in the books of the lessee company in situations where the lease "... transfers substantially all the risks and rewards of ownership of an asset to the lessee".

It should be presumed that such a transfer of risks and rewards occurs if at the inception of the lease the present value of the minimum lease payments, including any initial payment, amounts to substantially all (90 per cent) of the fair value of the leased asset. In effect, this means that there would normally be a non-cancellable contract between the parties over the life of the asset with a secondary period (at a peppercorn rent) to cover that life.

Thus, SSAP 21 ensures that the substance of the transaction is recorded as the economic reality in that the lessee has the full use of the asset over its useful life and has the responsibility of maintaining it, thus making it similar to an outright purchase using a long-term loan from a bank. The future economic benefits deriving from the use of that asset belong to the lessee and the risks attached to the asset are also clearly with the lessee.

Accounting for Goods Subject to Reservation of Title Clauses

The Romalpa case in 1976 focused attention on certain terms of sale whereby sellers could retain title to the goods sold until such time as they were paid for those goods.

In drafting the accounts of undertakings trading on such terms, it is necessary to decide at what stage they should be treated as sold by the supplier and purchased by the party to whom they are supplied (the customer). CCAB released a Technical Guidance Statement in 1976 and it considered that in reaching a decision on this point:

> ... the commercial substance of the transaction should take precedence over its legal form where they conflict. The substance of transactions of this nature has to be decided from consideration of all the surrounding circumstances.

It was provided in that Statement that where the customer was a going concern, and therefore likely to pay for the goods, the omission of the stock and of its corresponding liabilities from the balance sheet of the customer would prevent it from showing a true and fair view of its state of affairs. Similarly, the accounts of the supplier would also be distorted by the omission of such goods from sales and debtors. The recommendation is, therefore, that the goods be treated as purchases in the accounts of the customer and as sales in the accounts of the supplier.

Complex Financial Instruments

One of the most highly controversial issues of the 1990s has been the topic of complex capital instruments. The ASB decided to tackle this issue in 1993 because of the increasing number and variety of these instruments which became available on the market in recent years.

Accounting for these new financing instruments has developed on an ad-hoc basis and has not always been consistent across enterprises. FRS 4, *Capital Instruments*,[16] adopts the same definition for a liability from the *Statement of Principles* as does FRS 5.

FRS 4 therefore requires that a capital bond, issued at a substantial discount from face value, should be recorded as a liability initially at the value of the net cash proceeds received (say £60). (Subsequently, the bond will be redeemed at its face value (say £100) and bears a low rate of interest (say 2–3 per cent per annum). The legal form of the transaction would suggest recording the liability at £60 and charging interest payable to the profit and loss account when paid. However, this would ignore the economic substance of the transaction, in that the £40 of discount really represents a form of rolled-up interest charge which becomes payable on redemption of the bonds.

The economic substance should clearly reveal this fact, and to reflect that situation it is necessary to accrete the £40 gradually to the value of the liability each year so as to charge a fair expense against profits for the period and to record the liability at its fair value. For example, if the bond happened to have a 10-year life, the £40 could be spread over that 10-year period, and this would result in an additional notional interest charge of £4 per annum through the profit and loss account.

Because of the legal position enshrined in the Companies Acts, FRS 4 also requires shares to be accounted for in the balance sheet according to their legal status only. Convertible loan stock, for example, must be accounted for as debt until such time as the debt is converted into shares. It is argued that the balance sheet shows the resources of the business at a particular point in time and the conversion process should not be predicted. Also, preference share capital, which is in effect similar to debt, is legally classified as capital and should be recorded as such. FRS 4 does, however, attempt to present it separately by identifying it as non-equity interests and requiring separate disclosure from any equity interests in the balance sheet. This is one of the few examples where the strict legal form is being adhered to, but really only because preference shares usually have restricted rights to receive dividends and to recoup capital in a winding-up situation.

Related Party Transactions

In exposure draft ED 46,[17] the ASC was concerned that any abnormal transactions between the reporting entity and its related parties be disclosed so as not to mislead the readers of those accounts. In deciding on who should be considered to be related parties, paragraph 22 explained that this emerges where one party is able to exercise either direct or indirect control or influence over the other party, and, in making this decision, it is essential to consider the substance of the relationship between the parties. All the aspects and implications of the relationship should be investigated and the ED required that greater weight be placed on those factors likely to have a commercial effect in practice.

In practice, this control aspect could have had significant repercussions for some reporting entities. It was originally proposed in ED 46, for example, that, where a management contract existed and the reporting entity was either the managing or the managed partner, any abnormal transaction between the two parties should be disclosed. Examples 10 and 11 at the end of the Exposure Draft revealed two incidences where it was essential to report the fact of economic dependence of one party on another, particularly if a major proportion of sales is made to a single customer. In effect, that customer economically has considerable control over the affairs of the supplying company and has the ability often to dictate its own terms of trade. However, this was subsequently dropped from the definition of a related party in the standard FRS 8, *Related Party Disclosures*.[18] FRS 8 also requires all material transactions to be disclosed between related parties, whether abnormal or not.

Brand Accounting

The issue of brand accounting has become one of the "hottest potatoes" on the agenda of the ASB. It initially developed as an exercise in bolstering up the net assets in the balance sheet to discourage unwanted takeover bids. Including brands on the balance sheet was said to provide the existing shareholders with a better idea of the true value of the assets in the company in which they had invested, and thereby make them less willing to sell their shares.

It later developed as an attempt to get around the problem of accounting for goodwill under SSAP 22. By renaming "goodwill" as "brands" and by refusing to depreciate brands on the grounds that sufficient resources were being invested to maintain their value, companies could "protect" earnings.

A third reason for the growth in interest in brand accounting was the improvement it could bring about in the gearing ratios of companies. By including on their balance sheet home-grown brand names at a value of £678 million in 1988, RHM plc was able to increase its asset base by 68 per cent and to reduce its gearing considerably.

In terms of the concept of ensuring that financial statements record the economic substance of transactions, it is clear that if substantial brand names are acquired from other companies, these should be recorded in the balance sheet of the acquirer company. However, ED 52, *Accounting for Intangible Fixed Assets,*[19] and the Discussion Paper, *Goodwill and Intangible Assets,*[20] have taken the view that brand names are really synonymous with goodwill, and therefore their accounting treatment should be the same. As such, the rules of SSAP 22, *Accounting for Goodwill,* should apply and brands should either be written off directly to reserves or capitalised and subsequently amortised to the profit and loss account over the assets' economic useful life.

The position as regards home-grown brands is still unclear but the ASB has published a discussion paper on *The Role of Valuation in Financial Reporting,*[21] and as a result it is likely that the profession will eventually move away from strict historical cost accounting to a value-based approach with the "deprival value" concept forming the nucleus of the concept of capital maintenance. This will take place in the long term, but in the immediate future the proposal is that a number of valuable assets, whose market values are required for disclosure for balance-sheet purposes, should be compulsorily revalued on the face of the balance sheet, i.e. properties not specific to the reporting entity, commodities and investments with a ready market.

The move towards current-value reporting will undoubtedly provide more relevant information to the readers of financial statements, and this should also accord with the commercial reality of recording the net assets of the business at their true worth to the business and not at out-of-date historic costs.

Accounting for Subsidiary Undertakings

Prior to the recent Companies Acts implementing the Seventh European Directive, the definition of a subsidiary undertaking was one in which the parent effectively either owned more than 50 per cent of the shares in another entity or appointed a majority of the directors to the board. In the 1980s, a number of "special-purpose vehicles" were set up deliberately to get around this definition, and thus avoid the process of consolidation.

This could be achieved by assigning disproportionate voting rights either to the shares controlled by the "parent undertaking" or to the directors which it appointed, giving the parent effective control. The advent of these dependent controlled non-subsidiaries had led to a situation whereby consolidation had become optional in many instances.

The Seventh European Directive tried to solve this problem by extending the "net" of the definition of a subsidiary. This was expressed largely on the basis of the control that a parent might exercise over another entity. Emphasis was on ensuring that the commercial reality be recorded by requiring that any "vehicle" under the control of a parent undertaking be capitalised. There are now five legs to the definition of a parent/subsidiary relationship. Three of these emphasise voting rights as opposed to the percentages of shares or numbers of directors appointed as the key to establishing control over another entity. In addition, if a parent can exercise a dominant influence over another entity (that is, if it can control the operating and financial policies of that other entity), despite the fact that it may not at present own any shares in that company, then it should be consolidated.

Similarly, if a parent, holding at least 20 per cent of the shares, can exercise a dominant influence over another or is able to manage both companies effectively on a unified basis, a subsidiary relationship is assumed to exist.

It is often quite difficult in practice to identify these relationships, but it is important to discern that the parent actually exercises its influence over the other entity. This usually requires a written control contract to be drawn up between the two parties by which the "parent" effectively controls the operations of the other entity. It could in some instances also be covered by altering the articles or memorandum of association.

An example of this type of relationship should help to clarify the issue. In the US, a few years ago, a computer software company, Digilog Inc., set up a "subsidiary" in a new field of software development in which it owned none of the shares and ensured that the shares in that entity were held by trustee shareholders. In order to retain control over that entity, the "parent" provided 90 per cent of the working capital in return for convertible loan stock which could be converted at any time, at the option of the "parent", into ordinary stock. If the "subsidiary" turned out to be a loss maker, the loan stock would not be converted and the losses would be sheltered from the consolidated accounts. On the other hand, if the "subsidiary" were to report profits, then the loan stock could be immediately converted into stock and the profits brought into the consolidated profit and loss account as from that date. Clearly, consolidation had become optional in this situation and it is doubtful if a true and fair view could be expressed about the group's affairs.

The new legislation and FRS 2, *Accounting for Subsidiary Undertakings*,[22] would insist that, in Ireland and the UK, this would now constitute a subsidiary relationship and the special-purpose vehicle would need to be consolidated. This, of course, reflects the economic reality of the relationship between the two companies.

Securitisations

In some situations, an entity finances an item on terms that the provider of the finance has a limited recourse to the item it has financed and not to the other assets in the entity's balance sheet. It could be argued that the item is no longer an asset of the entity since it does not have access to all the future benefits generated by it, nor does it have a liability for the full amount of the finance. However, it still retains significant benefits and risks relating to that item.

An example of this is the securitisation of mortgages, but it applies equally well to a whole series of financing arrangements. For example, an entity might transfer title to a block of mortgage loans of £100 in exchange for non-returnable proceeds of £90, plus the rights to a further sum depending on when and whether the loans are repaid. Assuming that the entity does not have to repay the £90 in any circumstance, it does not have a liability of £90 nor an asset of £100 (as the first £90 must be passed on to the transferee). However, the entity's asset of £10 (rights to future benefits) depends principally on the performance of the whole portfolio of £100.

In order to reflect the economic substance and to show a true and fair view of the arrangement, the ASB in FRS 5 has come up with a unique solution called a "linked presentation".

In the above example this would be presented as follows:

Debts subject to financing arrangements:	
Debts (after bad debts provision £2)	£98
Less: non returnable amounts received	(£90)
	£8

This linked presentation shows both that the entity retains significant benefits and risks relating to those debts, and that the claim of the provider of the finance is limited solely to the funds generated by it.

CONCLUSION

When the accounting profession first attempted to identify some of the fundamental accounting concepts now inherent within financial accounting, the idea that economic substance should take precedence over legal title was not an issue. Most transactions up until the 1970s tended to incorporate both. It was really the advent of off-balance-sheet finance that saw the beginning of a divergence between the two.

The concept of substance was recognised fairly early in the life of the IASC, and in 1984 it became enshrined in IAS 1. In the US, as long ago as 1970, the concept was acknowledged in Accounting Principles Board Statement 4, where it was recognised that, in some instances, "accountants emphasise the substance of events rather than their form so that the information provided better reflects the economic activities represented".

In the UK and Ireland, the implementation of the concept in practice has emerged on a piecemeal basis, largely because of the negative reaction from the legal profession and an attempt by accountants to avoid a direct conflict with the Law Society. It is only since the advent of the European Seventh Directive on group accounts that the profession has been able to develop the concept fully.

The recent legal opinion of Justice Arden, expressed in an appendix to the *Foreword to Accounting Standards* (June 1993), suggests that with the strengthening of the standard-setting operation and the implementation of several of the main recommendations of the Dearing Report into company law, there is a clear road down which the profession can travel to implement this concept fully into practice. The release of FRS 5 is an important step in this direction and it appears that from the advent of these proposals into practice (September 1994), economic substance will play a full part in the recording of financial transactions.

The requirement for a set of financial statements to disclose a true and fair view and the fact that substance will be enshrined as an accounting standard means that the profession now must regard that concept as underlying the whole notion of giving a true and fair view.

The practical implications of embodying economic substance as a fundamental accounting concept are bound to result in varying interpretations between the auditor and the client. This will be in relation not only to the control or non-control that an entity has over an asset or another undertaking, but also in determining the expenses/income reported annually in the statements of financial performance. Financial reporting can only become more subjective as a result, but as long as the end product (that is, the financial report) is more relevant to the user, the loss in objectivity will be more than compensated for by the increase in its usefulness.

11
A Critical Afterword

Justice Ronan Keane

PMPA, Icarom, BCCI, the Maxwells, Barings — the litany of catastrophes seems never-ending and, every time, the ordinary newspaper readers brace themselves for even more superlatives. Will this be the disaster to end all disasters, the fraud which for villainy and effrontery is unrivalled, the ultimate in financial incompetence? At times, it is hard to remember that the fourth estate is famously uninterested in good news and that the energy, intelligence, creativity and old-fashioned hard work which are present in abundance in the commercial world in Ireland as elsewhere go largely unrecorded. Yet I am sure that the many distinguished accountants who have contributed to the discussion in the preceding pages would confirm that the spectacular disasters which occurred with such depressing regularity through the 1980s and into the 1990s are not a reason for pessimism and resignation. Rather, they have provided urgent warnings to those in a position to act of the need to ensure that our law and practice in the area of auditing are relevant to the economic and social realities of Ireland today.

Lawyers in general, and judges in particular, might be forgiven for taking a bleak view of the conduct of Irish business. The healthy firm does not want to spend a day, let alone several weeks, in the Four Courts. Least of all does it want to be a part of the funeral rites of the liquidations which absorb so much of the time of the commercial side of the High Court. Even more than the average newspaper reader, we have to remind ourselves that in the world beyond Courts 5 and 6 on Monday morning people are getting on with the work on which the future of our whole economy, and our children's prospects of employment and happiness, ultimately depend.

The lessons to be derived from those dramatic collapses are many and diverse, as this excellent collection of essays demonstrates. Does the function of auditing adequately meet the expectations reposed in it by the public today? Specifically, are the appropriate standards of the accountancy profession sufficiently reflected in the regulatory framework governing Irish companies? And does that regulatory framework take sufficient account of some important features of the Irish scene? Has our tendency to model our legislation on that of the UK and the close relationship between the accountancy professions and the financial markets in the two countries resulted in too little attention being paid to those features of our economy which are noticeably different?

As to the suggested lack of confidence of the public in the auditing process — to which the Minister for Finance's recent "whistle-blowing" legislation[1] was a reaction — Gerard McHugh's essay (Chapter 1) demonstrates that there are a number of factors at work here. Not least is the increase in the actions taken against accountants as a result of what are alleged to have been negligently conducted audits. He properly sounds a warning note as to whether the amount of such claims — as distinct from those arising from other accountancy functions — may not be exaggerated. But, undoubtedly, the huge scale of some of the claims made and the possible exposure of accountancy firms have led to significantly increased insurance premiums, a cost which presumably must ultimately be borne by the clients in the form of increased fees.

That development has led to a debate, reflected in the essays by Arthur Moran and Laurence Shields (Chapter 5) and Michael Forde (Chapter 6), as to whether the existing law achieves a satisfactory balance in this area. Should it depart from the famous aphorism of Lopes L.J., that auditors are watchdogs, not bloodhounds? More broadly, should it not recognise the reality of today's commercial world, in which fraud, particularly in its computerised form, is so widespread and can bring in its wake such tragic consequences for innocent people, be they creditors, pensioners, depositors or employees?

The extent of the problem is also highlighted in the contribution by Gerard McHugh and Eugene McMahon on "Fraud and the Auditor" (Chapter 4). At the time of writing, the government, in the light of the recommendations of the Law Reform Commission, is preparing new fraud legislation which will consolidate offences of dishonesty into one Act. Experience counsels against undue optimism, but it would be refreshing to find politicians reacting in a measured and balanced manner to this sort of problem by providing a carefully thought-out legislative scheme and not the excitable, media-driven response that we have become sadly familiar with, in, for

A Critical Afterword

example, the area of sexual crime.

As to the difficult topic of the liability of auditors, some of the contributors have rightly stressed the dangers of the "deep-pocket" approach. Not merely is that legally and morally dubious — its social implications are also disquieting, since it tends to exonerate the directors who should bear the primary responsibility for bad business decisions. Similarly, it relieves investors of the consequences of an imprudent reliance on an audit of accounts which has been carried out for defined statutory reasons, and not by way of giving a warranty of good health to the world at large.

Here I suppose I should proceed with caution: Irish law has yet to come to definitive conclusions on the extent of the auditors' liability in this area. But, while reserving the right to take an entirely different view in another context, I am inclined to think that the "duty of care" doctrine as defined by Irish courts in a number of recent decisions, should result not merely in the confining of the auditors' liability to those whom they might reasonably have foreseen would rely on their reports (the present position), but also in restricting the category of persons embraced in that formula on public-policy grounds. We are, I would hope, some way from realising the nightmare of Cardozo J: liability in an indeterminate amount for an indeterminate time to an indeterminate class.

That view is, of course, entirely consistent with the provision in Irish law of a statutory framework for accounting standards as recommended by the Ryan Commission and the Company Law Review Group. I would share Paul O'Connor's gloomy reaction to the suggestion emerging in some quarters that yet another commission should be established before ministers take the plunge (Chapter 3). Of the establishment of committees, commissions and task forces, there is, in Ireland, no end — what we significantly lack is decisive executive and legislative implementation of their recommendations.

That brings me finally to Cecil Donovan's thought-provoking discussion of the auditing of small companies (Chapter 9). There is clearly a fundamental disagreement to be resolved between "abolitionists" favouring the removal of all auditing requirements on business below a certain size, and "retentionists" who fear the consequences of such a drastic change and who significantly appear to have the support of the Revenue. But whatever the ultimate decision may be, the controversy is clearly useful in focusing attention on one of the crucial features of our economy distinguishing us from the UK with which we are naturally so closely linked in this whole area.

Our law has for too long been set in the aspic of Victorian and Edwardian legislation framed for a different business environment. The relatively small number of public companies in this jurisdiction renders singularly unsuitable a legislative framework which takes as its first axiom that the public company is the rule and the private company the exception. I would echo Michael Forde's call for a codification of our company law and would merely add the proviso that it should be a codification and not simply a consolidation — it should, in other words, recognise the reality of Irish commercial life.

That need not inhibit progress on the more immediate and pressing problems identified in this collection. But it would, in the medium term, be an immensely significant reform in our commercial law, and one that would surely have appealed to that fine and thoughtful man, Eddie Grace, to whom this collection is so impressive a tribute.

References

1: THE AUDIT ENVIRONMENT

[1] In interview with Gene Barrett reported in the *Journal of Accountancy*, 174 (6), December 1992, pp. 86–9.

[2] Ward, Graham (1994), "Towards a Fairer System for Auditors' Liability", *Accountancy*, April 1994, p. 80–81. A slight exaggeration. His precise words were:

> ... the knock-on effects of huge liability claims are already with us. For example, there are now many instances where the widows and orphans of deceased partners and former partners cannot get access to the estate because of the spectre of outstanding claims.

[3] Editorial comment, *Accountancy Ireland*, 25(6), December 1993, p. 4.

[4] The term was first used by Liggio in a 1974 article titled "The Expectations Gap: The Accountant's Waterloo", *Journal of Contemporary Business*, 3 (3) pp. 27–44. However, it received "institutional" approval from the AICPA in its terms of reference to the Commission on Auditors' Responsibilities (the Cohen Commission), which reported in 1978. In its terms of reference the Commission was charged *inter alia* "to consider whether a gap may exist between what the public expects or needs and what auditors can and should reasonably expect to accomplish".

[5] Gower, L.C.B. et al. (1979), *Principles of Modern Company Law*, 4th edition, Stevens, London.

[6] The Joint Stock Companies Act, 1844 was the first enactment to require all incorporated companies to have their annual financial statements audited. The Act did not require the auditor to be independent of management or to have any special qualification. The Joint Stock Companies Act, 1856 (which followed the Limited Liability Act, 1855, providing a form of general limited liability to shareholders) abandoned the audit provisions of the 1844 Act, effectively making it voluntary. The 1856 Act also gave companies *an option* about whether or not to present accounts to shareholders. Interestingly, this option was not given to the regulated companies such as railways, banks and gas companies. These companies were required to produce audited accounts and it is accepted that the rationale for this was essentially the protection of the public against monopoly pricing and inadequate safety measures. The belief in laissez faire meant that it was

assumed that shareholders could look after themselves. Sir George Jessel (later Lord Jessel, Master of the Rolls), in his evidence to the 1877 Company Law Amendment Committee, stated that there was no reason to compel directors to issue accounts to shareholders, since shareholders could call for them themselves if they wished.

For an excellent summary of this period in financial reporting history see: Parker, R.H. (1990), "Regulating British Corporate Financial Reporting in the Late Nineteenth Century", *Accounting, Business & Financial History*, 1(1), pp. 51–71.

[7] Cooper, V.R.V. (1971), *Student's Manual of Auditing*, Gee & Co., London.

[8] The strict legal position is that the auditor is appointed by the shareholders at the annual general meeting and can only be removed in the same way. In practice, it is the senior management who make the recommendation for shareholders to approve.

[9] The Institute of Chartered Accountants in Ireland was granted a Royal Charter upon its foundation in 1888, and retains this today. The Chartered Association of Certified Accountants is a UK-incorporated body and was granted a Royal Charter in 1974.

[10] There have been instances where audit firms have let go excess staff, but they are the exception rather than the rule.

[11] A survey by Stella Fearnley and Vivian Beattie of the University of Southampton, reported in *Accountancy*, August 1993, p. 12

[12] CIFAR (1991), Information Service, Princeton, NJ: Centre for International Financial Analysis and Research.

[13] Under partnership law, there is no requirement to file any financial information publicly and, as one might expect, little if any is made available. A recent survey conducted by *The Accountant* found that Irish accounting firms are more secretive than their European counterparts. Interestingly, this level of secrecy was rivalled only by those accounting firms in underdeveloped countries (reported in *Sunday Business Post*, 3 October 1993).

[14] Simon, D.T. and Francis, J.R. (1988), "The Effects of Auditor Change on Audit Fees: Tests of Price Cutting and Price Recovery", *The Accounting Review*, April, pp. 255–69.

[15] However, a British survey, conducted in 1993 by JHD Consultants, found that the top audit firms were charging their smaller clients more, to compensate for the downward pressure on fees from the larger clients.

[16] This was seriously proposed by one ICAI member in an article published in *Accountancy Ireland*. See: Lynch, Peter (1993), "Shall We Tell the President?", *Accountancy Ireland*, 25 (2), April 1993, pp. 14–15.

[17] Alderman, C.W. and Dietrick, J.W. (1982), "Auditors' Perceptions of Time Budget Pressures and Premature Sign-offs: A Replication and Extension", *Auditing: A Journal of Practice and Theory*, 1 (2), pp. 54–68.

Lightner, S.M. (1981), "An Examination of Underreporting of Hours by Auditors in Public Accounting Firms", *The Ohio CPA Journal*, Summer, pp. 97–100.

For an excellent Irish study of the extent of time-underreporting, see the study by Pierce B.J. and Otley, D.T. (1994), "The Operation of Control Systems in Large Audit Firms: An Empirical Investigation", presented to the Irish Accounting and Finance Association Annual Conference at

Queen's University Belfast, 28–29 March 1994.
18. There is, of course, an alternative interpretation, i.e., that partnership profits are reduced. However, the identity of the ultimate beneficiaries of staff accountants' uncharged hours is of little relevance — provided that we recognise that they themselves are not.
19. Report in *Accountancy*: "PW Defended", *Accountancy*, June 1991, p. 10.
20. See Briloff, A. (1990), "Accountancy and Society: A Covenant Desecrated", *Critical Perspectives on Accounting*, 1(1) 5–30.
21. Traynor, D., Chairman's statement to Shareholders, CRH plc, Annual Report 1992, p. 7.
22. The president's page, *Accountancy Ireland*, April 1991, William. H. deF. Smyth.
23. See *The Irish Times* Business Page, 25 November 1992.
24. At the time of writing, the US legislature was about to introduce legislation which would permit courts to apportion liability in proportion to responsibility.

2: FINANCIAL REPORTING REFORMS — RECENT DEVELOPMENTS IN THE UK

1. See, for example, Humphrey, C., Moizer, P. and Turley, S. (1992), *The Audit Expectations Gap in the United Kingdom*, Research Board of the Institute of Chartered Accountants in England and Wales, London.
2. For further details, see Nobes, C. and Parker, R. (1995), *Comparative International Accounting*, 4th edition, Prentice Hall, London.
3. The members of the CCAB are the Institute of Chartered Accountants in England and Wales, the Institute of Chartered Accountants of Scotland, the Institute of Chartered Accountants in Ireland, the Chartered Association of Certified Accountants and the Chartered Institute of Management Accountants.
4. See, for example, Davies, M., Paterson, R. and Wilson, A. (1994), *UK GAAP*, 4th edition, Ernst and Young/Macmillan, London, Chapter 1.
5. FRC (1991), *The State of Financial Reporting: A Review*, FRC, London, p.5.
6. Report of the Review Committee under the Chairmanship of Sir Ronald Dearing, *The Making of Accounting Standards*, ICAEW, London, September 1988.
7. FRC (1991), *op. cit.*, p.45.
8. FRC (1991), *op. cit.*, p.15.
9. FRC (1992), *The State of Financial Reporting: Second Annual Review*, London, p.24.
10. FRC (1991) *op. cit.*, p. 47.
11. Comprehensive coverage of accounting standards, together with comments on their application, can be found in, for example, Blake, J. (1995), *Accounting Standards*, 5th edition, Pitman, London; Sangster, A. (1995), *Workbook of Accounting Standards*, 3rd edition, Pitman, London. More detailed analysis and discussion of problem areas can be found in Davies, M., Paterson, R. and Wilson, A. (1994), *UK GAAP*, 4th edition, Ernst and Young/Macmillan, London.
12. ASSC (1975), *The Corporate Report* (discussion paper), ASSC, London.

[13] *Report of the Inflation Accounting Committee, Inflation Accounting* (1975), Cmnd. 6225, HMSO, London (The Sandilands Report).
[14] ASC (1978), *Setting Accounting Standards: A Consultative Document*, London, ASC (The Watts Report).
[15] Macve, R. (1981), *A Conceptual Framework for Financial Accounting and Reporting: The Possibilities for an Agreed Structure*, ICAEW, London.
[16] ICAS (1988), *Making Corporate Reports Valuable*, Kogan Page, London.
[17] Solomons, D. (1989), *Guidelines for Financial Reporting Standards*, ICAEW, London.
[18] Arnold, J. (1991), *The Future Shape of Financial Reports*, ICAEW/ICAS, London.
[19] For a more detailed exploration of conceptual framework projects, see Davies et al., *op. cit.*, Chapter 2; for a brief introduction to accounting theory and reporting standards, see Lewis, R. and Pendrill, D. (1994), *Advanced Financial Accounting*, Pitman, London, Chapter 1.
[20] ASC (1995), *Statement of Principles*, ASC, London.
[21] The Federal Accounting Standards Board (FASB) began consideration of a conceptual framework virtually from its outset, taking over the work begun by the American Institute of Certified Public Accountants (AICPA) in 1971 with the Wheat Committee (which resulted in the establishment of the FASB) and the Trueblood Committee. For further details, see Davies et al., *op. cit.*, Chapter 2.
[22] See for example Page, M. (1992), "Marching in Step Backwards", *British Accounting Review*, 24, pp. 77–85.
[23] ASB (1995), *Accounting for Tax*, ASB Discussion Paper.
[24] For a more detailed explanation of these inconsistencies, see, for example, Davies et al., *op. cit.*
[25] Davies et al., *op. cit.*, p. 32, note 55, lists five such studies.
[26] The Foreword to the ASB's draft *Statement of Principles* (June 1993) includes a legal opinion from Mary Arden QC which confirms this view, first given in the joint opinion expressed by Arden with Leonard Hoffman QC in 1983/4.
[27] Davies et al., *op. cit.*
[28] CCAB Consultative Document (1994), *Exemptions from standards on the grounds of size or public interest*, CCAB, November. (Note that since this chapter was written, the Working Party has published a further report in the light of responses received to their initial proposals. This now proposes that small companies should be exempt from all but five of the existing standards and that a special standard for small companies (Financial Reporting Standard for Smaller Enterprises) should be devised to cover all other reporting requirements.)
[29] Davies et al., *op cit.*, p. 23–4.
[30] ASB, Foreword to the draft *Statement of Principles*, *op.cit.*
[31] TR 690: *Statement by the Accounting Standards Committee on the Application of Accounting Standards to Small Companies*, February 1988.
[32] CCAB, *op. cit.*, p. 12.
[33] CCAB, *op. cit.*, p. 13.
[34] ASC, *Operating and Financial Review*, July 1993.
[35] FRC (1992), *op. cit.*, p. 34.

3: FINANCIAL REPORTING REFORMS — AN IRISH PERSPECTIVE

1. While many acquisitive Irish companies have had transactions such as these and in many instances might even justify such an accounting treatment, the problem for the user is that profits or losses arising on disposal of previously acquired assets were usually impossible to disentangle from underlying operating profit. See, for example, note 18: Acquisitions and Disposals in the 1993 Annual Report of the Jones Group plc.
2. Smith T. (1992), *Accounting for Growth: Stripping the Camouflage from Company Accounts*, Century, London.
3. The Institute of Chartered Accountants in England and Wales (1988), *The Making of Accounting Standards: The Report of the Review Committee (The Dearing Committee)*, ICAEW, London.
4. The Institute of Chartered Accountants in Ireland (1992), *The Report of the Commission of Enquiry into the Expectations of Users of Published Financial Statements*, ICAI, Dublin.
5. Accounting Standards Board (1993), *Operating and Financial Review*.
6. *The Report of the Committee on the Financial Aspects of Corporate Governance*, Gee & Co., London, 1991.
7. The Institute of Chartered Accountants in Ireland (1992), *Companies Reporting in the Republic of Ireland*, ICAI, Dublin.
8. The Institute of Chartered Accountants in Ireland (1992), *The Audit of Companies Reporting in the Republic of Ireland*, ICAI, Dublin.
9. The Institute of Chartered Accountants in Ireland (1992), *The Response of the Institute of Chartered Accountants in Ireland to the Recommendations of the Commission of Enquiry into the Expectations of Users of Published Financial Statements*, ICAI, Dublin.
10. Chartered Association of Certified Accountants (1993), *The Ryan Report: Proposals of Working Party Established by The Chartered Association of Certified Accountants to Supplement and Progress the Financial Reporting Commission's Report into the Expectations of Users of Published Financial Statements*, ACCA, Dublin.
11. Dublin Stationery Office (1994), *First Report of the Company Law Review Group* (December 1994).

4: FRAUD AND THE AUDITOR

1. Petersen, J.C. and Farrell, D. (1986), "Whistleblowing: Ethical and Legal Issues in Expressing Dissent", *Module Series in Applied Ethics,* Dubuque, IA: Kendall/Hunt.
2. Wells, J.T. (1990), "Six Common Myths about Fraud", *Journal of Accountancy*, 169(2), pp. 82–8.
3. Underwood, L. (1988), "The Discreet Harm of Bourgeois Crime", *Director*, 42(4), pp. 92–6.
4. KPMG Stokes Kennedy Crowley (1993), *Fraud Awareness Survey,* SKC Publications, Dublin. The Irish survey was conducted among Ireland's top 500 companies — there were 301 respondents.

[5] Robb, G. (1992), *White-Collar Crime in Modern England: Financial Fraud and Business Morality, 1845–1929*, Cambridge University Press, Cambridge.
[6] In this context it is worth noting that the EU intends to propose new legislation to tackle fraud, following the publication of official figures showing that detected fraud against the EU budget amounted to Ecu 1 billion in 1994. Reported in *The Financial Times*, 30 March 1995.
[7] Reported in the *Sunday Business Post*, 12 March 1995.
[8] Dublin Stationery Office (1993), *Report of the Government Advisory Committee on Fraud*.
[9] Collins, J.M. and Schmidt, F.L. (1993), "Personality, Integrity and White Collar Crime: A Construct Validity Study", *Personnel Psychology*, 46, pp. 295–311.
[10] Albrecht, S.W. and Williams, T. (1990), "Understanding Reactions to Fraud", *Internal Auditor*, August, pp. 45–51.
[11] Albrecht, W.S., McDermott E.A., and Williams, T. (1994), "Reducing the Cost of Fraud", *Internal Auditor*, February, pp. 29–34.
[12] *The Economist* (1994), "Savings and Loan Scandals: The Texas Tally", *The Economist*, 330 (7849), pp. 60–61.
[13] Staple, G. (1992), "Serious and Complex Fraud: A New Perspective", The Shimizu Lecture delivered at the London School of Economics and Political Science, 10 November 1992.
[14] Davies, J. and Warman, A. (1992), "Computer-aided Fraud: The Role of the Accountant", *Management Accounting*, London, September, pp. 26–30.
[15] National Commission on Fraudulent Financial Reporting (1987), *Report of the National Commission on Fraudulent Financial Reporting* (The Treadway Commission Report), Washington.
[16] Reported in *The Financial Times*, 6 March 1995.
[17] Badaracco, J.L. and Webb, A.P. (1995), "Business Ethics: A View from the Trenches", *California Management Review*, 37(2), pp. 8–28.
[18] Levi, M. (1987), *Regulating Fraud: White Collar Crime and the Criminal Process*, Tavistock, London.

5: AUDITORS AND THE LAW

[1] Auditing Practices Board (1995), *Statement of Auditing Standards 110: Fraud and Error*.

6: DIRECTORS AND THE LAW

[1] Companies Act, 1990, Section 27(1).
[2] Id. Part III.
[3] *Coubrough v. James Ponton & Co.* [1965] I.R. 272.
[4] *Healy v. Healy Homes Ltd.* [1973] I.R. 309.
[5] *Bishopsgate Investment Management Ltd (in liquidation) v. Maxwell* (1993) BCLC 814 at p. 832.
[6] *E.G. Regal (Hastings) Ltd. v. Sullivan* (1967) 2 AC 134 n.
[7] *Re Claridge's Patent Asphalt Co.* [1921] 1 Ch. 543.

[8] *Re Duomatic Ltd.* (1969) 2 Ch. 365.
[9] [1991] 1 A.C. 187, at p. 217.
[10] *Al Saudi Banque* v. *Clarke Pixley* [1990] Ch. 313.
[11] *Banque Financière/Kayser Ullman Case* [1989] 2 All E.R. 952 at p. 991.
[12] *West Mercia Safetywear Limited* v. *Dodd* [1988] B CLC 250.
[13] [1994] ICRM 387.
[14] [1993] 3 IR 191.

8: AUDIT FAILURE

[1] Woolf, E. (1990), *Auditing Today*, Prentice Hall, Hemel Hempstead, 4th Edition, p. 1.
[2] Lee, T.A. (1979), "A Brief History of Company Audits: 1840–1940", in Lee, T.A. and Parker, R.H. (Eds.), *The Evolution of Corporate Financial Reporting*, Nelson, London, 1979.
[3] *The Companies Act, 1990,* Section 193, requires an audit. The Minister "recognises" certain designated accountancy bodies, which have to satisfy the Minister regarding standards of training, qualification, ethics, independence, codes of conduct, disciplinary procedures, etc. (Section 191).
[4] Hopkins, L. (1984), *The Audit Report,* Butterworths, London.
[5] Part One, *Auditing and Reporting, 1993/94,* Accountancy Books, London.
[6] Brennan, N., O'Brien, F.J. and Pierce, A. (1992), *European Financial Reporting — Ireland,* Routledge, London, pp. 68–9.
[7] Definition taken from the "Explanatory Foreword" to *Auditing Standards and Guidelines* issued by the Auditing Practices Committee in 1980 (revised 1990), which has, since April 1991, been replaced by the Auditing Practices Board, whose objective is to develop auditing standards and guidelines for the United Kingdom and Ireland.
[8] Argenti, J. (1976), *Corporate Collapse,* McGraw Hill, London, p. 140.
[9] Merino, B.D. and Kenny, S.Y. (1994), "Auditor Liability and Culpability in the Savings and Loan Industry", *Critical Perspectives in Accounting,* 5(2), June 1994, pp. 179–94.
[10] Dunne, J. (1993), "Courts to Re-examine Insurance Debacle", *The Irish Times,* 2 October 1993, p. 5.
[11] "SKC asks Court to Dismiss Primor Claim for £175m Damages", *The Irish Times,* 30 October 1993, p. 2.
[12] Palmrose, Z.V. (1987), "Litigation and Independent Auditors: The Role of Business Failures and Management Fraud", *Auditing: A Journal of Practice and Theory,* 6(2), Spring 1987, pp. 90–103.
[13] Skousen, K.F. (1991), *An Introduction to the SEC,* South Western Publishing, Ohio, 5th Edition.
[14] Palmrose, *op. cit.*
[15] *Ibid.*
[16] Skousen, *op. cit.*
[17] Burton, J.C. (1975), "SEC Enforcement and Professional Accountants: Philosophy, Objectives and Approach" in Previts, G.D. (Ed.) (1981), *The Development of SEC Accounting,* Addison-Wesley, Reading, MA.
[18] United States Securities and Exchange Commission: *1990 Annual Report,* Washington, DC.

[19] Hopkins, op. cit.
[20] Cahill, E. (1991): *Professional Accountancy Regulation in the United Kingdom and the Public Interest — The Joint Disciplinary Scheme*, paper given at the first EIASM Auditing Research Workshop, Copenhagen Business School, 1991.
[21] Almost 2,000 DTI investigations undertaken between 1971 and 1987/88, with an average of 116 per year. Of these, 61 DTI inspectors' reports (generally external inspectors, a QC and a chartered accountant) were published — mainly in respect of publicly quoted companies with a public interest dimension. See: Russell, P. (1991), "Department of Trade and Industry Investigations" in Scherer, M. and Turley, S., *Current Issues in Auditing*, 2nd Edition, Paul Chapman Publishing, London.
[22] The Joint Disciplinary Scheme, *Annual Report, 1991*, Milton Keynes, p. 12.
[23] Rotaprint plc investigation under Section 432(2) and Section 442 of the Companies Act, 1985, HMSO, London, 1991.
[24] Atlantic Computers plc, and Atlantic Computer Systems plc, Investigation under Section 432(2) of the Companies Act, 1985, HMSO, London, 1994.
[25] O'Leary, C. (1994), "Audit Failure", *Accountancy Ireland*, October 1994.
[26] Gwilliam, D.R. (1987), "The Auditor, Third Parties and Contributory Negligence", *Accounting and Business Research*, 18(69).
[27] Cahill, op. cit.
[28] *The Sunday Tribune*.
[29] *Greencore plc. Report of Inspectors of Investigation under the Companies Act*, The Stationery Office, Dublin, 1992.
[30] *Finance*, March 1994.

9: THE AUDIT OF SMALL COMPANIES

[1] Department of Trade (1979), *Company Accounting and Disclosure*, A Consultative Document, London, HMS0 Cmnd. 7654.
[2] APC (1979), *Small Companies: The Need for Audit*.
[3] DTI (1985), *Burdens on Business*, London, HMSO, March.
[4] DTI, (1985), *Accounting and Audit Requirements for Small Firms*, A Consultative Document, London, HMS0.
[5] DTI, (1992), Consultative Document on amending the Fourth Company Law Directive on annual accounts, London: DTI, January 1992.
[6] ICAEW (1992) *The Statutory Audit of Small Companies: The Case for Reform*, FRAG 21/92, London ICAEW, 1992.
[7] Dublin Stationery Office (1994), *Report of the Task Force on Small Business*.
[8] Dublin Stationery Office (1994), *First Report of the Company Law Review Group*, December 1994.
[9] CCAB (1994), Draft Consultative Document: *Exemptions from Standards on Grounds of Size or Public Interest*.

10: SUBSTANCE OVER FORM

[1] ASC (1975), *The Corporate Report*, The Accounting Standards Committee.

² ASC (1984), SSAP 21 *Accounting for Leases and Hire Purchase Contracts*, The Accounting Standards Committee.
³ Brindle, I. (1987), "Off Balance Sheet Financing", Chapter 14, *ICAEW Financial Reporting 1986/87*, pp. 49–62. The Institute of Chartered Accountants in England and Wales.
⁴ ICAEW (1986), TR 603 *Off Balance Sheet Finance and Window Dressing*, The Institute of Chartered Accountants in England and Wales.
⁵ ASC (1983), *Foreword to Accounting Standards*, The Accounting Standards Committee.
⁶ ASB (1993), *Foreword to Accounting Standards*, The Accounting Standards Board.
⁷ IASC (1984), IAS 1 *Disclosure of Accounting Policies*, The International Accounting Standards Committee.
⁸ IASC (1989), *Framework for the Preparation and Presentation of Financial Statements*, The International Accounting Standards Committee.
⁹ The Law Society (1986), *Off Balance Sheet Finance and Window Dressing*, The Law Society.
¹⁰ ASC (1988), ED 42 *Accounting for Special Purpose Transactions*, The Accounting Standards Committee.
¹¹ ASC (1990), ED *49 Accounting for the Substance of Transactions in Assets and Liabilities*, The Accounting Standards Committee.
¹² ASB (1993), FRED 4 *Reporting the Substance of Transactions*, The Accounting Standards Board.
¹³ ASB (1994), FRS 5 *Reporting the Substance of Transactions*, The Accounting Standards Board.
¹⁴ CCAB (1976), "Accounting for Goods Subject to Reservation of Title".
¹⁵ The Financial Reporting Commission (1992), The Institute of Chartered Accountants in Ireland.
¹⁶ ASB (1993), FRS 4 *Capital Instruments*, The Accounting Standards Board.
¹⁷ ASC (1989), ED 46 *Disclosure of Related Party Transactions*, The Accounting Standards Committee.
¹⁸ ASB (1994) FRS 8, *Related Party Disclosures*, The Accounting Standards Board.
¹⁹ ASC (1990) ED 52 *Accounting for Intangible Assets*, The Accounting Standards Committee.
²⁰ ASB (1993), Discussion paper, "Goodwill and Intangible Assets", The Accounting Standards Board
²¹ ASB (1993), Discussion paper, "The Role of Valuation in Financial Reporting", The Accounting Standards Board.
²² ASB (1992), FRS 2 *Accounting for Subsidiary Undertakings*, The Accounting Standards Board.

11: A CRITICAL AFTERWORD
¹ Section 172 of the Finance Act, 1995 imposes a requirement on auditors and tax advisers to report material tax evasion in certain circumstances.